The Sociologist as Detective

An Introduction to Research Methods

Edited with Introduction and Exercises

by WILLIAM B. SANDERS

ctive

Familiarity with the techniques of researchers is essential for an understanding of many disciplines. Yet many students approach the subject of research methods with fear and trepidation or—more commonly—apathy and boredom. This innovative book meets the problem by demonstrating the parallels between the sociological researcher and more familiar investigator of social life, the detective, whose work is generally regarded as full of excitement and intrigue. Both the sociologist and the detective are interested in human behavior, and both investigate it through interviews, observations, experiments, and other information-gathering practices. By recognizing that the sociologist and the detective have much in common in their methods, the student will, it is hoped, come to regard sociological research as a fascinating opportunity to discover the mysteries of social action rather than as a series of mechanical processes that he is required to master. Further, the analogy can serve more than motivational purposes, for the sociologist can learn from the detective—among other things, how to combine several methods and sources of data in a single investigation.

The idea of considering detectives' methods for sociological purposes is not entirely new. After reading the work of Eugene J. Webb and his colleagues on "unobtrusive measures," Professor Sanders turned to the stories of Sherlock Holmes and other fictional detectives. He then read accounts by real detectives and, finally, began to interview them and to observe their activities firsthand. He became convinced that they knew a great deal about methods that sociologists have only begun to explore. Chapter 1 of this book contains

The Sociologist as Detective

AN INTRODUCTION TO
RESEARCH METHODS

Edited with Introduction and Exercises by
William B. Sanders

PRAEGER PUBLISHERS
New York • Washington

Published in the United States of America in 1974
by Praeger Publishers, Inc.
111 Fourth Avenue, New York, N.Y. 10003

Library of Congress Cataloging in Publication Data

Sanders, William B   comp.
  The sociologist as detective.
  Includes bibliographies.
  CONTENTS: Sanders, W. B. The methods and
evidence of detectives and sociologists.—The
critical perspective: Deutscher, I. Words and deeds:
social science and social policy. Sacks, H. Notes
on police assessment of moral character. [etc.]
  1. Sociological research—Addresses, essays,
lectures. 2. Social science research—Addresses,
essays, lectures. 3. Criminal investigation—Addresses,
essays, lectures. I. Title.

HM48.S24   301'.07'2   73-1912

Printed in the United States of America

To Eli and Billy

Contents

Preface and Acknowledgments

THIS BOOK IS INTENDED TO INTRODUCE SOCIAL-SCIENCE STUDENTS TO research techniques by providing both illustrations of and firsthand experience with several research methodologies. The sociologist is compared to a more familiar investigator of social life. the detective, whose work parallels that of the sociologist in that he also engages in interviews, observations, experiments, and other information-gathering practices. Detective work, however, is generally regarded as exciting and full of intrigue, while sociological research is more often seen as dull and drab. By recognizing that sociologists and detectives have much in common in their methods, the student may, it is hoped, approach sociological research as a fascinating opportunity to discover the mysteries of social action rather than as a mechanical process that he is required to master.

The idea of considering detectives' methods for sociological purposes is not new, but it has not been fully exploited. Eugene J. Webb, Donald T. Campbell, Richard D. Schwartz, and Lee Sechrest, in their unexcelled work *Unobtrusive Measures* (1966), suggest the use of multiple measurements and operations as a basic strategy in social-science research and give several examples of the sorts of things detectives routinely do. After reading their work, I read the stories of Sherlock Holmes and found that the Great Detective's methods had much to offer sociologists. Not satisfied with mere fiction, I began reading the accounts of real detectives and found that they were equally interesting as potential sources of techniques for sociological research. Finally, I began talking with real detectives and became convinced that they knew a great deal about methods that sociologists have only begun to explore. Eventually, I was able to observe firsthand how detectives worked, and from these observations I found that sociologists could learn from detectives. Chapter 1 contains much of what I learned.

The remainder of the book has been arranged into five parts. Part I deals with developing a critical perspective of social interviews and observations and is intended as a caution against overdependence on a single technique or point of view. Each of the other four parts deals with a single form of sociological research. The readings presented here were chosen because they are interesting as well as sound examples of research methods. Too often, students are asked to read works that contain excellent sociology but dull material; as a result, they do not read and they learn nothing.

Finally, exercises are included in each part to show the students that the research methods they have read about can be applied, and that they themselves can do so. The exercises are designed for individual and/or group research. By doing these exercises the students will learn about many contingencies of research that can never be explained in a textbook. Some of the exercises are designed as practical demonstrations of the use of more than one method for the investigation of a single problem. However, most exercises employ only a single method, so that the student can obtain focused experience in using it. It is hoped that the student and the instructor will feel free to use more than one method in doing the exercises and to alter the exercises to fit their particular community and research situation. I have deliberately not introduced the more sophisticated forms of analysis, such as Chi square and path analysis, but the exercises are arranged so that, if such analysis is considered desirable by the instructor, it can readily be done.

Several people assisted me in numerous ways in putting this book together, but most credit must be given to those detectives of the Santa Barbara County Sheriff's Office who tutored me in the art of investigation. Detectives Anthony Baker, Chip Marchbanks, Moorman Oliver, Jr., Frank Wright, Fred Holderman, William Harris, James Taylor, Don McCormick, Gil Chayra, Roger Best, William

Crook, William Baker, James Regan, Ed McCauley, Mike Kirk-
man, Ed Picento, Fred Ray, Roy Rosales, Larry Gold, and others
put up with my questions, my tape recorder, and my presence,
often underfoot, while they carried out investigations, and to them
I am sincerely grateful. I am also grateful to Jay Moore and Dave
Hershman for their introductions to the detectives and to Sheriff
John Carpenter for allowing me access to the detective bureau for
my research.

Thanks are also due to Donald R. Cressey and Howard Daudistel, who helped me to organize the material and offered suggestions, editing, and needed encouragement. Clinton Terry, Michael
Williams, Don Zimmerman, and D. Lawrence Wieder also gave
suggestions and other assistance. Patty Terry typed the manuscript,
transcribing it all correctly despite the staples, tape, coffee stains,
and tobacco burns that littered the pages. Gladys Topkis and
Svein Arber of Praeger Publishers were constantly encouraging and
patient. I am also extremely grateful to the various authors and
publishers who allowed me to reprint their work. Finally, I want to
thank my wife, Eli, and my son, Billy, for tolerating me during
this period, and to them I dedicate this book.

WILLIAM B. SANDERS

Santa Barbara, California
October, 1973

some of Professor Sanders' observations regarding what detectives have to teach the social scientist.

The book is no less innovative in its format and organization than in its approach to its subject. The four sections that constitute the heart of the book deal, respectively, with the interview, the survey, the ethnography, and content analysis. Following an introduction to each part, which presents the distinctive aspects of the method covered and the types of problems for which it is best suited, Professor Sanders offers two or three reading selections describing variants of the method in action— e.g., observation and questionnaire surveys, field and laboratory experiments, participant observation and intensive interviews, conversation analysis and content analysis. Each reading selection, chosen because it is interesting as well as a sound example of research method, is followed by a set of exercises designed to show students that they themselves can apply the methods they have read about and thereby learn a great deal about research that can never be explained in a textbook. The exercises can be used for individual or group projects. Some of them are designed as practical demonstrations of the use of more than one method to investigate a single problem. Others employ only a single method, so that students can obtain a more focused experience by using it.

The book thus combines an introduction to research, descriptions of several methods, examples of each method in use, and exercises requiring application of the methods in new situations. It is, therefore, a field manual as well as a textbook, invaluable for the beginning student researcher.

THE EDITOR: William B. Sanders is currently Assistant Professor of Sociology and Criminal Justice at California State College, Stanislaus. He holds a Ph.D. degree from the University of California, Santa Barbara.

1. Introduction

THE METHODS
AND EVIDENCE
OF DETECTIVES
AND SOCIOLOGISTS
—William B. Sanders

IN THE COURSE OF THEIR WORK, both detectives and sociologists must gather and analyze information. For detectives, the object is to identify and locate criminals and to collect evidence to ensure that the identification is correct. Sociologists, on the other hand, develop theories and methods to help them understand social behavior. Although their specific goals differ, both sociologists and detectives formulate theories and develop methods in an attempt to answer two general questions: "Why did it happen?" and "In what circumstances is it likely to happen again?"— that is, to explain and predict. Detectives' theories consider such questions as: "What motives would explain a specific type of crime?" "What do certain crimes have in common?" "Where is a given type of crime likely to occur?" Sociological theories are developed around such questions as: "How is social order possible?" "How is social conflict regulated?" "What forms are displayed in social interaction?"

To test their theories, detectives and sociologists rely on empirical evidence and logical modes of analysis as well as on their imagination. Both employ observation techniques, interviews, experiments, and other empirical methods to test the validity of their theories. Nevertheless, there are differences in their methods of gathering and analyzing information, and each can profit from techniques developed by the other. Sociologists, for example, rarely if ever employ such devices as the polygraph machine (lie detector), and detectives do not use multivariate analysis (charting several causal variables). Detectives have made much more use of physical evidence than have sociologists, who have seldom bothered to analyze the physical features of social phenomena. (The work of Webb and his associates [1966] stands as a notable exception.)*

In investigating a crime, detectives interview victims, witnesses, informants, and suspects. They compare these interviews with physical evidence that they gather in order to piece together a consistent account of what took place and to determine whether the people they interviewed were telling the truth. They may conduct an experiment to see whether a crime could have occurred in the way suggested by the accounts and the physical evidence. Finally, the detectives may discern a pattern from several cases involving crimes of the same sort. (A pattern would include the typical method used to commit the crime, the type of place in which the crime occurred, and the time the crime occurred.) Knowing this pattern, the detectives would then observe ("stake out") certain areas during the times the crime is likely to occur.

Sociologists, on the other hand, generally use only a single method and only a single source of data. Survey researchers will use only the data gathered in interviews, experimental researchers will only conduct an experiment, and participant observers will conduct no surveys or experiments and will report their findings solely in terms of their field notes. Moreover, it is unlikely that any of them will use available physical evidence. However, the sociologist could greatly profit from using multiple methods and measurements in a single study. Each method or source of data has its strengths and weaknesses. Experiments have questionable external validity, attitudes elicited by interviews often have no relation to people's actual behavior, and observational studies lack control. By using more than one method and source of data in a single study,

* Modern detectives use more sophisticated modes of analysis than did Sherlock Holmes, who was able to detect that Dr. Watson had been in Afghanistan after merely shaking hands with him, or Charlie Chan, who could tell whether a person was left- or right-handed by noting how matches had been torn from a matchbook, but they devote the same attention to details and basic reasoning.

as detectives do, sociologists can discover and compensate for the weaknesses of the various methods and will multiply their strengths (Webb et al., 1966:3).

THEORY

The stereotype of the detective who asks for "just the facts" is inaccurate, for detectives are always working with and testing theory. In any investigation a detective would be at a loss for questions to ask and interviewees without at least a rudimentary theory. For instance, in homicide cases, the first people generally contacted by detectives are friends, relatives, or acquaintances of the victim. Behind such investigative procedures is the theory that most homicides are committed by people who are socially close to the victim. Theory even determines what facts are noted. For example, in "Silver Blaze," a case of a stolen racehorse, Sherlock Holmes's observation of the fact that a dog was not barking was directed by the theory that dogs do not bark at people they know. The "fact" that the thief must have been known to the dog was overlooked by Dr. Watson and readers who were not guided by that theory.

Similarly, sociologists develop theories that lead them to ask certain questions and not others, and these questions in turn lead them to notice certain "facts" and not others (Parsons, 1937). For example, Max Weber's theory of the relationship between religious belief systems and economic systems led him to formulate certain questions concerning the economic structures of societies with and without predominantly Protestant beliefs (Weber, 1958). Likewise, Durkheim's theory of anomic suicide led him to examine suicide rates in various countries in terms of each country's dominant religion (Durkheim, 1951). In both of these theories, religion was a fact to be noticed. In Goffman's examination of mental hospitals (1961), on the other hand, the focus of his theory on the social world of patients in a mental hospital as they developed and sustained it led him to ignore the issue of what bearing their religious background had on their being committed. Problems relevant to certain theories are not relevant to others, and certain questions are relevant to certain problems and not to others. The facts that are located in research stem from the researcher's theory.

Central to theories and research are concepts, which Blumer (1969:155) calls "fashioners of perception," in that they direct the researcher to "see" the world in certain terms and configurations. For instance, the concept of "social class" directs the researcher to look at elements that give some people power and deny it to others. The concept of "the situation" directs the observer's attention to the context of encounters between people rather than just to the individuals in interaction. Concepts provide the crucial link between theory and research, in that they tell the researcher what is of theoretical interest and what to look for. If a theory states, for example, that there is a relationship between associations and criminal behavior, the researcher will not look at head shapes, economic position, or family size, but will concentrate on whom criminals associate with.

Detectives' investigations are also guided by certain concepts. The concept of "motive," for example, plays a central role in many investigations. Assuming that people are generally rational, detectives attempt to identify those who would benefit from a crime. This conceptual view leads them to certain people as possible suspects and away from others. For example, in an arson case, detectives try to determine whether the owner of the house or business or anyone else would benefit more from the building's absence than its presence. Without such a guiding concept, there would be no starting point for an investigation and no grounds on which to build a theory or finish an investigation.

EVIDENCE

Just as theories direct researchers to facts and give meaning and relevance to facts, so facts in turn give validity and shape to theories. And since sociology, like detecting, is an empirical enterprise, sociological theories require evidence for them to be considered valid, just as detectives' theories do.

Beginning with a hypothesis, the researcher gathers concrete evidence to either substantiate or disprove it. For example, detectives may hypothesize that the butler was responsible for the murder of the lord of the manor. Before they can arrest him, however, they must locate evidence to show that there is "probable cause" for considering him a suspect. For conviction, they must show that the butler was guilty beyond a reasonable doubt. If the butler's fingerprints are found on the murder weapon, for example, this would stand as cause for arresting him; however, if the murder weapon is found to be something the butler normally handled, such as a poker for tending the fire, other corroborating evidence would have to be located to prove the hypothesis that he was guilty.

Similarly, sociologists must prove their hypotheses. For example, in attempting to discover whether there is a relationship between amount of education and income, the sociologist might hypothesize that the more education an individual has, the greater his income will be. But he gathers evidence to prove or disprove this hypothesis, not by showing that one person with a college degree has a greater income than another person with less education, but by taking the average amount of education of several people and comparing it with their average income. Thus, instead of working with single cases, sociologists typically work with several cases.

An important feature of detective investigations is the practices involved in recognizing evidence as evidence. At a crime scene and in the course of an investigation, there are numerous elements that may or may not be regarded as evidence. Physical artifacts, statements by witnesses, and written documents can all turn out to be evidence, but whether they are so treated depends on the formulated circumstances of the case. For example, in an investigation of a burglary with attempted homicide, detectives searched an area around the crime scene for evidence. Overlooked but quite visible was a plastic bleach bottle that had been partially ripped apart. Later, when a suspect was arrested, a similar piece of plastic was found in his possession.* The old bleach bottle was now seen retrospectively in an entirely new light. If the piece of plastic found on the suspect could be matched to the piece missing from the bottle found on the crime scene, the suspect could be linked to the crime. Thus, from being merely a piece of trash, the bleach bottle was elevated to a piece of evidence.

Because what comes to be seen as evidence depends on the context of the situation and what will be evidence is often unclear until a context has been provided or a hypothesis is more fully developed, detectives keep everything that appears to be potentially useful (Stukey, 1968:21). Intelligence units, for instance, keep all sorts of information in their files. Much of it is never used or even seen as useful at the time it is collected, but if a situation comes up where they need the information, they will have it. In a crude way, much of what is collected by detectives is like using seat belts.

---

* Credit cards, plastic playing cards, and other flat, thin pieces of plastic are commonly used by burglars to slip open door locks.

They do nothing for the driver until he has an accident, but, for the value they have on the occasions when they are needed, they are worth the little inconvenience they cause.

Similarly, sociologists know that concepts may be indicated in different ways, depending on the research situation. Using the concept of social status, the sociologist cannot assume that the status symbols of one group will be the same for another group. For example, having a big, expensive automobile may indicate status among most Americans, but status among environmentalists may be indicated by the lack of such a car. Thus, before specifying big cars as an indicator for social status, the sociologist sensitizes the concept to the research situation. In this way he ensures that what is taken to indicate an instance of a conceptual phenomenon actually does so.

Related to this is the issue of contextual embeddedness of meaning and evidence. That is to say, what something means and whether or not it is seen as evidence depend on the context of the situation. For instance, consider the question "Do you have a match?" If the sociologist is studying pickup strategies in bars (cf. Cavan, 1966), this would be taken as an indicator of an attempt to initiate a conversation. In the context of male-female bar interaction, the question has a certain meaning. However, in another context—say, in a conversation between two old friends or in a gymnasium where boxers train—it has an entirely different sense. In a study of pinball players (Sanders, 1973), the author found that the term "match" generally refers to a free game. Hence, what is defined as evidence for the sociologist as well as for the detective depends on the context of the situation.*

PURPOSES AND PROBLEMS OF RESEARCH

In the very broadest sense, the purpose of sociological research is to test and develop sociological theory. Theory, in turn, explains and predicts social behavior. However, there is a good deal of sociological research that only indirectly tests or develops theory. A researcher may collect data to determine the *frequency and distribution* of various features of social life. For example, a researcher may conduct a survey to find how many students smoke marijuana.

* For a full discussion of the contextual embeddedness of social phenomena, see Wilson (1970) and Garfinkel (1967).

On the other hand, a sociologist may want to conduct a study simply in order to *describe* the forms of behavior in a given setting, such as bars, airports, laundromats, or department stores. Both of these types of studies, though, are related to theory. In looking at the frequency and distribution of marijuana smokers, the researcher may find that students who live in urban areas are more likely to smoke marijuana than are rural students. Such findings would serve as tests for a theory linking crime with population density. Similarly, by describing typical forms of behavior in various social settings, the researcher may test the theory that social settings determine the type of behavior to be found in a given setting.

Let us turn now to some of the problems in sociological research. Some of these issues are specific to certain kinds of research, and they will be explained in other parts of the book. Here only the general problems common to all research will be considered.

Validity.　Simply stated, validity refers to the correspondence between the researcher's collected data and the real world. The extent to which the collected data reflect naturally occurring social behavior and processes determines its validity. For example, if for some reason respondents to a questionnaire elected not to tell the truth, the data collected by the researcher would not reflect the real world and would be considered invalid. (See Chapter 2 for a full discussion of this point.) *Internal validity* is generally considered in the context of measurement (Campbell, 1963), but here it will be used to entail description as well. If data have internal validity, any significant differences observed in a comparison can be attributed to a predicted cause, and not to measurement or description error. For example, in a study of assembly workers (Roethlisberger and Dickson, 1939), the researchers predicted that the workers would increase production if the lighting were heightened. As the lighting improved, so did production; however, work production also went up when the lights were dimmed. The researchers concluded that the assembly workers increased their efforts as a result of the presence of the researchers. The increased production had nothing to do with the lights. Thus, the prediction that work production increased with lighting proved to be erroneous. Similarly, in descriptive studies, notably participant-observation research (Chapter 8), often what the researcher describes is due to the researcher's presence rather than being a picture of normal behavior that occurs in the researcher's absence. Field experiments (Chapter 7) and unobtrusive measures (Chapter 10) have features that avoid some of the problems of internal validity.

External validity, on the other hand, refers to the generalizability of the findings. If the data cannot be generalized to other, theoretically similar settings, situations, organizations, or populations, then the study lacks external validity. For example, if a researcher were interested in finding out the attitudes of a given community but interviewed only members of the upper class, he would have no way of knowing whether the attitudes he found were truly representative of the entire community. Thus, he could not generalize his findings to the entire community, and the study would lack external validity.

In order to increase external validity, researchers employ *randomization* procedures. Used mainly in surveys but occasionally in other methods as well, randomization is a procedure that gives every unit in the universe of interest an equal chance of being included in the sample to be interviewed, tested, or observed. The *universe* is the population in which the researcher is interested, and the *sample* is that part of the universe that will be researched. If the sample is random, it is assumed that all of the various relevant aspects of the universe will be proportionately represented; therefore, the findings can be generalized to the entire universe and be considered externally valid. In Part II, the procedure of drawing a random sample will be explained fully.

Reliability.   Another problem encountered in research is that of reliability (Forcese and Richer, 1973). Reliability is the ability of a method to replicate results when it is used by different researchers. For example, a researcher in California conducts an experiment and finds that individuals under a specific set of conditions will conform to group norms even though they do not personally agree with them. The researcher sends his experimental design to a researcher in New York who conducts the same experiment under the same conditions and finds the same results. The experiment is then considered reliable, since different researchers using the same instrument found the same thing. Fixed-choice questionnaires are considered highly reliable, whereas participant-observation studies are considered to have lower reliability.

Ethics. A final problem that should be discussed here involves research on human beings. This problem is in part an interactional one pertaining to such issues as soliciting subjects to participate in experiments, gaining access to an observation setting, and getting people to respond to interviews. This aspect of the problem will be developed in the readings and exercises, since the problem differs depending on the nature of the research topic and method. Here we will deal with ethical problems.

Unlike the detective, the sociologist does not face legal constraints in gathering evidence. The sociologist's data will not be invalidated if he does not warn his subjects that what they say may be used against them, nor do defense lawyers instruct subjects not to speak to sociologists. However, sociologists do have an unwritten code by which they attempt to abide.

Sociological researchers should not invade the privacy of others without their permission. For instance, even if they were legally able to do so, sociologists should not plant bugs in people's homes or locate themselves so that they can secretly observe others in private places. Similarly, sociologists should avoid lying, cheating, and stealing as resources for gathering data. Often it may seem that the only way to get information is by using techniques that are unethical and rationalizing their use in the name of sociology. Not only is such behavior unethical, but if sociologists began to engage regularly in these practices, they would soon lose their position of trust and would find it difficult to persuade informants to reveal information.

While sociologists are not ethically required to announce their research intentions in public places, in some situations it may be difficult to differentiate between private and public settings; some very private business takes place in public. An excellent example is the research by Laud Humphreys (1970) in which Humphreys, in the role of a "watch queen," or voyeur, observed impersonal sex between men in public toilets. On the one hand, Humphreys was not invading a private space, and that criterion alone justified his presence without announcing that he was a sociologist engaging in research. On the other hand, the sexual activity was private, and it was not the type of behavior with which most of the participants would want their names associated; therefore, in this sense the research can be taken as an invasion of privacy. The resolution of where the invasion of privacy begins and where the public domain ends must be in terms of the general standards of the members' understanding of public and private places. Thus, since no one needs special permission to enter a public toilet as one would need for entering a private home, it can be argued that observation of such domains should not be forbidden to the unannounced researcher.

This does not, however, exclude the sociologist from using data from private places that have been discarded and from which inferences can be made as to what takes place in those places. By analyzing what people put in their trash, for example, sociologists have found certain private activities that, although unseen, are easily inferred. Sawyer (1961), for example, estimated drinking habits from the frequency and distribution of liquor bottles found in trash cans. Thus, like detectives, who are barred from invading privacy without permission, either in the form of a search warrant or by the controller of the private space, sociologists need to develop methods for *seeing more than that to which they have access.*

A final ethical consideration lies in the confidentiality of the sociologist's subjects. Much of the information gathered by sociologists may be harmful to those who were observed or questioned. In order to protect their subjects, sociologists do not reveal the names of their subjects, the names of the organizations, or (sometimes) even the location of the study. Confidentiality, besides having ethical implications, has practical ones as well. Much of the information gathered by detectives is based on what their informants tell them. If detectives revealed the names of their informants, soon there would be no informants. Similarly, if sociologists made public the names and places of their studies that uncovered adverse information, soon no one would speak to them.

CHOOSING A METHOD: THE PLAN OF THIS BOOK

For testing their theories, propositions, and hypotheses, sociologists have a vast array of methods from which to choose. The choice of method depends on the type of information the researcher needs to resolve his problem. For example, if the problem is to find what people think about correctional programs in the criminal-justice system, the researcher will want to employ a method that includes interviews or questionnaires. On the other hand, if the researcher wants to know how people handle crisis situations, he will either design an experiment to simulate a crisis and observe what the subjects do or he will go to places that typically involve crises, such as emergency receiving rooms in hospitals, and observe behavior there. In the first case, the researcher is interested in *beliefs*; in the second case, in *action*. To elicit beliefs in research, as in everyday interaction, researchers generally ask questions. To discover how people act in various situations, they use experimental or observation techniques.

The general considerations for any research are: *What information is necessary? What sources of information are available? What methods are there for gathering the information?* Determining the various sources of data necessary for resolving a problem is called *theoretical sampling*. Even though sociologists typically use only a single method, usually information from a variety of sources is necessary and available. For example, if a researcher wants to find out about the public's reaction to crime, he might decide simply to interview people. However, his findings would be more substantial if, in addition to interviewing, he observed whether people, especially old people and women, ventured out alone after dark, the number and quantity of locks people employed, and the number of people who had large dogs. In other words, if the researcher took a proper theoretical sample, more than a single source of data would be tapped.

Perspective. The first section of this book deals with the researcher's perspective. The perspective suggested is that of the detective, who does not believe everything he hears or sees. Broadly speaking, a *perspective* refers to an *angle of observation*, and a "critical perspective" refers here to several angles of observation (Schatzman and Strauss, 1973). Such a perspective not only prevents one from jumping to unwarranted conclusions based on a single source of information but also forces the researcher to look at a problem from several angles. In researching any social phenomenon, the first consideration is the perspective from which the researcher will view the issue.

Surveys. More than any other single method, sociologists have been identified with survey research. Essentially, a survey entails interviewing or observing people in terms of a specified set of dimensions. Various polls, such as the Gallup Poll, in which the researcher may want to find out about the population's views toward presidential candidates, the economy, the military, and similar dimensions of society, are the best-known examples of a survey. Surveys are used most efficiently when the researcher's problem pertains to the frequency and distribution of a relatively few aspects of a population (Zelditch, 1962). In the survey by Ennis (Chapter 4), the problem deals with the frequency and distribution of crime victims; in Wiseman's survey (Chapter 5), social types are surveyed in terms of court dispositions.

Experiments. Experiments are the prototype of the scientific model. They are designed to find what causes a given behavior by controlling the situation so that only the causal variable is present to affect the behavior in question. The two types explained in Part III involve introducing an *experimental variable* to determine what change occurs as a result of the variable. Middleton (Chapter 6) introduces a film denouncing anti-Semitism as an experimental variable to see if it leads to any changes in anti-Semitic attitudes among those who watched the film. The *field experiment* by Russo and Sommer (Chapter 7) introduces "sitting too close" as a unique experiment of personal space.

Ethnographies. Ethnographic research has traditionally been the prime tool of anthropologists, and it actually refers to more than a single method. Ethnographies are basically analytic descriptions of cultures (including subcultures), organizations, or settings. They involve *participant observation,* wherein the researcher spends a great deal of time observing and listening to those of interest. In the study by Sanders and Daudistel (Chapter 8), the authors went on cases with detectives, observing and participating in the detectives' day-to-day activities. *Intensive interviewing* entails long, unstructured talks with subjects and is generally used in all ethnographies in addition to whatever other method is employed. Cressey (Chapter 9) explains how, using intensive interviews, he developed an explanation of embezzlement. A third method used by ethnographers involves *unobtrusive measures.* This means the use of various physical artifacts to infer social behavior in a given setting or community. Webb and his associates (Chapter 10) offer numerous ingenious suggestions as to how valuable data can be gathered by noting such artifacts.

Content Analysis. The last section deals with a method that indirectly serves an information-gathering function and is often used in conjunction with other methods. Content analysis is employed to find underlying forms and structures in social communication. By analyzing the content of written or transcribed documents, the researcher hopes to find themes, forms, and structures that will account for the pattern of the communication. For example, Winick (Chapter 11) analyzed a dominant form of humor among teen-agers by studying the themes used in *Mad* magazine. A newer form of content analysis is *conversation analysis*, in which transcriptions of conversations are analyzed in terms of their structure. The final reading (Chapter 12) is an analysis of police interrogation, in which the author shows how the conversational structure is subtly used to get suspects to talk.

Multiple Methods. Several of the readings deal with more than a single method. Deutscher (Chapter 2), in his discussion of the relationship between what people say and what they do, shows that by using only a survey, a researcher may be led to erroneous conclusions. Likewise, Sanders and Daudistel (Chapter 8) use interviews and participant observation as well as content analysis, and Winick (Chapter 11) employs a questionnaire along with content analysis.

Besides being a means by which the researcher can get the necessary information in terms of a theoretical sample, the use of multiple methods serves to "triangulate" the findings (Webb *et al.*, 1966; Denzin, 1970). That is, each method serves to "correct out" erroneous data supplied by the other methods; thus, the findings represent only those data that have been shown to be valid in terms of all the methods used. This puts the researcher in a much stronger position to claim validity for his findings.

ANALYSIS

Once the researcher has collected his data, he has to ask, "What does all this mean?" Do the data prove or disprove the hypothesis?

Does the experimental variable really cause a change? What structures, forms, and patterns does this group display, and why? All these questions depend on analysis of the data, for analysis is the process of extracting information (Simon, 1969:333).

The information necessary for most research boils down to the relationship between variables. If one variable can be shown to change when another variable does and a causal link can be shown to exist (or not), then the analysis is successful. The variable that produces the change is referred to as the *independent variable* and the variable that is changed with the action of the independent variable is called the *dependent variable*. When a batter hits a ball, the movement of the bat (independent variable) causes the movement of the ball (dependent variable). Similarly, in sociological research, if it can be shown that crime (dependent variable) increases with association with criminals (independent variable) and no other variable (intervening variable) can be shown to vary to the same extent, then it can be said that association with criminals increases the likelihood that one will engage in crime.

Quantitative Analysis. Quantitative analysis, used primarily in survey and experimental research, is based on assigning numerical values to measured social variables. The numbers assigned to the variables are then compared in statistical tests to determine whether or not there is a causal relationship between the independent and dependent variables. Some of the statistics involved are quite simple; others are extremely complex. Here, and in the readings and exercises that follow, only the more simple statistics will be presented.

Suppose that you have collected data from urban and rural areas and you want to know whether people living in cities are more likely to be graduated from college than those living in the country. The problem is that you have more data from the city than from the country; therefore, comparing the actual number of college graduates will only reflect the larger sample taken from the city. A simple statistic to make such a comparison is the *percentage*. To find the percentage of college graduates, the number of college graduates is divided by the total sample and then multiplied by 100. For example, if your urban sample contained 500 cases and 200 had been graduated from college, 200 would be divided by 500 to get .40. Multiplying .40 by 100 would give you a percentage of 40. Similarly, if your rural sample contained 200 cases and 80 had been graduated from college, 40 per cent would have been graduated from college. By comparing the percentages, the researcher can now see that there is no difference between college graduation and living in the city or country. Both have 40 per cent college graduates.

The following formula can be used for computing percentages where N equals the total number in the sample and n equals the number in the category:

$$\frac{n}{N} \times 100 = \text{percentage}$$

A second group of basic statistics involves *means, medians, and modes*. These statistics are used to locate center points and are used for comparisons and in determining amount of change. Using the following data as an example, each will be explained.

Monthly Income

Group 1		Group 2		Group 3	
1.	$1,000	1.	$2,000	1.	$700
2.	900	2.	1,800	2.	700
3.	800	3.	1,000	3.	700
4.	700	4.	100	4.	700
5.	700	5.	100	5.	700
6.	500	6.	100	6.	700
7.	400	7.	100	7.	700
8.	200	8.	100	8.	700
9.	200	9.	100	9.	700
	$5,400		$5,400		$6,300

Each group has nine members, and they have been arranged in descending order according to monthly income. To find the mean income of any of the groups, simply divide the total of all incomes by the number of cases. Group 1 has 9 cases totaling $5,400, and by dividing $5,400 by 9 we find the mean of $600. Group 2 also has a mean of $600, and Group 3 has a mean of $700. Thus, based on mean income, Group 1 and Group 2 are the same.

A *median* is the value of the middle item when the items have been arranged in increasing or decreasing order (Freund, 1960:54). In the three groups presented, Item 5 is the median, since it is midway between the first and last items. Thus groups 1 and 3 have a median income of $700, and Group 2 has a median income of $100. Now, based on the median, groups 1 and 3 are the same.

A final measure of location is the *mode*, and it is based on the category with the highest frequency. In Group 2, $100 is the modal income, since it is more frequent than any other income figure. That is, more members earn $100 than any other amount. Group 1 has two modes, since there are an equal number of members who earn $700 and $200. Finally, since all of the items in Group 3 are $700, its mode is $700. (Note that the mean, median, and mode in Group 3 are all $700).

Before making comparisons using any one of these statistics, the student is cautioned to first look at the distribution. For example, even though Group 1 and Group 2 have the same mean, the groups are different in that they are differently distributed. Similarly, Group 1 and Group 3 have the same median, but Group 3 has an equal distribution, whereas Group 1 has an unequal distribution. In making comparisons or in looking for changes, the analysis will be much better if more than one statistic is employed.

Qualitative Analysis. Qualitative analysis is much less systematized than quantitative analysis and involves much more complexity and subtlety. The basic elements are relatively clear. It entails a description of social patterns and processes as well as an explanation of the patterns and processes from the social actor's point of view. For example, in Chapter 8, the authors describe the exigencies in detectives' decisions to work or not to work a case. Similarly, in Cressey's discussion of how he formulated hypotheses based on his interviews with embezzlers (Chapter 9), the process of qualitative analysis is outlined. In the readings and exercises that follow, the various nuances of qualitative analysis will be explained.

REFERENCES

BLUMER, H. 1969. *Symbolic Interactionism: Perspective and Method.* Englewood Cliffs, N.J.: Prentice-Hall.

CAMPBELL, DONALD T. 1963. "From Description to Experimentation: Interpreting Trends as Quasi-Experiments." In *Problems in Measuring Change*, Chester W. Harris (ed.), pp. 212–42. Madison: University of Wisconsin Press.

CAVAN, SHERRI. 1963. "Interaction in Home Territories," *Berkeley Journal of Sociology*, Vol. 8, pp. 17–32.

DENZIN, NORMAN K. 1970. *The Research Act*. Chicago: Aldine.

DOYLE, SIR ARTHUR CONAN. "Silver Blaze." In *The Annotated Sherlock Holmes*. Vol. II. William S. Baring-Gould (ed.), pp. 261–81. New York: Clarkson N. Potter.

DURKHEIM, E. 1951. *Suicide*. New York: Macmillan.

FORCESE, D. P., and S. RICHER. 1973. *Social Research Methods*. Englewood Cliffs, N.J.: Prentice-Hall.

FREUND, J. E. 1960. *Modern Elementary Statistics*. Englewood Cliffs, N.J.: Prentice-Hall.

GARFINKEL, H. 1967. *Studies in Ethnomethodology*. Englewood Cliffs, N.J.: Prentice-Hall.

GOFFMAN, ERVING. 1961. *Asylums*. Garden City, N.Y.: Doubleday.

HUMPHREYS, L. 1970. *Tearoom Trade: Impersonal Sex in Public Places*. Chicago: Aldine.

PARSONS, T. 1937. *The Structure of Social Action: Volume I*. New York: The Free Press.

ROETHLISBERGER, F. J., and WILLIAM J. DICKSON. 1939. *Management and the Worker*. Cambridge, Mass.: Harvard University Press.

SANDERS, W. B. 1973. "Pinball Occasions." In *People in Places: The Sociology of the Familiar*, Edward Sagarin and Arnold Birenbaum (eds.). New York: Praeger Publishers.

SAWYER, H. G. 1961. "The Meaning of Numbers." Speech before the American Association of Advertising Agencies.

SCHATZMAN, L., and ANSELM STRAUSS. 1973. *Field Research*. Englewood Cliffs, N.J.: Prentice-Hall.

SIMON, J. L. 1969. *Basic Research Methods in Social Science*. New York: Random House.

STUKEY, G. B. 1968. *Evidence for the Law Enforcement Officer*. New York: McGraw-Hill.

THOMAS, W. I., and D. S. THOMAS. 1928. *The Child in America*. New York: Alfred A. Knopf.

WEBB, EUGENE, D. T. CAMPBELL, R. D. SCHWARTZ, and L. SECHREST. 1966. *Unobtrusive Measures: Nonreactive Research in the Social Sciences*. Chicago: Rand McNally.

WEBER, MAX. 1958. *The Protestant Ethic and the Spirit of Capitalism*. New York: Charles Scribner's Sons.

WILSON, T. 1970. "Conceptions of Interaction and Forms of Sociological Explanation," *American Sociological Review*, Vol. 35, No. 4, pp. 697–709.

I: THE CRITICAL PERSPECTIVE

THE TWO READINGS IN THIS SECTION ARE INTENDED TO SENSITIZE THE student to a critical perspective and to point out that what the researcher will come to see depends on what perspective he takes. On the one hand, Deutscher shows that there is an unknown relationship between what people say and what they do. This is a somewhat cynical point of view in that it suggests that people don't always tell the truth. More importantly, it suggests that a truer picture of social life is gained by using more than a single method or viewing device.

Sacks, on the other hand, is dealing with the perspective of a special group, namely the police. The problem for the police is to keep an eye on criminals while not bothering law-abiding citizens. In order to do this, they must pick out cues that with a high degree of probability will reveal potential or actual criminals. The criminals, for their part, attempt to conceal any cues that will give them away, and the police know that criminals attempt to do so. Thus, the police must look for the smallest cue the criminal has not concealed.

Depending on one's point of view, certain things will be noticed and other things ignored. Moreover, if something is ignored, it is, for all intents and purposes, invisible. Thus, if the police are looking carefully for criminal cues, which they know criminals attempt to hide, what they see—what is visible—is very different from what others, with a different perspective, can see. For example, as Sacks points out, a girl getting out of a cab may be seen by police to be a call girl going to or returning from her business, whereas to non-police observers such comings and goings are seen in such a way to be unnoticed or, if noticed, not in the same way.

Other lines of work also highlight certain features of the world while playing down others. For instance, the shoe repairman notices people's shoes, the jeweler notices their watches and jewels, the pickpocket notices bulges in pockets and straps on purses. Their interest leads them to attend to and notice these things while ignoring other things outside their immediate or general concern. To put this in another way, a person's perspective leads him to experience the world in a particular fashion.

For sociological research this has two important implications. On the one hand, since a perspective determines what will be noticed and what will be ignored, what will and what will not be recognized as data are determined by the point of view the researcher takes. If the method used for the viewing leads to erroneous data, as Deutscher points out, or if a given perspective leads to a skewed picture of a totality, it may be that the use of several methods or perspectives will lead to a more valid conclusion and picture of the phenomenon being researched. On the other hand, sociologists are interested in the actor's point of view and in his constructed reality. In any social-research situation, there are bound to be several positions and roles, each generating a perspective. What the reality of the social unit is depends on the totality of these different perspectives. Thus, by investigating the multiple points of view generated in a social milieu, the researcher comes to form a relatively complete picture of the phenomenon.

No exercises are provided to accompany this section of the book. Rather, these two readings should be taken as a point of departure for an attitude toward research. In later exercises, using either single or multiple methods, the reader should keep in mind that a useful perspective for him, the researcher, is one that leads beyond superficial appearances or one-sided opinions and viewpoints.

2. Words Versus Deeds

WORDS AND DEEDS:
SOCIAL SCIENCE
AND SOCIAL POLICY
—Irwin Deutscher

THE SOCIETY FOR THE STUDY
of Social Problems was established by and continues to
attract sociologists with a dual
commitment. We seek, on the
one hand, to achieve a better understanding of the problems society
creates for some of the people within it and, on the other, more
effective application of socially relevant knowledge to the solution
of those problems. Ultimately most of us are concerned with finding ways to alter this world in such a manner that more people
may find it a better place in which to live. Our orientation leads us
to search for effective alterations of the society rather than effective adjustments of individuals to the society. We tend, therefore,
to shun efforts to improve treatment of individuals who reflect
symptomatically the malfunctionings of the society—whether they
be defined as sick, deviant, pathological, nonconformists, outsiders,
or whatever. Since our focus is upon the society rather than the
individual, whatever changes we have to recommend, whatever
advice and criticism we have to offer, must be directed toward
those who make or influence policy in our society.

My point of departure is the basic research, the evaluative
studies, and the demonstration projects which are the "scientific"
materials from which social scientists generally derive their recom-

From *Social Problems*, Vol. 13, No. 3 (1966), pp. 233–54. Reprinted by permission of the author and The Society for the Study of Social Problems.

mendations to policy makers. Our scientific conclusions, for the most part, are based on analyses of verbal responses to questions put by an interviewer. Those responses may be written or oral and the questions may range from forced choice to open ended, but the fact remains that what we obtain from such methods are state ments of attitude, opinion, norms, values, anticipation, or recall. The policy maker is interested in none of these things; as a man of action, he is interested in overt *behavior*. Although we rarely study such behavior, we do insist that the object of our discipline is to understand and even to predict it. Therefore, to oblige the policy maker, as well as ourselves, the assumption must be made that verbal responses reflect behavioral tendencies.

In his definitive volume on interviewing, Hyman (1954:17–8) makes this assumption explicit: "If one could wait around indefi- nitely," he writes, "the natural environment would ultimately lib- erate behavior relevant to a given inference. However, practical limitations preclude such lengthy procedures. As Vernon puts it (1938): 'Words are actions in miniature. Hence by the use of questions and answers we can obtain information about a vast number of actions in a short space of time, the actual observation and measurement of which would be impracticable.' " This inferen- tial jump from verbal behavior to overt behavior appears to be tenuous under some conditions.

Acting out a relationship is not necessarily the same as talking about a relationship. We have known this for a long time and we have known why for a long time, but we proceed as if we did not know. With the advantage of hindsight, I intend to suggest that we began to make incorrect choices in the early 1930's, and once having begun, managed easily to build error upon error. Although we have frequently proceeded with rigor and precision, we have, nevertheless, been on an erratic course. In restrospect, we may well have had a thirty-year moratorium in social science.

THE LAPIERE EXPERIMENT

Symbolizing the period during which we had the choice to make is a classic experiment designed by Richard LaPiere and reported in 1934. LaPiere's quest for answers to a haunting methodological problem can be traced through a trilogy of his papers, the last of which is "Attitudes vs. Actions." If such quests can be thought of as being initiated at a specific point in time, LaPiere's probably began while he was attending a seminar with Malinowski at the London School in 1927. During the course of that seminar, the term "verbalization" was employed to indicate a distinction between what informants may say and what may be the actual custom of the primitive society. LaPiere (1928) was formulating a comparative survey of race prejudice in France and England. Interested in the concept of "verbalization," he attempted to check his questionnaire findings against actual practices. This he accomplished by questioning hotel proprietors about their policy. The results left LaPiere satisfied at the time that he had found a fair concordance between verbal responses and nonverbal responses and, consequently, that his survey results were sufficiently valid.

Upon his return to the United States, LaPiere undertook a study of an Armenian community (1936), as a result of which he writes, "I began again to doubt the certain value of verbal evidence." Perhaps as a result of this doubt, LaPiere (1934:231) reconsidered the evidence from his French study and realized that "at that time I overlooked the fact that what I was obtaining from the hotel proprietors was still a 'verbalized' reaction to a symbolic situation." He had not compared verbal and nonverbal behavior. What he had done was to compare attitudes with self-reports of behavior. His concern resulted in the carefully designed and controlled experiment which consumed two years in the field and over 10,000 miles of driving and culminated in the publication of "Attitudes vs. Actions."

Traveling with a Chinese couple, twice across country and up and down the West Coast, the investigator recorded the treatment they received in hotels, auto camps, tourist homes, and restaurants. Of the 251 establishments approached in this manner, one auto camp refused to accommodate them. Here then was an estimate of Caucasian-Oriental integroup behavior.

Allowing a time-lapse of six months after being served by an establishment, a questionnaire was sent to each. Half of them were asked only, "Would you accept members of the Chinese race as guests in your establishment?" The other half were asked additional questions about other ethnic groups. Only one "yes" response was received—this from a lady who reminisced about the nice Chinese couple she had put up six months earlier. Here then was an estimate of Caucasian attitudes toward Orientals.

Most important is the juxtapositioning of these two estimates.

We have, then, in 1934, strong empirical evidence, not only that there may be no relationship between what people say and what they do, but that under some conditions there may be a high inverse relationship between the two.

LaPiere's conclusions are primarily theoretical and methodological. With scientific caution he restricts *empirical* conclusions to the empirical data and warns against careless generalization. He reminds us that the conventional questionnaire is a valuable tool for identifying such phenomena as political or religious *beliefs* (1934:235). But, he continues, "if we would know the extent to which [his belief] restrains his behavior, it is to his behavior that we must look, not to his questionnaire response:

> Sitting at my desk in California I can predict with a high degree of certainty what an "average" businessman in an average Mid-Western city will reply to the question, Would you engage in sexual intercourse with a prostitute in a Paris brothel? Yet no one, least of all the man himself, can predict what he would actually do should he by some misfortune find himself face-to-face with the situation in question [1934:235–36].

In LaPiere's work we find a line of continuity leading toward new theoretical insights into human behavior, new methods for attaining knowledge, and new kinds of evidence which could be used with confidence by policy makers bent on reducing some of the problems of the contemporary world. But that line of continuity has hardly extended beyond the publication of "Attitudes vs. Actions" in March, 1934. . . . For the most part social science proceeded in other directions.

LaPiere contends that no one has ever challenged his argument that what men say and what they do are not always in concordance. "On the other hand," he writes, "it seems to have had no effect at all on the sociological faith in the value of data gathered via opinion, attitude, and other kinds of questionnaires. The 'Attitude vs. Action' paper was," he continues, "cited for years by almost everyone who wrote on attitudes or opinions as a sort of caution not to take their data too seriously; whereupon each author promptly ignored the caution and proceeded to assume that his data was indicative of what people would actually do in real-life circumstances."

LaPiere was certainly not alone; there were other voices crying in the wilderness. In the late thirties some of the best young minds in American sociology were clearly concerned with the problem. Reading a paper at the 1938 meetings of the American Sociological Society, Robert K. Merton was critical of his own recently acquired survey data on attitudes toward Negroes. He wondered if it wasn't possible that Northerners treat Negroes less favorably than they talk about them and that Southerners talk about Negroes less favorably than they treat them. He asks, "May we assume the amount and direction of spread between opinion and action to be relatively constant for members of different groups? To my knowledge," Merton (1940:21–22) continues, "no systematic research on this problem has been carried out."

At about the same time, C. Wright Mills (1940) argued, "Perhaps the central methodological problem of the social sciences springs from recognition that often there is a disparity between lingual and social-motor types of behavior." Mills suggested that we need to know *"how much and in what direction* disparities between talk and action will probably go."

Herbert Blumer has been the most consistent spokesman for the point of view suggested by LaPiere's data. For the past thirty-five years in at least a half-dozen articles, Blumer has argued the logic of this position, in terms of theory (1954, 1940, 1931), in terms of method (1956), and in terms of substantive fields such as Industrial Relations (1947) and Public Opinion Polling (1948). In his presidential address to the American Sociological Society in 1956, Blumer suggests that, not only do we know nothing about behavior or the relation between attitudes and behavior, but we don't know much about attitudes either: "The thousands of 'variable' studies of attitudes, for instance, have not contributed to our knowledge of the abstract nature of an attitude; in a similar way the studies of 'social cohesion,' 'social integration,' 'authority,' or 'group morale' have done nothing so far as I can detect, to clarify or augment generic knowledge of these categories." Yet, in the closing lines of his address, after thirty-five years of persistence, Blumer acknowledges defeat with the wistful hope that people at least know what they are doing. He concludes, "In view, however, of the current tendency of variable analysis to become the norm and model for sociological analysis, I believe it important to recognize its shortcomings and its limitations."

Why have both the empirical evidence and the theoretical

rationale been ignored? There is adequate reason to suspect that behavior toward words about social or cultural objects (i.e., responses to questions) may not provide an adequate basis for imputing behavior toward the objects themselves (i.e., responses to the people or situations to which the words refer). Three decades ago LaPiere's explanation was couched in terms of economy and reliability: "The questionnaire," he observed, "is cheap, easy, and mechanical. The study of human behavior is time consuming, intellectually fatiguing, and depends for its success upon the ability of the investigator. The former method gives quantitative results, the latter mainly qualitative. Quantitative measurements are quantitatively accurate; qualitative evaluations are always subject to the errors of human judgment. Yet," he concludes, "it would seem far more worthwhile to make a shrewd guess regarding that which is essential than to accurately measure that which is likely to prove quite irrelevant" (1934:237).

Others, like Mills, have assumed a more cynical explanation. Turning to the sources of research finance, he suggests that: "Many foundation administrators like to give money for projects that are thought to be safe from political or public attack, that are large-scale, hence easier 'to administer' than more numerous handicraft projects, and that are scientific with a capital S, which often only means made 'safe' by trivialization. Accordingly," Mills (1954) concludes, "the big money tends to encourage the large-scale bureaucratic style of research into small-scale problems as carried on by The Scientists."

These explanations have persisted and most of them remain as valid today as they were in the past, but I suspect that they reflect a deeper and perhaps more basic problem. It is possible that the apparent anomaly of acknowledging the correctness of one position while pursuing another can best be explained in terms of the sociology of knowledge.

EPISTEMOLOGY AND RESEARCH METHODS

It has been suggested that the sociology of knowledge "is devoted to digging up the social roots of knowledge, to searching out the ways in which knowledge and thought are affected by the environing social structure" (Merton, 1957:440). We may indeed have some roots to dig in our attempt to understand the directions taken by American sociology during the last three or four decades. The perceptions of knowledge—notions of the proper or appropriate ways of knowing—which were fashionable during the late twenties and early thirties, when sociology had its choices to make, surely impinged upon those choices.

Men like LaPiere, Blumer, and, later, Mills were arguing from a basically anti-positivistic position at a time when a century or more of cumulative positivistic science was resulting in a massive payoff in our knowledge and control of physical forces. And sociology had its alternatives. L. L. Thurstone was giving birth to what was to become modern scaling. Emery Bogardus was translating some of these ideas into sociological scales of contemporary relevance. And the intellectual brilliance of men like George Lundberg and Stuart Chapin was creating the theoretical and methodological rationale for the new "science." Incisive critiques of the new sociology and the logic of its quantitative methods were plentiful (cf. Merton, 1940; Cohen and Nagel, 1934: Ch. 15; Johnson, 1936; Kirkpatrick, 1936), but if we listen to Richard LaPiere's recollections of the temper of the times it becomes apparent that logic may not have been the deciding factor:

> What you may not know, or at least not fully appreciate, is that well into the 1930's the status of sociology and hence of sociologists was abominable, both within and outside the academic community. The public image of the sociologist was of a blue-nosed reformer, ever ready to pronounce moral judgments, and against all pleasurable forms of social conduct. In the universities, sociology was generally thought of as an uneasy mixture of social philosophy and social work. . . . Through the 1920's the department at Chicago was the real center of sociology in the United States [but] . . . the men who were to shape sociology during the 1930's were, for the most part, products of one- or two-men departments (e.g., Columbia) of low status within their universities; they were, therefore, to a considerable degree self-trained and without a doctrinaire viewpoint, and they were exceedingly conscious of the low esteem in which sociology was held. Such men, and I was one among them, were determined to prove—at least to themselves—that sociology is a science, that sociologists are not moralists, and that sociology deserves recognition and support comparable to that being given psychology and economics. It was, I think, to this end that toward the end of the '20's, scientific sociology came to be identified with quantitative methods

... and by the mid-thirties American sociologists were split into two antagonistic camps—the moralists . . . and the scientists. . . . Now as to my own uncertain part in all this. I was one of the Young Turks, and I shared with Lundberg, Bain, Stouffer, etc., the distaste for sociology as it had been and the hurt of its lowly status. But unlike the majority of the rebels, I did not share their belief that the cure for bad sociology was quantification [although] I did set off in that direction.

LaPiere sees the history of American sociology between the two world wars as an effort, not to build knowledge, but to achieve respectability and acceptability. In terms of this goal we have been successful. "For it has in considerable measure been sociological reliance on quantitative methods that has won for sociology the repute and financial support that it now enjoys. That in gaining fame, sociology may have become a pseudo-science is another, and quite different, matter. Now that sociology is well-established, it may be possible for a new generation of young Turks to evaluate the means through which sociology has won respectability."

With the security of respectability perhaps now we can afford to take a more critical look at alternatives which were neglected at other times for reasons which are no longer cogent. Perhaps now we can begin again to achieve some understanding of the tenuous relationships between men's thoughts and their actions. One strategic point of departure for such a re-evaluation is an examination of some of the consequences of the choices we have made. In attempting to assume the stance of physical science, we have necessarily assumed its epistemology—its assumptions about the nature of knowledge and the appropriate means of knowing, including the rules of scientific evidence. The requirement of clean empirical demonstration of the effects of isolated factors or variables, in a manner which can be replicated, led us to create, by definition, such factors or variables. We knew that human behavior was rarely if ever directly influenced or explained by an isolated variable; we knew that it was impossible to assume that any set of such variables was additive (with or without weighting); we knew that the complex mathematics of the interaction among any set of variables, much less their interaction with external variables, was incomprehensible to us. In effect, although we knew they did not exist, we defined them into being.

But it was not enough just to create sets of variables. They had to be stripped of what little meaning they had in order that they might be operational, i.e., that they have their measurement built into their definition. One consequence, then, was to break down human behavior in a way that was not only artificial but which did not jibe with the manner in which that behavior was observed.

Having laid these foundations and because the accretion of knowledge is a cumulative affair, we began to construct layer upon layer. For example, in three decades we "advanced" from Bogardus to Guttman (1959). Merton (1951) suggests that the cumulative nature of science requires a high degree of consensus among scientists and leads, therefore, to an inevitable enchantment with problems of reliability. He is wrong in his equation of scientific method with maximum concern for problems of reliability: *all* knowledge, whether scientific or not, is cumulative and all men who think or write stand on the shoulders of those who have thought or have written before. It does, nevertheless, appear that the adoption of the scientific model in the social sciences has resulted in an uncommon concern for methodological problems centering on issues of reliability and to the concomitant neglect of problems of validity.

We have been absorbed in measuring the amounts of error which results from inconsistency among interviewers or inconsistency among items on our instruments. We concentrate on consistency without much concern with what it is we are being consistent about or whether we are consistently right or wrong. As a consequence we may have been learning a great deal about how to pursue an incorrect course with a maximum of precision.

It is not my intent to disparage the importance of reliability per *se*; it is the obsession with it to which I refer. Certainly zero reliability must result in zero validity. But the relationship is not linear, since infinite perfection of reliability (zero error) may also be associated with zero validity. Whether or not one wishes to emulate the scientist and whatever methods may be applied to the quest for knowledge, we must make estimates of, allowances for, and attempts to reduce the extent to which our methods distort our findings.

This is precisely why C. Wright Mills identifies the "disparities between talk and action" as "the central *methodological* problem of the social sciences" (1940; italics added). Mills's plea for systematic investigations into the differences between words and deeds is based on the need for the "methodologist to build into his methods standard margins of error"—to learn how to appropriately discount variously located sources of data. Just as Mills is concerned about reliability in the historical method, Hyman (1954) has documented the need for estimates of reliability in social anthropological and clinical psychiatric observations. He reminds us, for example, that the village of Tepoztlan as described by Lewis is quite different from the same village as it was described earlier by Robert Redfield. Hyman cites Kluckhohn's lament (1945) that "the limited extent to which ethnologists have been articulate about their field techniques is astonishing to scholars in other disciplines."

One of the few positive consequences of our decades of "scientific" orientation is the incorporation into the sociological mentality of a self-consciousness about methods—regardless of what methods are employed. As a result, those few sociologists who bring ethnological field techniques to bear on their problems are constrained to contemplate methodological issues and to publish methodological observations. I have in mind, specifically, the continuing series of articles by Howard S. Becker and Blanche Geer (e.g., Becker and Geer, 1957; Becker, 1958; Becker and Geer, 1960; Geer, 1964). Regardless of the importance of reliability, there remains a danger that in our obsession with it, the goals—the purposes for which we seek knowledge—and the phenomena about which we seek knowledge, may become obscured.

One of the more regretful consequences of our neglect of the relationship between words and deeds has been the development of a technology which is inappropriate to the understanding of human behavior, and conversely, the almost complete absence of a technology which can facilitate our learning about the conditions under which people in various categories do or do not "put their monies where their mouths are." We still do not know much about the relationship between what people say and what they do —attitudes and behavior, sentiments and acts, verbalizations and interactions, words and deeds. *We know so little that I can't even find an adequate vocabulary to make the distinction!*

Under what conditions will people behave as they talk? Under what conditions is there no relationship? And under what conditions do they say one thing and behave exactly the opposite? In spite of the fact that all of these combinations have been empirically observed and reported few efforts have been made to order such observations. Furthermore, and perhaps of even greater importance, we do not know under what conditions a change in attitude anticipates a change in behavior or under what conditions a change in behavior anticipates a change in attitude. Again, both phenomena have been empirically observed and recorded.

It is important that my comments not be misunderstood as a plea for the simple study of simple behavioral items. This would be a duplication of the same kinds of mistakes we have made in the simple study of simple attitudinal items. Overt action can be understood and interpreted only within the context of its meaning to the actors, just as verbal reports can be understood and interpreted only within the context of their meaning to the respondents. And in large part, the context of each is the other. But the fact remains that one of the methodological consequences of our recent history is that we have not developed a technology for observing, ordering, analyzing, and interpreting *overt behavior*— especially as it relates to attitudes, norms, opinions, and values.

The development of a new technology could take any of a number of directions. Ideally, we should seek to refine the model provided by LaPiere, whereby we obtain information from the same population on verbal behavior and interaction behavior under natural social conditions. Surely, the kind of cleverness which creates situational apparati for the psychological laboratory could also create refined situational designs for research under conditions which have meaning for the actors. The theoretical and methodological rationalization of participant-observer field techniques, begun by Becker and Geer, is a promising alternative. There may be as yet untapped possibilities in contrived laboratory experiments —if we can learn how to contrive them in such a way that their results are not denuded of any general meaning by the artificial specificity of the situations. If someday reliable and valid projective instruments are developed, we may have made a significant technological step forward. There is considerable developmental work under way at present on instruments which facilitate self-reporting of overt behavior and allow comparisons to be made between attitudes and behavior on the same people, although still on a verbal level (Hardt and Bodine, 1964).

There was a time earlier in this century when we had a choice to make, a choice on the one hand of undertaking neat, orderly studies of measurable phenomena. This alternative carried with it all of the gratifications of conforming to the prestigious methods of pursuing knowledge then in vogue, of having access to considerable sums of monies through the granting procedures of large foundations and governmental agencies, of a comfortable sense of satisfaction derived from dealing rigorously and precisely with small isolated problems which were cleanly defined, of moving for thirty years down one track in an increasingly rigorous, refined, and reliable manner, while simultaneously disposing of the problems of validity by the semantic trickery of operational definitions. On the other hand, we could have tackled the messy world as we knew it to exist, a world where the same people will make different utterances under different conditions and will behave differently in different situations and will say one thing while doing another. We could have tackled a world where control of relevant variables was impossible not only because we didn't know what they were but because we didn't know how they interacted with each other. We could have accepted the conclusion of almost every variant of contemporary philosophy of science, that the notion of cause and effect (and therefore of stimulus and response or of independent and dependent variables) is untenable. We eschewed this formidable challenge. This was the hard way. We chose the easy way.

Yet the easy way provides one set of results and the hard way provides another. The easy way for LaPiere in 1934 would have been to conduct as rigorous as possible a survey of attitudes of hotel and restaurant managers toward Orientals. But this leads to a set of conclusions which are the opposite of what he finds when he does it the hard way, i.e., traveling thousands of miles in order to confront those managers with Orientals. One of our graduate students (Hanson, 1965), after reviewing some of the literature on the relationship between attitudes and overt behavior, concluded that laboratory experimental studies such as those by Scott (1957, 1959), King and Janis (1956), and DeFleur and Westie (1958) tend to show a positive correlation between attitude and behavior, while observational field studies such as those by LaPiere, Kutner, Wilkins, and Yarrow (1952) and Saenger and Gilbert (1950) tend to show no such correlation. Although there are important exceptions to this rule, it serves as a reminder that our choice of methods may not be unrelated to our conclusions.

EMPIRICAL EVIDENCE AND THEORETICAL SUPPORT

Why do I fuss so, largely on the basis of a primitive field study on a Chinese couple done over thirty years ago and the stubborn polemics of a Herbert Blumer? Frankly, that would be sufficient to cause me considerable concern! But there is other empirical evidence as well as a variety of theoretical support for the argument that more attention needs to be directed toward the relationship between what men say and what they do.

There is reason to believe that this problem transcends American attitudes toward Chinese tourists thirty years ago. There is evidence that interracial attitudes and behavior are not identical in Brazil (Bastide and van den Berghe, 1957), that sentiments about Negroes in northern American communities do not coincide with behavior toward Negroes in those communities (Brookover and Holland, 1952), that interracial attitudes and behavior between customers and department store clerks are inconsistent, and that divergences between interracial attitudes and behaviors persist in 1965 as they did in 1934 (Linn, 1965).

Perhaps of even greater importance are the bits of empirical evidence that this discrepancy between what people say and what they do is not limited to the area of racial or ethnic relations: it has been observed that trade union members talk one game and play another (Dean, 1958), that there is no relationship between college students' attitudes toward cheating and their actual cheating behavior (Freeman and Ataov, 1960), that urban teachers' descriptions of classroom behavior are sometimes unrelated to the way teachers behave in the classroom (Henry, 1959), that what rural Missourians say about their health behavior has little connection with their actual health practices (Hassinger and McNamara, 1957), and that the moral and ethical beliefs of students do not conform to their behavior (Putney and Middleton, 1962a, 1962b).

It has also been reported that Kansans who vote for prohibition maintain and use well-equipped bars in their homes (Warriner, 1958), that small-time steel wholesalers mouth patriotism while undercutting the national economy in wartime (Kriesberg, 1956), that employers' attitudes toward hiring the handicapped are not reflected in their hiring practices (Schletzer et al., 1961), and that the behavior of mothers toward their children is unrelated to their attitudes toward them (Zunich, 1962). If it were possible to observe bedroom behavior, I wonder what would be the relationship between Kinsey's survey results and such observations? I don't know, nor does anyone else, but a contemporary novelist has a confused fictional respondent muse about a sex survey, "But what do they expect of me? Do they want to know how I feel or how I act?" (Wallace, 1961).

Students of aging suspect that what older people have to say about retirement has little relationship to their life during that stage of the life cycle (Breen, 1963; Henry and Cumming, 1961) A pair of industrial psychologists, interested in assessing the current state of knowledge regarding the relationship between employee attitudes and employee performance, covered all of the literature in that area through 1954 (Brayfield and Crockett, 1955). Treating various classes of studies separately, they find in every category "minimal or no relationship between employee attitudes and performance."

It would be a serious selective distortion of the existing evidence to suggest that all of it indicates an incongruence between what people say and what they do. Consumers sometimes do change their buying habits in ways that they say they will (Martin, 1963), people frequently do vote as they tell pollsters they will, urban relocation populations may accurately predict to interviewers the type of housing they will obtain (Deutscher and Cagle, 1964), local party politicians do in fact employ the campaign tactics which they believe to be most effective (Frost, 1961), and youngsters will provide survey researchers with reports of their own contact or lack of contact with the police which are borne out by police records.

The empirical evidence can best be summarized as reflecting wide variation in the relationships between attitudes and behaviors. As a result of their review all of the studies on employee attitudes and performance, Brayfield and Crockett (1955) observe, "The scarcity of relationships, either positive or negative, demonstrated to date even among the best designed of the available studies leads us to question whether or not methodological changes alone would lead to a substantial increase in the magnitude of the obtained relationships." Having arrived at the point where they are able to question the assumption that a relationship must obtain between what people say and what they do, these authors can now question whether or not the failure to observe such a relationship is necessarily a consequence of the inefficiency of the measuring instruments. This is an important breakthrough, since it permits them, and us, to look at alternative explanations—especially at conceptual considerations.

A cursory review of the conceptual frameworks within which most of us work suggests that *no matter what one's theoretical orientation may be, he has no reason to expect to find congruence between attitudes and actions and every reason to expect to find discrepancies between them.* The popular varieties of balance theory in current social science, such as functionalism in sociology and anthropology and cognitive dissonance in psychology, posit a drive or strain toward consistency. This image of man and society must carry with it the assumption that at any given point in time a condition of imbalance or dissonance or inconsistency obtains.

The psychoanalytic concepts of the unconscious and the subconscious assume that people cannot themselves know how they might behave under specified conditions and such mechanisms as repression suggest that they may not be able to tell an interviewer how they have behaved in the past. Such dissimilar sociological ancestors as Charles H. Cooley and Emile Durkheim built their conceptions of man in society around the assumption that human nature is such that it requires the constraints of society. Under such conditions there is an inherent conflict between man's private self and his social self and the area of role theory is developed to help us understand some of the mechanisms by which man is constrained to act as he "ought."

On the gross societal level, such concepts as social disorganization and cultural lag suggest that people can be caught up in discrepant little worlds which make conflicting demands upon them. The immigrant to a new world has been described as assuming new forms of behavior while clinging to older attitudes and beliefs. In the developing countries of Africa, the idea of cultural lag leads us to expect that the rapid acceptance of new behaviors may outrun, at least for a while, the rejection of old norms. Or perhaps behavioral changes may not be able to keep pace with the rapid acceptance of new norms. Either way, the outcome must be inconsistent attitudes and behaviors!

When we consider the behavior of individuals in groups smaller than societies, we frequently think in such terms as situational contingencies, the definition of the situation, public and private behavior, or reference-group theory—all of which relate what one does or what one says to the immediate context, both as it exists objectively and as it exists in the mind of the actor. Do we not expect attitudes and behaviors to vary as the definition of the situation is altered or as different reference groups are brought to bear?

The symbolic interactionists have traditionally exhibited the greatest sensitivity to this problem in sociology. Among others, both Blumer and LaPiere have insisted that we act, either verbally or overtly, in response to the symbolic meaning the confronting object has for us in the given situation. A question put to me by an interviewer concerning how I feel about Armenian women forces me to respond to the words and to the interviewer; standing face-to-face with a real flesh and blood Armenian woman, I find myself constrained to act toward a very different set of symbols. Is there any reason to assume that my behavior should be the same in these two radically different symbolic situations? Arnold Rose (1956) has developed a vigorous symbolic interactionist argument regarding the theoretical independence of attitudes and behaviors.

One conceptual framework which we tend to neglect lies in the undeveloped field of *sociolinguistics*. Although it may be many other things, sociolinguistics should also deal with an analysis of the meanings of verbal communications. It provides an untapped potential for understanding the relation between what people say and what they do. What differences in meaning can be conveyed by different people with the same words? The eloquent teen-age Negro prostitute, Kitten, can find herself involved in a $100 misunderstanding only because she thinks she is listening to someone who speaks the same language (Gover, 1963). The truth of the matter is that, unfortunately, she and her Babbitt-like college sophomore protagonist employ the same vocabulary to speak different languages. Might this not also occur occasionally between interviewer and interviewee? What is the relationship between language and thought and between language and action? Should we assume that a response of "yah," "da," "si," "oui," or "yes" all really mean exactly the same thing in response to the same question? Or may there not be different kinds of affirmative connotations in different languages? And, of course, can we assume that the question itself means the same thing simply because it translates accurately?

We have a great deal to learn from comparative linguistics if we can bring ourselves to view language from the perspective of the symbolic interactionist—as social and cultural symbolism—rather than from the perspective of those psycholinguists who reduce language to mathematical symbols and thus effectively denude it of its socio-cultural context. I would suggest that it is impossible to translate any word in any language to any word in any other language. Words are fragments of linguistic configurations; they mean nothing in isolation from the configuration. The basic linguistic problems of cross-cultural and cross-class survey research have hardly been recognized, much less dealt with.

Let me suggest that, as an intellectual exercise, you take whatever other conceptual frameworks you may be partial to or comfortable with and determine whether or not they permit you to assume that you can expect people to act in accordance with their words. Meanwhile, I will return to Brayfield and Crockett (1955), who helped me earlier with the transition from method to theory: "Foremost among [the] implications," of their review of research, "is the conclusion that it is time to question the strategic and ethical merits of selling to industrial concerns an assumed relationship between employee attitudes and employee performance." It is but a slight extension of this conclusion to question the strategic and ethical merits of selling anything to anyone or to any establishment based on the dubious assumption that what people say is related directly to what they do.

Social Research and Social Policy

If I appear to have belabored some obvious points, it is because it is necessary to build as strong a backdrop as possible to the implications of all of this for the role of social science research in policy recommendations. Research aimed at demonstration and evaluation tends to make precisely the assumption which I have been challenging: the notion that what people *say* is a predictor of what they will *do*.

Thus far, I have tried to restrict my attention to the relatively simple question of the relations between attitudes and behaviors —simple as compared to the issues raised when we turn to the relationship between attitudinal and behavioral changes. If we are to be relevant to social policy, then we must consider this more complex question. Can we assume that if we are attempting to alter behavior through a training program, an educational campaign, or some sort of information intervention, a measured change in attitude in the "right" direction results in a change in behavior?

Leon Festinger (1964:405), encountering a statement in an unpublished manuscript, reports that he was "slightly skeptical about the assertion that there is a dearth of studies relating attitude or opinion change to behavior." Although no examples occurred to him, he was certain that there must be many such studies. "After prolonged search," he writes, "with the help of many others, I succeeded in locating only three relevant studies, one of which is of dubious relevance and one of which required reanalysis of data. The absence of research and of theoretical thinking, about the effect of attitude change on subsequent behavior is," Festinger concludes, "indeed astonishing."

The three relevant studies all involve study and control populations and pre- and post-tests of attitude. Some form of persuasive communication was injected into the study groups and either self-reports or behavioral observations are obtained. The studies deal with attitudes of mothers of infants toward the age at which toilet training should begin; the training of industrial foremen in human relations; and attitudes of high school students toward proper dental care. *In all three cases the process of persuasive communication resulted in a significant change of attitude in the desired direction. In all three cases there is no evidence of a change in behavior in the desired direction.* To the contrary, Festinger (1964:416) concedes that he has not "grappled with the perplexing question raised by the persistent hint of a slightly inverse relationship," and he confesses his inability to explain the possibility of such a reversal.

It seems to me that we have sufficient grounds to reject any evaluation of an action program which employs attitudinal change as a criterion of "success," except in the unlikely event that the goal of the program is solely to change attitudes without concern for subsequent behavioral changes. And even under these conditions, the validity of our attitudinal measurements can be seriously challenged. For example, Ehrlich and Rinehart (1965) recently reported the results of their analysis of a stereotype-measuring instrument which has been used in identical or slightly modified form in dozens of studies since 1933. They observe that the results achieved in these studies have all been roughly consistent and then proceed to demonstrate that these reliable results are of doubtful validity. In effect, we have achieved over thirty years' worth of cumulative, consistent, and misleading information about prejudice.

If we do not know enough about the behavioral consequences of attitude change to make policy recommendations with confidence in their validity, what do we know about the attitudinal consequences of behavioral change? There is some evidence in the American Soldier studies that the integration of army units may lead to more favorable attitudes toward Negroes on the part of the integrated white soldiers (Stouffer et al., 1949). Integrated public housing projects are reported to increase friendly contacts between races and to reduce stereotyping and prejudice among the white occupants (Deutsch and Collins, 1956; Wilner et al., 1952). In Yarrow's report (1958) of a controlled experiment in a children's camp, the experimental (desegregated) cabins did produce a significant reduction in prejudice as measured by pre- and post-sociometric interviews. But another study in an integrated camp concludes that four weeks of intimate contact on the part of the children produced no change in attitude (Mussen, 1950). Similarly, Bettelheim and Janowitz (1964) found in their study of veterans that intimate contact with members of the minority group does not seem to disintegrate prejudices.

These bits of evidence concerning the attitudinal consequences of behavioral change are all limited to the specific case of coercively integrated residential enclaves, i.e., army units, public housing projects, and children's camps. Although it has been reported that interracial occupational contacts may also result in changed attitudes, the evidence is limited. The invasion-succession process which occurs when people are not coerced in their residential arrangements suggests that, by and large, they prefer flight (avoidance) to attitudinal change. Furthermore, there is some evidence that even when attitudinal changes appear to have occurred in one area, such as the work situation or the housing situation, they are not necessarily generalized to other interactional areas (Lohman and Reitzes, 1954; Rose, 1961; Minard, 1952).

Aside from the case of interracial attitudes and behaviors, there are an infinite number of situations where attitudinal consequences of behavioral change can be studied. In a country such as Britain, where employers are coerced by law under certain conditions to employ handicapped workers, do their attitudes toward such workers change? If a group of Jaycees can be induced to undertake work with delinquent boys, does the experience alter their attitude toward such boys? Does a relatively indifferent adolescent drafted and shipped to Viet Nam consequently develop hostile attitudes toward the Viet Cong?

There can, of course, be no simple "yes" or "no" answer to such simple questions. To polarize attention upon two variables labeled "attitude" and "behavior" and to operationally define them so that we can measure their relationship is to continue down the same track. It is what goes on in between—the process—toward which we must direct our attention. We need to ask what intervenes between the change in behavior and the change in attitude. Such questions need to be reformulated and qualified so that we ask "under what conditions do what kinds of people change their attitudes as a consequence of induced behavior?" We need to recognize that change probably occurs in both directions—from thought to act and from act to thought—sometimes separately, sometimes simultaneously, and sometimes sequentially.

Taking such a balanced position, Bettelheim and Janowitz (1964) reject on theoretical grounds "the view that social practice must invariably precede attitude or personality changes." They argue, "It is a serious oversimplification to assume that changes in overt behavior necessarily bring about desired changes toward increased tolerance," and that "attitude changes often anticipate overt political and social behavior. Thus," they conclude, "it becomes necessary to assess the policy implications of our research on both the levels of social and personal controls."

It would seem that, in spite of our facile use of such concepts as socialization, internalization, re-enforcement—all of which imply attitudinal development as a consequence of behavioral experience—we cannot blandly suggest to the policy maker that if he changes behavior, a change in attitude will follow. Nor can we lead him to assume that if he can alter attitudes, he need only wait patiently for the appropriate behavior to develop.

In view of the arguments and evidence reviewed, I should allude to the possibility that changes in policy are not necessarily related to subsequent changes in behavior. It follows that the process of influencing policy makers may at times have negligible impact on the resolution of social problems. Nevertheless, I am concerned with the consequences of doling out to policy makers wrong advice, based on bad research and justified in the name of science. How many good programs are halted and bad ones continued because of "scientific" evaluations? There are increasing demands being made upon social science. There are expectations that we can be helpful—and we ought to be. We do not know the current extent of our influence or its future limits. No doubt it will increase. It may be that as consultants or advisors or sources of information we are used by policy makers only when our knowledge is expedient to bolster positions they have already arrived at for other reasons. But the fact remains that we are used.

We are all aware of the psychological, sociological, and anthropological documentation of the Supreme Court's historic decisions on segregated education in 1954. We know of the intimate involvement of sociologists as architects of President Kennedy's Committee on Juvenile Delinquency and Youth Crime. We realize the multiple influences of social scientists on President Johnson's "War on Poverty." And our role in local school systems, urban renewal and relocation programs, social agency programs, hospitals, and prisons is probably more pervasive than anyone—including ourselves—realizes.

There are new terms in the language we use to describe ourselves and we ought to be self-conscious about their implications. To what new phenomenon are we referring when we invent the phrase "behavioral science"—and why? What are the implications of beginning to refer to selected disciplines as the "policy sciences"? Why is a new magazine launched in 1965 which is described as concerning itself with "problems of public policy especially," on the grounds "that the social sciences (particularly economics, politics and sociology) have become inextricably linked to issues of public policy?"

The myth of a value-free social science was exploded with finality by Alvin Gouldner (1962). To make such a pretext reflects either hypocrisy or self-delusion. As social scientists, we have responsibility for encouraging and working for social change. The theme of these meetings is based in part upon that assumption and upon the consequent requirement we place upon ourselves to ask, "change for what and why?" The sacred political documents of the United States refer repeatedly to certain kinds of equality and freedoms from constraints in our kind of democracy. There is a discrepancy between the words which most of us honor and the deeds which we all observe. I have no reluctance—in fact, feel an obligation—to bring about a maximum congruence between the word and the deed.

I think that, in large part, this is what the so-called current social revolution in the Untied States (and probably elsewhere) is all about. It is not a revolution in the sense of seeking to replace existing political and social values with new ones; it is the opposite—a conservative movement which demands that we live by old values. It is rebellion, if at all, only against an hypocrisy which claims that there are no inequitable social, political, educational, or economic barriers in our kind of democracy, while in fact there are. It is rebelling against an hypocrisy which claims that universities are establishments where highest values are placed upon teaching and learning, while in fact they are not.

Actually, it makes no difference whether we view the nature of man through the dark lenses of a Hume or a Hobbes—"beastly," with each warring against all others—or through the rose colored glasses of a Locke or Rousseau—as essentially "good" but corrupted by society. It makes no difference since either way man is constrained to behave in ways which are contrary to his supposed nature; either way, the dialect between man's private self and his social self must create occasional and sometimes radical inconsistencies between what he says and what he does; either way, inconsistency between attitudes and behavior may be assumed.

The dilemma of words and deeds is not peculiarly American, as Gunnar Myrdal would have it, nor is it peculiar to the race question. It is a universal condition of human nature. If our inability to recognize and contend with this condition between World War I and World War II was largely a consequence of the scientific temper of the times, perhaps one day it will be written that in the temper of the new times between World War II and World War III, sociology did flourish and come of age.

REFERENCES

BASTIDE, R., and P. L. VAN DEN BERGHE. 1957. "Stereotypes, Norms, and Interracial Behavior in São Paulo, Brazil," *American Sociological Review*, 22 (December), pp. 689–94.

BECKER, HOWARD S. 1958. "Problems of Inference and Proof in Participant Observation," *American Sociological Review*, 23 (December), pp. 652–60.

BECKER, HOWARD S., and BLANCHE GEER. 1957. "Participant Observation and Interviewing: A Comparison," *Human Organization*, 16 (Fall), pp. 28–32.

————. 1960. "Participant Observation: The Analysis of Qualitative Field Data." In R. N. Adams and J. L. Preiss (eds.), *Human Organization Research*. Homewood, Ill.: The Dorsey Press.

BETTELHEIM, BRUNO, and MORRIS JANOWITZ. 1964. *Social Change and Prejudice Including Dynamics of Prejudice*. New York: The Free Press of Glencoe.

BLUMER, HERBERT. 1931. "Science Without Concepts," *American Journal of Sociology*, 36 (May), pp. 515–33.

————. 1940. "The Problem of the Concept in Social Psychology," *American Journal of Sociology*, 45 (May), pp. 707–19.

————. 1947. "Sociological Theory in Industrial Relations," *American Sociological Review*, 12 (February), pp. 271–77.

————. 1948. "Public Opinion and Public Opinion Polling," *American Sociological Review*, 13 (March), pp. 542–49.

————. 1954." What Is Wrong with Social Theory," *American Sociological Review*, 19 (February), pp. 3–10.

————. 1956. "Sociological Analysis and the Variable," *American Sociological Review*, 21 (December).

————. 1966. "Sociological Implications of the Thought of George Herbert Mead," *American Journal of Sociology*, 71.

BRAYFIELD, A., and D. M. CROCKETT. 1956. "Employee Attitudes and Employee Performance," *Psychological Bulletin*, 52 (September), pp. 396–428.

BREEN, LEONARD Z. 1963. "Retirement: Norms, Behavior, and Functional Aspects of Normative Behavior. In R. H. Williams, C. Tibbetts, and W. Donahue (eds.), *Processes of Aging*. Vol. 2. New York: Atherton Press.

BROOKOVER, WILBUR B., and JOHN B. HOLLAND. 1952. "An Inquiry into the Meaning of Minority Group Attitude Expressions," *American Sociological Review*, 17 (April), pp. 196–202.

COHEN, MORRIS, and ERNEST NAGEL. 1934. *An Introduction to Logic and Scientific Method*. New York: Harcourt, Brace.

DEAN, LOIS. 1958. "Interaction, Reported and Observed: The Case of One Local Union," *Human Organization*, 17 (Fall).

DeFLEUR, MELVIN L., and FRANK R. WESTIE. 1958. "Verbal Attitudes and Overt Acts: An Experiment in the Salience of Attitudes," *American Sociological Review*, 23 (December), pp. 667–73.

DEUTSCH, MORTON, and MAY EVANS COLLINS. 1956. "Interracial Housing." In William Petersen (ed.), *American Social Patterns*. New York: Doubleday Anchor Books.

DEUTSCHER, IRWIN, and LAURENCE CAGLE. 1964. "Housing Aspirations of Low Income Fatherless Families." Syracuse, N.Y.: Syracuse University Youth Development Center. Mimeo.

EHRLICH, HOWARD J., and JAMES W. RINEHART. 1965. "A Brief Report on the Methodology of Stereotype Research," *Social Forces*, 43 (May).

FESTINGER, LEON. 1964. "Behavioral Support for Opinion Change," *Public Opinion Quarterly*, 28 (Fall).

FREEMAN, LINTON C., and TURKOZ ATAOV. 1960. "Invalidity of Indirect and Direct Measures Toward Cheating," *Journal of Personality*, 28 (December), pp. 443–47.

GEER, BLANCHE. 1964. "First Days in the Field." In P. E. Hammond (ed.), *Sociologists at Work*, pp. 322–44. New York: Basic Books.

GOULDNER, ALVIN. 1962. "Anti-Minotaur: The Myth of a Value-Free Sociology," *Social Problems*, 9 (Winter).

GOVER, ROBERT. 1963. *The One Hundred Dollar Misunderstanding*. New York: Ballantine Books.

GUTTMAN, LOUIS. 1959. "A Structural Theory for Intergroup Beliefs and Action," *American Sociological Review*, 24 (June), pp. 318–28.

HANSON, DAVID J. "Notes on a Bibliography on Attitudes and Behavior," unpublished manuscript.

HARDT, ROBERT H., and GEORGE E. BODINE. 1964. *Development of Self-Report Instruments in Delinquency Research*. Syracuse, N.Y.: Syracuse University Youth Development Center.

HASSINGER, EDWARD, and ROBERT L. McNAMARA. 1957. "Stated Opinion and Actual Practice in Health Behavior in a Rural Area," *The Midwest Sociologist* (May), pp. 93–97.

HENRY, JULES. 1959. "Spontaneity, Initiative, and Creativity in Suburban Classrooms," *American Journal of Orthopsychiatry*, 29, pp. 266–79.

HENRY, WILLIAM E., and ELAINE CUMMING. 1961. *Growing Old: The Process of Disengagement*. New York: Basic Books.

HYMAN, HERBERT, et al. 1954. *Interviewing in Social Research*. Chicago: University of Chicago Press.

JOHNSON, H. M. 1936. "Pseudo-Mathematics in the Mental and Social Sciences," *American Journal of Psychology*, 48, pp. 342–51.

KING, B. T., and I. L. JANIS. 1956. "Comparison of the Effectiveness of Improvised Versus Non-improvised Role-Playing in Producing Opinion Changes," *Human Relations*, 9, pp. 177–86.

KIRKPATRICK, CLIFFORD. 1936. "Assumptions and Methods in Attitude Measurements," *American Sociological Review*, 1, pp. 75–88.

KLUCKHOHN, CLYDE. 1945. "The Personal Document in Anthropological Science," Social Research Council Bulletin, No. 53. New York: SSRC.

KRIESBERG, LOUIS. 1956. "National Security and Conduct in the Steel Gray Market," *Social Forces*, 34 (March), pp. 268–77.

KUTNER, B., C. WILKINS, and P. B. YARROW. 1952. "Verbal Attitudes and Overt Behavior Involving Racial Prejudice," *Journal of Abnormal and Social Psychology*, 47, pp. 649–52.

LAPIERE, RICHARD T. 1928. "Race Prejudice: France and England," *Social Forces*, 7 (September), pp. 102–11.

————. 1934. "Attitudes vs. Actions," *Social Forces*, 13 (March), pp. 230–37.

————. 1936. "Type-Rationalizations of Group Antipathy," *Social Forces*, 15 (December), pp. 232–37.

LINN, LAWRENCE S. 1965. "Verbal Attitude and Overt Behavior: A Study of Racial Discrimination," *Social Forces*, 43 (March), pp. 353–64.

LOHMAN, JOSEPH, and DIETRICK C. REITZES. 1954. "Deliberately Organized

Groups and Racial Behavior," *American Sociological Review*, 19 (June), pp. 342–48.

MARTIN, HAROLD H. 1963. "Why She Really Goes to Market," *Saturday Evening Post* (September 28), pp. 40–43.

MERTON, ROBERT K. 1940. "Fact and Factitiousness in Ethnic Opinionnaires," *American Sociological Review*, 5 (February).

——————. 1957. *Social Theory and Social Structure* (rev. ed.). Glencoe, Ill.: The Free Press.

MILLS, C. WRIGHT. 1940. "Methodological Consequences of the Sociology of Knowledge," *American Journal of Sociology*, 46, pp. 316–30.

——————. 1954. "IBM Plus Reality Plus Humanism = Sociology," *Saturday Review* (May 1).

MINARD, R. D. 1952. "Race Relationships in the Pocahontas Coal Field," *Journal of Social Issues*, 9, pp. 29–44.

MUSSEN, PAUL H. 1950. "Some Personality and Social Factors Related to Changes in Children's Attitudes Toward Negroes," *Journal of Abnormal and Social Psychology*, 45 (July), pp. 423–41.

PUTNEY, SNELL, and RUSSELL MIDDLETON. 1962a. "Ethical Relativism and Anomia," *American Journal of Sociology*, 67 (January), pp. 430–38.

——————. 1962b. "Religion, Normative Standards, and Behavior," *Sociometry*, 25, pp. 141–52.

ROSE, ARNOLD. 1956. "Intergroup Relations vs. Prejudice: Pertinent Theory for the Study of Social Change," *Social Problems*, 4 (October).

——————. 1961. "Inconsistencies in Attitudes Toward Negro Housing," *Social Problems*, 8 (Spring), pp. 286–92.

SAENGER, GERHART, and EMILY GILBERT. 1950. "Customer Reactions to the Integration of Negro Sales Personnel," *International Journal of Opinion and Attitude Research*, 4 (Spring), pp. 57–76.

SCHLETZER, VERA MEYERS, et al. 1961. "Attitudinal Barriers to Employment," *Minnesota Studies in Vocational Rehabilitation: XI*, Industrial Relations Center, Bulletin No. 32. Minneapolis: University of Minnesota.

SCOTT, W. A. 1957 "Attitude Change Through Reward of Verbal Behavior," *Journal of Abnormal and Social Psychology*, 55, pp. 72–75.

——————. 1959. "Attitude Change by Response Reinforcement: Replication and Extension," *Sociometry*, 22, pp. 328–35.

STOUFFER, SAMUEL A., et al. 1949. *The American Soldier; Adjustment During Army Life*, Studies in Social Psychology in World War II. Vol. 1. Princeton, N.J.: Princeton University Press.

VERNON, P. E. 1938. *The Assessment of Psychological Qualities by Verbal Methods*, Medical Research Council, Industrial Health Research Board, Report No. 83. London: H. M. Stationery.

WALLACE, IRVING. 1961. *The Chapman Report*. New York: New American Library.

WARRINER, CHARLES K. 1958. "The Nature and Functions of Official Morality," *American Journal of Sociology*, 64 (September), pp. 165–68.

WILNER, DANIEL M., ROSABELLE P. WALKLEY, and STUART W. COOK. 1952. "Residential Proximity and Inter-group Relations in Public Housing Projects," *Journal of Social Issues*, 8:1, pp. 45–69.

YARROW, MARIAN RADKE. 1958. "Interpersonal Dynamics in a Desegregation Process," Special Issue, *Journal of Social Issues*, 14:1.

ZUNICH, MICHAEL. 1962. "Relationship Between Maternal Behavior and Attitudes Toward Children," *Journal of Genetic Psychology*, pp. 155–65.

3. Selective Attention

NOTES ON POLICE
ASSESSMENT OF
MORAL CHARACTER
—Harvey Sacks

INTRODUCTION

1. FOR WESTERN SOCIETIES, AT least, being noticeable and being deviant seem intimately related. The notions that one is suspect whose appearance is such that he stands out, and correlatively that the sinner can be seen, have the deepest of foundations. Indeed, in Judeo-Christian mythology, human history proper begins with the awareness by Adam and Eve that they are observables.[1] The next bit of social information they thereupon learn is: To be observable is to be embarrassable.[2] The first social technique they

---

[1] By this term I mean having, and being aware of having, an appearance that permits warrantable inferences about one's moral character. This use conforms with a usual use of the term.

[2] The central sociological status of the "possibility of embarrassment" is strongly suggested by its prominence in *Genesis*. Not only is it that the first human encounter with God begins with embarrassment, but the treatment of Cain suggests that, if only to avoid embarrassment alone, a conforming life is recommended. He, we recall, is condemned not to death, but to "observability for life."

That these are not merely arcane issues is accentuated by the concerns of modern literature. For example, each of the major works of the great social analyst Franz Kafka begins with, then develops a description of, what life is procedurally like after the transformation of the hero into an observable.

Reprinted with permission of Macmillan Publishing Co., Inc. from David Sunow (ed.), *Studies in Social Interactions*, pp. 280–93. Copyright © 1972 by The Free Press, a division of The Macmillan Company.

learn is: They can by mutual regard achieve privacy.[3] And then they learn the first terrible norm: The retention of privacy is conditioned on *naive* conformity.[4]

1.a   If, in American society, it is the case that the inferences as to moral character which particular appearances may warrant are a matter of central concern, then: We expect that there are specialized methods for producing from the appearances persons present such inferences as to moral character as can warrant the propriety of particular treatments of the persons observed.

1.b   It is the case that the relation of observability to deviance is of central concern. In public places persons are required to use the appearances others present as grounds for treating them. Persons using public places are concurrently expected by others to present appearances which can be readily so used, and expect others to treat their own appearances at face value.

1.c   While the regulation of inferences (hence of treatments) by reference to appearances determines an elegant means for routinizing casual public interaction, it obviously has characteristic problems. *First*, what is to be done about those persons whose appearance suggests no clear inferences, i.e., whose appearance does not warrant particular treatments?

Second, what is to be done about those persons whose appear-

---

[3] For the society under consideration, giving a public accounting is about as serious a situation as one can face. Furthermore, given the concern to use the appearances persons present in public as the materials for deciding their proper treatment, privacy is not merely valued but enforced. In routine interaction others need not attend to one's actual grounds of conduct. Indeed, within the bulk of legal situations "actual grounds" are enforceably excluded; one enforceably attends only to the typical grounds appearances suggest.

[4] Conformity is not sufficient. It is the comfort with which one wears conformity that seems critical, as the ensuing shall suggest. If this is so, it may lead to the development of an explanation for such data as Messinger's *Sociometry*, v. 25, 1962, pp. 98–109, where the trouble ex-mental patients felt was a lack of comfort with their conformity.

The position noted in the text has been expressed most dramatically by Emerson:

Commit a crime, and the earth is made of glass. Commit a crime, and it seems as if a coat of snow fell on the ground, such as reveals in the woods the track of every partridge and fox and squirrel.

Quoted in *Nightstick*, by L. J. Valentine, 1947, New York

ance is projected to take advantage of the enforced inferences others make in order to do the latter ill?

Third, what is to be done about those persons who consistently or blatantly fail to properly read appearances, who consequently produce inappropriate treatments?

Fourth, what is to be done about those persons for whom the problem of properly reading appearances is dramatically tortuous?

In this chapter I shall not consider "what is to be done." Rather, I am concerned with how those about whom that question may properly be raised are located.[5]

1.d As the appearances persons present are of central concern, so too are there specialized methods for producing the inferences that appearances warrant.

The concern of this essay is to move towards their description. I shall proceed in this direction by attempting a description of a method used by specialists—the police—for inferring from appearances such a probability of criminality as warrants the treatment of search and arrest.

My grounds for the choice of the police are as follows. First, the police are engaged, with others, in locating persons about whom the question may properly be raised: can they give a legitimate accounting for their appearance?

---

[5] Let me note, however, that the question "what is to be done" is handled quite widely by requiring of a properly located candidate that he offer an accounting for his appearance. If a person is competent to reasonably answer "why" questions, then that seems to stand as an indicator of his competence to regulate his affairs.

While one might suppose that the term "reasonably" is the sticker here, it does seem to be the case, perhaps curiously so, that even when persons are under interrogation for possibly serious offenses, ones for which their lives may be at stake, confessions can be garnered by saying to them that what they have said at some point is inconsistent with what they have said at another point. One might imagine them to say "How can it be inconsistent; I said both those things," or et cetera. A preliminary investigation of the method of interrogation suggests that while in exploration of what goes on in such situations is of great interest, it is by no means to be supposed that persons take lightly the reasonableness, consistency, clarity, and so on, of their answers, and may well be more concerned with preserving their claim to consistency than their claim to innocence.

Persons whose competency is denied, i.e., who are not given the right to state the sense of their actions seem to find the situation of interrogation tremendously frustrating.

Second, they are, in contrast to others so engaged, specialized in the locating of candidates on the basis of the appearances presented in public places.

Third, as specialists, certain problems of the relation of the first two and the last two problems of 1.c above need not be examined. That the police are specialists means that they are accredited for regularly recognizing possible deviants. Since the regular recognition of possible deviants, quite as much as the failure to produce a proper appearance, constitutes evidence for deviance (e.g., paranoia), the professional accreditation of the police provides a quick and easy test as to whether a claimed recognizer of deviants should be given diagnostic examination. The "public-spirited" citizen receives special and ambivalent attention.[6] Since, then, I want only to deal with the location of persons presenting improper appearances, choice of the police avoids in general the question of the possibly symptomatic status of recognizances. Fourth, as specialists their methods ought to be reasonably easy to discover.

1.e Since I am only interested in the police instantially, I shall restrict the investigation to a domain of their work involving a special concern for matters with which persons in general are, albeit less intensively, also concerned. I shall describe a method used for recognizing "suspicious persons," and shall not be concerned with methods used for recognizing either "wanted persons" or those seen in the commission of an offense. While some evi-

[6] The public-spirited citizen is not simply someone who responds with moral indignation towards perceived offenses; he is one who adopts an organization of observations—and indeed attends the world—so as to produce and explain with respect to legal system notions, the behavior of his neighbors. Below are some excerpts of what seems to have seemed strange.

A complaint was received to the effect that neighbors suspected that a woman was a "bookie." The complainant, who remained anonymous, indicated that this woman has been boasting of her winnings on the horse races and has been purchasing clothes and furnishings in excess of what she is capable of purchasing on her husband's earnings as a mail carrier. Neighbors also indicated that a man visited the house each morning and left something in the mailbox.

Some patrons of a bar reported to the local police that they believed gambling was going on there because two or three other patrons seemed to have quite a bit of money and no visible means of support.

These quotes are from pp. 61 and 62 of volume II, *The Administration of Criminal Justice in the United States*, Pilot Project Report, American Bar Foundation. This study will hereafter be referred to as ABF.

dence will be offered that the method the police use for recognizing suspicious persons is in general use, a demonstration of its general use will not be presented in this chapter.

A First Simplified Statement of the Policeman's Problem

2.   Among the Americans, the police are occupational specialists on inferring the probability of criminality from the appearances persons present in public places. Since a mutual orientation to appearances defines a means for producing and accepting the appropriate properties by which casual public encounters are routinized, it is important that these means be protected from exploitation. One central role of the police involves protecting the viability of these means. Patrolmen are intensively oriented to the possibly improper appearances persons may present.

2.a   The decisional problem faced has the following form: Maximize the likelihood that those who will turn out to be criminals and who pass in view are selected, while minimizing the likelihood that those who would not turn out to be criminals and who pass in view are selected. This problem is faced under the conditions:

1. that the persons seen are (differentially, to be sure) oriented to the character of their own appearances as grounds of inference as to probable criminality;
2. that the value of correct and incorrect inferences are neither equal nor uniformly calculable prior to a treatment decision.[7]

2.b   Others—for example, homosexuals while cruising—face a similar problem. For our purposes the latter differ from the police in the following way: The police are concerned to recognize persons concerned to make themselves unrecognizable as criminals. The homosexual is concerned to recognize homosexuals and to inform them of the presence of a colleague; he is also concerned not to be recognized as homosexual by others, particularly by the police. The issue reaches maximal complexity when police seek to have homosexuals recognize them as colleagues for the purpose of having the latter engage in a move that constitutes grounds for arrest.

[7] This feature is of course crucial to the problem of bribery. Failures to arrest may have low visibility. The surprise situation of halting for interrogation prominent citizens and officials, and the generally negative but occasionally positive gains to the policemen are well known.

The police face a similar problem with prostitutes, junkies, and the like, and that class of persons also faces the problem of differentially communicating, by way of their appearances, with potential clients, the public and the police.

THE METHOD IN USE: AN INCONGRUITY PROCEDURE: ITS BASIS

3. The method that the police are trained to employ may be called an "incongruity procedure." It constitutes an attempt to refine a method for observing persons based on the wisdom noted above (1).

3.a It begins with the fact that persons within the society are trained to naively present and naively employ presented appearances as the grounds of treatment of the persons they encounter in public places.

The treatments for which appearances are ordinarily used as grounds of selection vary widely, from, for example, deciding whether "that one" is such a one as one can pass in the street without fear of attack, illegitimate approach, etc., to how it is that one may properly pass, follow, or approach "that one."

3.b Since mutual orientation to appearances determines a means for producing and accepting the appropriate proprieties by which casual public encounters are routinized, it is important for the continuing viability of these means that they be protected from exploitation.[8] The incongruity procedure takes recognizance that the facts of 3.a determine a weapon by which inappropriate treatments may be garnered. Persons may exploit an ability to present appearances to which they are not otherwise entitled.

3.c If a group can be trained to (1) avoid routinely treating appearances at face value, and (2) alternatively to view the persons they see as presenting possibly improper appearances, they can (3) attend to a variety of features, such as the ease with which an appearance is presented, which may (4) warrant empirical investi-

[8] It is perhaps because of this orientation of the police that the most dangerous of persons are felt to be the person who uses his appearance as a policeman to cover his crooked acts. The members of the Denver police force who were also thieves used police cars as look-outs. Gosling, in *The Ghost Squad*, 1959, notes that criminals who presented the appearance of detectives were a matter of tremendous concern because of their effect in undermining public certainty about the import of apparent police status.

gation of the propriety of the presented appearance. Some comment on these points is appropriate.

First, that a warrant is necessary, i.e., that conditions are restricted under which an empirical investigation may be pursued as to the propriety of a presented appearance, is expectable.[9] The elegance of the use of appearances depends primarily on the fact that appearances in general are not to be questioned.

Second, users of the method do not propose that they are able to state definitively what features they will use to decide that an appearance may be improper, i.e., does warrant investigation. It is perhaps obvious why this should be so. As the police are oriented to using appearances as evidence of criminality, so criminals are oriented to using appearances as fronts, i.e., as hindrances to recognition. Were a definitive list compiled, one to which the police would themselves be bound, it would provide criminals with definitive information on the appearances to avoid in order to assure safe passage across the policeman's line of vision.

Given the latter two points, one central problem of the use of the procedure may be exposed: How is the proper use of the procedure to be decided in any particular case?

While I shall consider this problem further below, because of their general relation to the above discussion I note here the general features of its solution. Instead of the proper use of the procedure being decided by reference to the correctness of the inference of probable criminality, the propriety of the inference constitutes the condition for determining whether the persons selected are

[9] While, given the means of routinizing casual public interaction it is expectable that persons need good grounds in order to make the explanations of appearances a project for empirical investigation, this fact that they do need good grounds is by no means of trivial status. The norm "do not investigate, unless a problem is warrantable" may be the practical theorists' correlate of the scientist's norm of elegance. Theorists who warrant their investigations on the grounds that they will have no practical import are perhaps producing a warrant of the sort although there are no good grounds for investigating this, it is investigatable because nothing practical will come of it. If something practical will come of it, then good grounds may be needed. Cf. the emergence of sociology from the study of recognized social problems.

The normative import of knowledge of the world held in common seems such that those who will make of this knowledge a problem must first suggest the troubles we now have with its use.

possibly criminal. And whether the inference was proper is decided in the courts by having the policeman state what it was that aroused his suspicions; the judge (or jury) then considers whether an ordinary person would have been roused to suspicion on such grounds. Only if so is the person selected by the policeman convictable.

THE INCONGRUITY PROCEDURE IN USE

4. Given that police ply a route, they must, in order to use the incongruity procedure, learn to treat their beat as a territory of normal appearances. The learned normal appearances are to constitute background expectancies in terms of which the beat is observed during particular patrols. Given these expectancies the patrolman must so sensitize himself as to be arousable by whatsoever *slight variations* appear which seem to be warrantable bases for making of the explanation of presented appearances a matter for investigation.

4.a The novice policeman is obviously not in position to use the procedure. First he must learn how to see as a patrolman. By having a novice patrol with a mature officer, the former can be shown what it is that one can see by way of the method. The demonstration that may be offered can have a quite considerable charm.[10]

As he walks through his beat with a mature officer, persons who to him appear legit are cast in the light of the illicit activities in which the latter knows they are engaged. The novice is shown that he ought to see persons passing him in terms of the activities in which they are engaged. And the activities in which they are engaged are often more prurient than he might suppose. The lovely young lady alighting from a cab is now observable as a call girl arriving for a session. The novice is shown how to see the streets as, so to speak, scenes from pornographic films. And what is more, he is able to see the illicitnesses under the conditions that few, if any, who observe him passing through the streets are able to see either that the officer is in such a scene or what it is that he is indeed observing. The policeman, then, has the privacy of the stag

[10] See R. McAllister, *The Kind of Guy I Am*, New York, 1957.

show theatre, while parading the streets in full uniform, and, further, there is no noticeable entry or exit at which, if he is seen, embarrassment might be called forth.

4.b   Training manuals provide the novice with lists of features constituting good grounds for treating persons who pass in his view.[11] As we have noted, these lists are intendedly not definitive. They have an extremely interesting status. Aside from providing examples of the sorts of features any policeman ought to be attuned to,[12] they operate as records in an expandable history of police success and failure. The import of those parts of the lists that consist of "great recognizances" or "great boners" is, to use Moore's term, autotelic.[13] The policeman can attend to his route with an awareness that he can, by making an especially subtle recognizance, take a place within department history. That is to say, he is encouraged to engage, even when patrolling alone, in playing observation games; for example, glance at a store window, note to himself all the items that he can recall within it, then check back to see what he has missed or noted incorrectly. While such games are more readily played when police patrol in pairs, the attended history of recognizances permits the lone patrolman to play the games against the department's historical figures.

The persons on his beat can also reinforce the playing of observation games by expressing their amusement at his awareness when they make slight deviations from their normal habits. Then, too, the fact that one cannot pre-determine what information may turn out to be useful encourages the collection of seemingly trivial details because awareness of such details has occasionally paid off with an unexpected arrest which was heavily rewarded.

4.c   What is normal for a place is normal for the place at a time. The meaning of an event to the policeman at a place depends on the time it occurs. The time at which it occurs is furthermore a matter of an overlapping and changing group of cycles—that is, the meaning of an event is not merely a matter of the hour, but

[11] See, e.g., ABF vol. 5, pp. 1–19 to 1–29, or Callan, G. D., *Police Methods for Today and Tomorrow*, ch. 3, Newark, 1939.

[12] "Milwaukee recruits are instructed that if they observe a young man crossing the street with an overcoat on, collar up, and hat pulled down, in warm weather, they are to suspect that he is a burglar." ABF vol. 5, 1–19.

[13] Anderson and Moore, "Autotelic Folk Models," *The Sociological Quarterly*, Vol. 1, pp. 203–16.

the day too is involved in deciding its significance; furthermore, the season counts, and then finally "while it didn't used to be that way here," now "such a thing is typical."

While in a sense these facts are obvious, it is obvious as well that sociological theories of deviance are not now constructed to deal with them. Yet even for demographic analysis such facts may be of real importance. For example, given the use of learned normal appearances as the grounds of locating suspect persons, we would expect that territories in transition will have higher crime rates than stabler territories simply because the policeman geared to the normal appearances of a beat may, not adjusting exactly to the rate and character of transition, be ready to see newer arrivals as suspicious for the beat seen as an area in which they are not normal features.[14]

The time-ordered character of normal appearances poses a touchy strategic problem for the police. A patrolman can best be attuned to normal appearances by so scheduling his route such that he appears at places at the same significant time.[15] In doing so he gets the closest awareness of the constancies and variances at that time for that place. But if his behavior is so scheduled, it provides criminals with definitive information about where he will be at a particular time, and consequently permits the scheduling of illegal events. In order to reduce the information criminals can gain by observing his course, the policeman is therefore concerned to randomize his path through a beat, i.e., to proceed through different ways each time, to double back occasionally, to take his breaks at different times and in different places. But doing this of course reduces his sensitivity to the normal appearances he uses to detect the presence of something awry or, to avoid that perhaps unfortunate phrasing, reduces his confidence that he can discriminate the peculiar because the range of what he uses as normal becomes more extended.

[14] If one feels that it is strange that the rate of crime varies with the suspiciousness of the police, one probably has in mind crimes of violence or robbery as typical crimes. And these might be expected to be reported by the public. However, such matters as gambling, prostitution, dope selling depend for being listed in statistics on the ability of the police to locate arrestable persons.

[15] By significant time I mean only that "the same time" may not be the same clock time. It may be "closing time" or "dinner time" or the like.

4.d The police treat the normal ecology of territories as a normative ecology. As sociologists describe them, cities typically consist of discrete ecological areas of socio-economic segregation. Juvenile gangs tend to treat the borders of ecological areas as boundaries. Persons who "don't belong" are seen as foreigners, and are subject to treatment as such. Their safe passage depends on the deference of the local lords. The police too treat ecological borders as of normative import. Persons whose appearance indicates that they are not normal members of an ecological area, e.g., whites in negro areas, the apparently poor in wealthy areas, etc., are subject to having a request made for "their papers" and an interrogatory made as to the reason for their presence.[16]

Furthermore, as the police treat territories as a set of normal appearances, so they expect others to treat them.[17]

> Coming to a street intersection, the officers observed a man crossing the intersection who did not appear to know where he was going. The officers alighted from the car, questioned this man, and searched him. He provided the police with full credentials and indicated that was the first occasion on which he had ever been questioned by a police officer. His answers satisfied the officers that this man was quite "legitimate." They thanked him for his cooperation and sent him on his way.

4.e Two related features of the use of the procedure involve the policeman's appearance.

First, those who treat the presence of the police as other than normal are seen as other than normal themselves.[18]

> They were in search of "house jumpers"—who are individuals collecting current bet slips and who turn them in at a "drop" station. ... The officers indicate that they can determine who a collector is as a result of their experiences in dealing with these people. As an example, they indicate that if an individual gives them a "double look," they'll check him. By this the officers mean that if an individual sees them in their unmarked car and then turns to look at them once again, chances are the individual has some gambling paraphernalia on his person. In such cases, the officers leave their

[16] Anderson and Moore, *op. cit.*, pp. 115, 123.
[17] ABF vol. 2, p. 118.
[18] *Ibid.*, p. 120; see too Gosling, *op. cit.*, p. 56.

car and search the person in an attempt to uncover the current bet slips.

Conversely, as the police enforce on the persons that they treat their presence as normal, so it is enforced on the police that they appear as they are expected to appear, i.e., that if they are present, their presence be apparent.[19]

An officer attempted to develop an accosting and soliciting case through the use of a private and expensive vehicle. This case was thrown out of court upon the basis that "everyone knows that the police officers use cheap cars," and for a police officer to resort to the use of a Cadillac in order to develop an accosting and soliciting case constitutes entrapment.

Some time ago a handbook operation was going on in a downtown building. Since the handbook was located near the medical building, doctors dressed in white jackets sometimes frequented the place. An officer therefore disguised himself in a white coat and managed to place a bet. The case was thrown out of court on the ground that entrapment was involved.

4.f   Given the orientation of the police to the beat as a territory of normal appearances, a notion of "*normal crime*" may be constructed. We may talk of the normal crime of an area not in terms of the statistical constancy of certain crimes for time units, but as that crime that is so managed within an area that those so engaged appear while so engaged as features of its normal appearance.

The notion of normal crime has the following import: given the orientation of the police, those routinely engaged in illegal activities will attempt to construct a front such that their routine appearance in a territory will (or can) be treated as a normal appearance of the territory by its patrolmen. Organizers of the numbers racket will, for example, employ those who have a reason for going through a neighborhood several times a day and stopping at a wide range of places. The newspaper deliverers and the mailmen are ideal.

Whether or not those in the numbers racket have fixed the patrolmen, they must adopt a front for their routine collections and dispersals so that (a) public-spirited citizens and (b) various detective groups do not on observing the area interpret their routine

[19] *Ibid.*, pp. 137, 138.

presence as "numbers men making pick-up and deliveries." They must adopt this front simply to avoid being noticed, but because if by some chance they happen to be noticed, the beat patrolman who has failed to arrest must be able to reasonably claim that they simply appeared to him to be routine features of the territory, i.e., that they gave him no good grounds for an aroused suspicion.

4.g We have noted above (3.c) that it is not the case that the proper use of the method is determined by the demonstrable correctness of the inferences produced.

The general warrant of the method is not based on the professional status of the police; its general warrant is that anyone can see its plausibility. Its warrant in particular cases is that the inference made is one which ordinary persons would make. This means that the policeman is not simply concerned to develop his sensitivity. He must balance his sensitivity against his ability to verbalize, i.e., to present descriptions of how he became aroused. And what is more, though he is a specialist on the normal appearances of his beat, his inferences are judged by those who lack both his special knowledge and his developed sense of the unusual.

While the police would like their special skills in observation to constitute grounds of a recognition of their professional status, and their professional status to then operate as a preliminary warrant of their observations, the fact that the warrant of their observations is decided by a test of reasonableness for an ordinary man is not only irking but also places them in a severe bind.

Apart from the fact that they then tend to see the courts as hindering them in their work and in their search for professional status, they feel required to adopt a series of unpleasant adaptations.

First, the method of recognition and the method of presentation may become separate issues. The policeman may feel himself forced to "rationally reconstruct" what happened.[20]

A court officer noted that a particular police officer would behave in the following manner:
He would state that he saw defendant come down the street, knew him as a long time police game operator, stopped him, searched him, found policy tickets, and brought him in. The prosecutor would advise he had no case as the search was not legal, and unless

the search was made pursuant to a lawful arrest, the evidence was inadmissible. The officer would then say "put me on the stand." When on the witness stand, he would testify he was standing under a street light when the defendant came by, a man known to him to have been previously convicted of policy violation, and that he saw his policy ticket sticking out of the defendant's coat pocket. Thereupon he arrested him, searched him, and found a number of such tickets and brought this prosecution.

The court officer noted, in this case, that in one year two individuals each obtained $5,000 damages against this officer for false arrest. He was encouraged to resign from the force with his pension rights intact.

Then, once information has been gathered about criminal activities, the police may engage in staging observable crimes. For example, if the police know that someone is selling dope, they may—because they cannot say that the fellow was seen selling dope, only that an exchange of something was seen—arrange through the use of hired addicts for a purchase to take place which is sufficiently observable for recounting in court.

The staging of crimes is especially messy. First, the police may have to employ persons who would otherwise be institutionalized. In doing so they assure these persons at least a temporary freedom, sometimes indeed to pursue their illegal endeavors.[21] Second, where they are unable to get hired hands, they may themselves have to spend time in such activities as smiling in public toilets, making time with the lonely women who frequent bars, etc.

A Second Simplified Statement of the Policeman's Problem

5. A policeman takes it that the persons he sees engaged in passing through the streets are oriented to a social order in terms of whose features they select the proper or improper courses of action which bring them to use the streets. His aim is to find a way of making activities observable in the particular sense of

---

[21] For example: After an unsuccessful effort to contact a source of supply for narcotics, the following occurred: The agents took Myra to A Street, somewhere near B Street where she was to begin hustling. Myra mentioned that she had not been picked up by the police for the past two weeks for some reason she could not explain, but facetiously guessed that the Detroit police "must know I've been copping for the Feds." *Ibid.,* p. 90.

allowing him to see the passing of persons in terms of the courses they have selected.

Typically, he is in a position merely to observe persons passing in the street and does not engage in fully tracking their paths from entry to the streets to exit therefrom. In locating persons who are to be candidates in a test of their possible criminality he does not begin with information about the courses in which they are engaged. That they are possibly engaged in illegal activities must first be decided by way of the incongruity procedure, i.e., by way of a device for locating candidates from the set of observed persons.

Once located, his concern is to produce information about the paths candidates select and then to transform the information about the paths they select into evidence of the courses they have selected. He seeks, that is, to transform information about the paths candidates select into a description of a set of acts which may be seen as the assembly of a crime.

His problem then seems to be:

Given that
1. he encounters persons in and by way of the streets, persons engaged in undetermined activities;
2. the activities are taken to be parts of selected courses of action constructed with an orientation to their propriety;
3. candidates for investigation are located prior to tracking their paths or knowing the course of action in which they are engaged.

Then:
How, by way of their street activities, can one look at persons so as to be able to use their appearances to isolate candidates for investigation? and

How can one then use what candidates do both as materials for discovering the courses of action in which they are engaged, and for determining in terms of those courses that sense of their observable acts on the basis of which a strategy may be generated for demonstrating the observable character of their activities as the assembly of a crime?

5.a   While the police might treat the streets as merely incidental locales of the persons they encounter, in fact they treat the streets with great seriousness. The police take it that what takes place in the streets stands in a determinable relation to that organization of concerted courses of action which involves persons in using the streets. If they discover whom to investigate, then by tracking him they can at least determine the strategic problem that exposing the course to which he is oriented poses. Exposing the course itself will not be a problem patrolmen will be concerned with. But it is their job to determine who is to be tracked.

5.b As the police take it that those engaged in illegal activities do not randomly use the streets, so too persons routinely engaged in illegal activities are concerned to regulate the activities of those of their agents who use the streets in the course of work so that the use does appear random. Persons who organize illegal activities are concerned to minimize the clues that use provides to those who might, by analyzing street activities, expose the organization regulating those activities.

However, the strategic problem they face in doing so involves them in a bind similar to that the police were shown to face (4.c). Organizers of a numbers operation will, for example, regularly move the stations to which route-men go in delivering their slips. They may also attempt to have route-men vary the way they proceed through a territory. But the attempt to randomize has its drawbacks. Persons making purchases are kept in a far more viable mood if those they deal with keep a regular schedule. Then, too, those who keep a regular schedule will, if they are not held in suspicion, be less likely to arouse suspicion.

For the police, the problem of locating the persons using the streets as parts of coordinated illegal activities has a different purport than that of locating persons engaged in solo crimes. In the former case it is the organizers they seek to make observable, and the persons using the streets constitute not the sought-for criminals but possible resources by which organizers may be located. The police are oriented to the organizers, and are by and large willing to let the street operatives alone, because they are aware that those who use the streets are readily replaceable, and because, insofar as the organizers are not located, arrest of street operatives means only that the work of exposing the organization must begin again from the beginning, i.e., with an attempt to locate and track their replacements. Organizers, on the other hand, cannot rest content with the fact that their street operatives are not being bothered. For, even if this is so, it may be the case that the police are accumulating information that may soon be sufficient to crack the organization itself.

5.c.   Encountering by way of the streets what is taken to be a managed social order has a wide range of other imports.

Police seem often to treat an area as an "expressive unit." Suppose they see a group of persons standing on a street corner. The meaning they attach may be neither behavioral (e.g., how crowded they are) nor be conceived in terms of the conduct of those persons (e.g., what *they* are up to). A group of persons on a street corner may be seen as "the neighborhood is restless tonight," i.e., as a gesture of the territory. Conversely, in producing their own responses to neighborhood gestures they see their own actions as an answer to the neighborhood. Thus a policeman, having felt that the young toughs are getting over-rowdy, may pick one out and rough him up, taking it that this will be seen as instantial, as a remark that such persons had better get back in line. While such remarks often seem to be understood, i.e., the one that was beaten up takes it that he is incidental, and the others take it that police intend them to calm down, it seems also to be the case that when communication failures occur, the recipients of a gesture may experience both puzzlement ("why me, I was just standing on the corner?") and may have a hostility toward the police reinforced ("they have to maintain a quota of arrests, and don't care who they take in" or "they just pick on us, so what is the use of playing straight?").[22]

They also take it that the appearance of a neighborhood is attended to by those who pass within it as the shape in which it is maintained by the police. Thus, they may feel called on to make arrests because they feel that persons passing can see that the police see unshapely activities going on.[23]

> The wretched man positively insisted on being arrested. I'd been watching for a long time. And I didn't see how I could let him carry on much longer like that. He might get killed. Or someone might make a complaint at the police station. Then where would I be? There were a lot of people watching him and I thought most of

---

[22] See Len O'Conner, *They Talked to a Stranger*, 1957, *passim*.
[23] A. Thorp, *Calling Scotland Yard*, 1954, p. 9.

them knew I had seen him. They would be thinking it was time I did something about it. They couldn't be expected to realize that I was a policeman who had never made an arrest. I could almost feel them looking at me, wondering how long it would be before I went into action.

If only he would actually get on to a bus it would be all right. He would be whirled away, out of my uncomfortable little world, in no time at all. But he never did get on to a bus. He tried often enough, but usually the conductor waved him off, or he waited too long, grabbed wildly at the handrail as the vehicle drew away and, losing his balance, went reeling into the gutter. What a skinful he must have had! He was as tight as an owl.

For the police, the range of sights, sounds and the like which they observe while going through the streets is conceived in terms of the access these might give to private places. If the private places of a territory are the dominant setting for its activities, then the police attend to the streets with a highly refined sensitivity. Persons living in suburban areas report that "the only way" they can walk in the streets at night without being stopped by the police is if they can get a dog to accompany them. And the police chief of Beverly Hills notes that even this may not be sufficient, since his police are familiar with the persons and dogs who make a habit of walking at night.[24]

For the police, objects and places having routine uses are conceived in terms of favorite misuses. Garbage cans are places in which dead babies are thrown, schoolyards are places where molesters hang out, stores are places where shoplifters go, etc.

5.d For the police, each patrol of a beat is conceived as potentially adding items to a cumulative set of values; they want a patrol to count. What any patrol may, however, add to (or subtract from) an assembled body of knowledge, reputation, security, opportunity, etc., may vary considerably.

Given that some sort of mathematics seems attended to in the patrol as an occasion within a continuing set of occasions, we can appreciate the police concern with the matters that are seen as unordered, for example, the fact that "breaks," i.e., unexpected large accumulations (or losses) of units occur at undetermined

[24] C. H. Anderson, *Beverly Hills Is My Beat*, 1960, pp. 33–34.

points within a career. A policeman may, whether rookie or oldster, happen upon a crime in its course which, because of the public attention it gets, assures him then and there of fame and promotion. Or an old policeman, having assembled a large collection of units of value, may suddenly be caught in a compromising situation, and see himself stripped at a point when re-assembly cannot be looked forward to. Or a policeman who knows the habits of the crooks he usually deals with may encounter a young hood who, being unaware of the business relations regular crooks and regular cops arduously establish, on being caught, fires and kills the cop.

The import of these unordered contingencies are, quite simply, that talk of the "course of a policeman's career" must recognize that the policeman is never able to say at what point he currently is in his career. Where he is now is radically a matter of where he will have turned out to be. This corner he approaches may be the corner at which he will have been killed.

5.e   That the police seek to be professionals is well known.[25] While this might be accounted for in terms of a general search for status, one basis for the status seems to be their concern, and the concern of those they deal with, i.e., criminals, to develop means for establishing their relation as businesslike, i.e., as impersonal, code-governed, etc.

The police claim that crime is a business is not merely a cry on their part for more adequate means to attack crime. It is as well an attempt to suggest, given quite limited means, that if criminals behave reasonably the police, too, will try to do so. The persons feared most by either side are the green groups of the other. The new criminal is felt to be most dangerous; the old pro, trustable, almost a partner. And the criminal, too, is much more afraid of the rookie cop than of the veteran.

Throughout this century, each generation of oldsters seems to see the young members of the other as over-ready to engage in unwarranted violence, and to remark to their co-generationists about the businesslike relation they might have were it not for the

[25] One training manual states the matter neatly: "Once a man has chosen police work as a career, he should do his part to make it a profession." Towler, *Practical Police Knowledge*, 1959, p. 58.

young hot-heads.[26] A businesslike relation need imply no bribery, of course; merely that minimizable risks may be minimized.

[26] "Once or twice he had gotten close to Sutton, but the wily bank robber seemed to have a second sense that told him Phillips was closing in. Phillips had picked up a former partner of Sutton's, and hoping for a lighter term than he faced, he had told Frank a lot about the fugitive. 'I seen Bill Sutton six weeks ago,' the prisoner said earnestly. 'He knows you're after him and he don't like it. Sutton never used a gun in his life, but he swears he'll kill you if he ever catches up with you. He's never forgotten what you did to Eddie Wilson.'

"He didn't tell her about this, but one of his partners did. When she mentioned it to him he laughed, "Sutton is a professional like I am. He knows I have nothing personal against him. He's a crook; I'm a cop. He knows the rules of the game as well as I do. To Sutton I'm a business rival—nothing more. That punk I collared who sang about Sutton was just trying to make things easy for himself.'

"And so it proved. When Sutton was finally caught he told Phillips about the rumors he had heard about his reported personal vendetta against the detective. 'That bothered me,' Sutton said. 'Sure I was afraid you'd make me some day and grab me, but I knew there was nothing personal about you trying to collar me. Shooting a cop is for these trigger-happy young punks who are loaded with junk. I'm a bank robber, not a killer, Frank. Believe that. Of course,' he added with a grin, 'there were some days when I didn't like you so much.'"

Q. Reynolds, *Headquarters*, 1955, pp. 15–16.

II: THE SURVEY

DETECTIVES EMPLOY SURVEYS OF A SORT IN DETERMINING WHERE crime is likely to occur. Burglary detectives, for example, place pins on maps for every burglary in a given geographical area. Eventually certain blocks can be identified as being more burglary-prone than others, and various prevention measures can be taken to lower the number of crimes there. Sociological surveys, in the same way, are methods of finding the frequency and distribution of given dimensions in a specified population. *Frequency* refers to the number of times a given dimension can be found, *distribution* refers to where the dimension is found, and *population* or *universe* refers to the group of interest. Thus, the detective in the example above is interested in the dimension of burglary in terms of how often burglaries occur (frequency) in various places (distribution) among various groups (population) in the city where he works (universe).

Surveys are generally characterized by highly structured measurement instruments, most often questionnaires. The questionnaires direct the researcher to ask specific questions about the dimensions of interest or, in the case of an observation survey, to observe specific events and processes. This design serves at least two purposes. On the one hand, by determining the frequency and distribution of certain characteristics in a given population or universe, surveys *describe* social phenomenon (Simon, 1969:244). For example, the researcher can describe a city in terms of its crime rate, birth rate, divorce rate, suicide rate, religious preferences, or any other dimension of interest. Such descriptions can be used in comparing a given society to other societies or to compare the same society at different times, as an indicator of social change. A second use of surveys is a quasi-experimental one (Denzin, 1970:171). Various aspects may be surveyed to find out if there is a *relation* between them. For example, members of various social classes might be questioned about their political preferences. If the researcher finds that members of a lower socio-economic background are more likely to have liberal political preferences than are those of a higher socio-economic class, then he has found a relation between social class and political preferences.

To conduct a survey of a given universe, the researcher rarely observes or interviews every unit in the universe. Rather, he attempts to survey a *sample* that is representative of the entire universe (Goode and Hatt, 1952:209–31). It has been found that if the sample is correctly drawn, what is true for the sample will be true for the entire universe. Thus, instead of having to spend a good deal of time and money surveying the whole population of interest, the researcher can achieve the same results with only a sample of that population.

In order to maximize the probability that the sample is representative of the universe, researchers attempt to ensure that every significant aspect of the universe is proportionately represented. The more nearly homogeneous the population is, the easier it is to draw a representative sample, since most of the members of the population are similar in terms of the aspects of interest. In a heterogeneous and large population, it is more difficult to ensure that all viewpoints and groupings have been proportionately represented in the sample, and the researcher will need a larger sample in order to do so. In either type of universe, however, researchers employ *randomizing* techniques to draw the sample so that every unit, grouping, and variation in a universe is proportionately represented, since they all have the same chance of being part of the sample.

There are a number of sampling techniques employing random sampling (Freund, 1960), and three will be presented here. The *simple random sample* entails determining the number desired for your sample, and selecting all the desired numbers randomly from the units of the universe. If the universe is relatively small, such as all the students in a given major at a given university, you can write each name on a slip of paper, put the slips in a container, and choose the desired number. For a larger universe, such as those listed in a telephone directory, a list of automobile owners, voting registration, or a city directory, you can assign each unit (e.g., name or household) a number and then select a number that, divided into the total number of units, will give you the desired sample size. Then you can take every nth number to be included in your sample. For example, if you have a list of 1,000 names and want 100 in your sample, you take every tenth number on the list. A third method is to use a prepared table of random numbers such as that one provided by L. H. C. Tippett.* After assigning a number to each unit, you draw the units for the sample by going down, across, or diagonally through the table, taking the number corresponding to those in the list.

A second commonly used sample is the *stratified sample.* If you know the different groupings in your universe and you know what proportion of the universe each one represents, you can use a stratified sample effectively. For example, if you know from examining census data that your community is made up of four ethnic groups and you want to draw a sample in which each group is proportionately represented, instead of having to draw a relatively large simple random sample you can draw a relatively small stratified sample. If 40 per cent of the community is of European origin, 20 per cent Asian, 30 per cent African, and 10 per cent Indian, then by randomly selecting a number proportionate to each group's representation in the community, you will have a sample reflecting the ethnic backgrounds of the entire universe without having to take a large simple random sample. Each ethnic group is treated as a subuniverse, and a proportionate simple random sample is taken from each subuniverse.

In the *area* or *cluster sample,* the universe for the research is located geographically and is divided into areas, such as blocks, neighborhoods, or census tracts (Denzin, 1970:88). Each area is assigned a number and the areas to be included in the sample are randomly selected. The assumption is that there is a high degree of homogeneity within each of the areas sampled, and that those

---

* *Tracts for Computers,* Number XV, Karl Pearson (ed.). New York: Cambridge University Press, 1947.

who live in a given area are likely to interact with one another. Thus, for comparative and descriptive purposes, area samples are highly useful, for each grouping can be treated as a real cohort, in that those in the sample are likely to have social relationships with one another rather than simply similar social characteristics.

In order to gather the necessary information from his sample, the survey researcher needs an instrument that will give him answers to his questions. This may seem obvious, but many inexperienced researchers construct questionnaires, interview schedules, or observation schedules without giving any thought to the question they are trying to answer. For example, some will automatically include questions about income, marital status, and ethnic background in any survey regardless of whether such information will answer their questions or not. Thus, before choosing or constructing an instrument for a survey, first determine what information is necessary and what questions will need to be asked or observations made to provide it.

Three of the most popular survey instruments are the questionnaire, the interview schedule, and the observation schedule.

The *questionnaire* is a self-administered set of questions that the researcher gives to the subjects in his sample. The items can either be *open-ended* (the respondent can give any answer he chooses, of any length he likes) or *closed-ended* (the respondent chooses from a limited number of responses, such as "true-false," or multiple choice) (Forcese & Richer, 1973:160). For example, a question about the subject's income that provided no categories of income to choose from would be open-ended. If the question asked the respondent to check one of five income groupings, the question would be closed-ended. Generally, open-ended questions are used to elicit new information when the researcher has no firm idea of what the answers might be. In the Ennis survey (Chapter 4), the researchers asked respondents who had been victims of crimes why they had not reported the crimes to the police. From the answers to this open-ended question they were able to derive certain categories that could be used in future surveys as closed-ended questions. In this manner, fixed-choice responses are developed from open-ended questions.

The *interview schedule* is like the questionnaire except that it is administered by an interviewer (Forcese and Richer, 1973:168–69). The advantage of the interview schedule over the questionnaire is that the interviewer can rephrase or explain a question that a respondent does not understand to ensure that the answer he gives is a response to the question intended. Also, an interview schedule can elicit feedback from the respondents. For example, if the interview schedule has a closed-ended question with a set of fixed-choice responses that are not reflective of what the respondents would normally choose as answers, the respondents can tell the interviewer; whereas with a questionnaire the subjects may simply fill in the fixed choices and offer no feedback.

The *observation schedule* is an instrument that directs the researcher to observe certain events in terms of fixed or open categories (Reiss, 1968). For example, in the Wiseman study of a drunk court (Chapter 5), the observer recorded the observed events in terms of a set of social types. Each social type was described in terms of a set of criteria, and the observer noticed the category each defendant fit best. Many items on an observation schedule can be phrased as questions, just like the items on interview schedules. For example, an observation schedule used in observing a court might include such questions as: "What tone of voice did the defendant use?" "What kind of reaction did the judge have to the defendant's story?"

All items on survey instruments should be constructed so that the responses can be compiled and analyzed once the data have been gathered. Generally this involves *coding* the responses and developing items in such a way that they can be coded. If the researcher has a good idea of what typical responses to questions might be, closed-ended questions greatly facilitate coding. For example, consider the following question:

What do you think of the drug laws?
> a. Too strict
> b. About right
> c. Too lenient
> d. Don't know

The researcher can simply compile the number and percentages of replies in terms of the four categories "a," "b," "c," or "d" and compare the responses with other items. However, with open-ended questions the researcher must develop categories after he has gathered the responses and then code the responses in terms of the categories he has developed. For example, if the question

"What do you think of women's liberation?" were asked without a set of fixed-choice responses, the content of the responses might vary greatly. By examining the specific responses, the researcher may find that all or most fit one of the categories "Approve and support actively," "Agree with goals but do not actively support," "Agree with some goals but not all," "Few good points, but generally disapprove," "Totally disapprove," "It's funny," "Don't know that much about it," or "Unsure."

Once the items are coded and compiled, the researcher can describe his universe in terms of the items. If the survey included items pertaining to socio-economic class and the classes are coded in terms of upper class, middle class, working class, and lower class, the population might be described socio-economically as follows:

Upper class	5%
Middle class	40%
Working class	40%
Lower class	10%

In addition to describing his population, the researcher may want to find whether there is any relationship between certain items—for example, between social class and attitudes toward socialized medicine. When the researcher analyzes more than one variable and tries to see if one variable changes when the other changes, the procedure is called *multivariate analysis* (Denzin, 1970:165). To find the effect, if any, of one variable on others, he *holds constant* one variable. That is, the researcher keeps the value of one variable unchanged, then looks to see the values of other variables in relation to the one held constant. In comparing middle- and working-class respondents in their attitudes toward socialized medicine, for example, he first determines the frequency of attitudes for and against socialized medicine in each class, thus holding social class constant (at the values of middle and working class). The findings may look something like this:

Middle Class
    Favor socialized medicine   30%
    Oppose socialized medicine 70%
Working Class
    Favor socialized medicine   70%
    Oppose socialized medicine 30%

From these figures, the researcher can see that more people who are working-class favor socialized medicine. To get a clearer picture of the relationship, the findings may be charted on a table, with the *independent variable* (the one that is held constant) making up the columns and the *dependent variable* making up the rows. In this case social class is the independent variable and attitudes toward socialized medicine make up the dependent variable.

Attitude Toward Socialized Medicine	SOCIAL CLASS	
	Working	Middle
Pro	70%	30%
Con	30%	70%

Now it can be seen that there is a relationship between social class and attitudes toward socialized medicine. As the class changes (varies) from working class to middle class, so do attitudes.

The two studies that follow show two different uses for the survey. The study by Ennis describes a universe in terms of crime rates and at the same time shows that the police have a biased sample of crime, in that they record only those crimes that are reported. On the other hand, the observation survey by Wiseman shows a relationship between social type and type of court disposition.

REFERENCES

DENZIN, NORMAN K. 1970. *The Research Act*. Chicago: Aldine.

FORCESE, D. P., and STEPHEN RICHER. 1973. *Social Research Methods*. Englewood Cliffs, N.J.: Prentice-Hall.

FREUND, J. E., 1960. *Modern Elementary Statistics*. Englewood Cliffs, N.J.: Prentice-Hall.

GOODE, WILLIAM J., and PAUL K. HATT. 1952. *Methods in Social Research*. New York: McGraw-Hill.

REISS, ALBERT J., JR. 1968. "Stuff and Nonsense About Social Surveys and Observations." In Howard S. Becker et al. (eds.) *Institutions and the Person*. Chicago: Aldine.

SIMON, J. L. 1969. *Basic Research Methods in Social Science*. New York: Random House.

4. Questionnaire Survey

CRIMES, VICTIMS, AND THE POLICE
—Phillip H. Ennis

"A SKID ROW DRUNK LYING IN A gutter is crime. So is the killing of an unfaithful wife. A Cosa Nostra conspiracy to bribe public officials is crime. So is a strong-arm robbery." So states the report of the President's Commission on Law Enforcement and Administration of Justice, commonly known as the Crime Commission report, in pointing out the diversity of crime. Our recent investigation at Chicago's National Opinion Research Center reveals that Americans are also frequent prey to incidents which may not fall firmly within the jurisdiction of criminal law, but which still leave the ordinary citizen with a strong sense of victimization—consumer frauds, landlord-tenant violations, and injury or property damage due to someone else's negligent driving.

With the aid of a new research method for estimating national crime rates, the Crime Commission study has now confirmed what many have claimed all along—that the rates for a wide range of personal crimes and property offenses are considerably higher than previous figures would indicate. Traditional studies have relied on the police blotter for information. The present research, devised and carried out by the National Opinion Research Center (NORC), tried a survey approach instead. Taking a random sam-

Published by permission of Transaction Inc. from *transaction*, Vol. 4 (June, 1967). © 1967 by Transaction Inc.

ple of 10,000 households during the summer of 1965, we asked people what crimes had been committed against them during the preceding year. The results—roughly 2,100 verified incidents—indicated that as many as half of the people interviewed were victims of offenses which they did not report to the police.

This finding raised several questions. How much did this very high incidence of unreported offenses alter the picture presented by the standard measures, notably the FBI's Uniform Crime Reports (UCR) index, based only on reported incidents? What was the situation with minor offenses, those not considered in the UCR index? What sorts of crimes tended to go unreported? And why did so many victims fail to contact the authorities? These were some of the issues we attempted to probe.

THE UNKNOWN VICTIMS

More than 20 per cent of the households surveyed were criminally victimized during the preceding year. This figure includes about *twice as much* major crime as reported by the UCR index. The incidence of minor crimes—simple assaults, petty larcenies, malicious mischiefs, frauds, and so on—is even greater. According to our research, these are at least twice as frequent as major crimes. The UCR index includes seven major crimes, so the proliferation of petty offenses not taken into account by the index makes the discrepancy between that index and the real crime picture even greater than a consideration of major offenses alone would indicate.

Table I compares our figures with the UCR rates for the seven major crimes upon which the index is based—homicide, forcible rape, robbery, aggravated assault, burglary. larceny (over $50), and auto theft. The homicide rate projected by the survey is very close to the UCR rate—not surprising since murder is the crime most likely to be discovered and reported.

The survey estimate of the car-theft rate is puzzlingly low. This could be because people report their cars as stolen to the police and then find that they themselves have "misplaced" the car or that someone else has merely "borrowed" it. They may either forget the incident when interviewed or be too embarrassed to mention it. The relatively high rate of auto thefts reported to the police confirms other studies which show that people are more likely to notify the police in this case than if they are victims of most other

TABLE I   ESTIMATED RATES OF MAJOR CRIMES: 1965–66

Crime	NORC sample: estimated rate per 100,000	UCR, 1965: individual or residential rates per 100,000
Homicide	3.0	5.1
Forcible rape	42.5	11.6
Robbery	94.0	61.4*
Aggravated assault	218.3	106.6
Burglary	949.1	296.6*
Larceny ($50+)	606.5	267.4*
Car theft	206.2	226.0†
Total	2,119.6	974.7

* The 1965 UCR show for burglary and larcenies the number of residential and individual crimes. The over-all rate per 100,000 population is therefore reduced by the proportion of these crimes that occurred to individuals. Since all robberies to individuals were included in the NORC sample regardless of whether the victim was acting as an individual or as part of an organization, the *total* UCR figure was used for comparison.
† The reduction of the UCR auto theft rate by 10 per cent is based on the figures of the Automobile Manufacturers Association, showing that 10 per cent of all cars are owned by leasing-rental agencies and private and governmental fleets. The Chicago Police Department's auto theft personnel confirmed that about 7-10 per cent of stolen cars recovered were from fleet, rental, and other nonindividually owned sources.

crimes. It may also indicate that people think the police can or will do more about a car theft than about many other offenses.

The startling frequency of reported forcible rape—four times that of the UCR index—underscores the peculiar nature of this crime. It occurs very often among people who know each other—at the extreme, estranged husband and wife—and there appears to be some stigma attached to the victim. Yet among the cases discovered in the survey, too few to be statistically reliable, most were reported to the police. Do the police tend to downgrade the offense into an assault or a minor sex case or put it into some miscellaneous category? This is a well-known practice for certain other kinds of crime.

To what extent is crime concentrated in the urban environment? To what extent are there regional differences in crime rates? And to what extent are the poor, and especially Negroes, more or less likely to be victims of crime? Behind these questions lie alternative remedial measures, measures which range from city planning and antipoverty programs to the training and organization of police departments and the allocation of their resources throughout the nation.

THE WILD, WILD WEST

The NORC findings presented in Table I give an overview of the crime rates for central cities in metropolitan areas, for their suburban environs, and for nonmetropolitan areas in the four main regions of the country. Figure 1 shows the crime rate (per 100,000 population) for serious crimes against the person (homicide, rape, robbery, and aggravated assault) and against property (burglary, larceny over $50, and vehicle theft).

The legend of the wild West is borne out by our data. Its present crime rate, for both property and personal crimes, is higher than that of any other region of the country. The West has almost twice the rates of the Northeast for all three types of communities. The South, in contrast, does not appear to have the high rate of violent crime that is sometimes alleged.

As one moves from the central city to the suburbs and out into the smaller towns and rural areas, the crime rates decline, but much more drastically for crimes against the person than for property crimes. The metropolitan center has a violent crime rate about five times as high as the smaller city and rural areas, but a property crime rate only twice as high.

Evidently the city is a more dangerous place than the suburbs or a small town. Yet these figures require some qualification: About 40 per cent of the aggravated assaults and rapes (constituting most of the serious crimes against the person) takes place within the victim's home; and about 45 per cent of all the serious crimes against the person are committed by someone familiar to the victim. Random "crime in the streets" by strangers is clearly not the main picture that emerges from these figures, even in the urban setting.

Who are the victims? Among lower income groups (under $6,000 per year) Negroes are almost twice as likely as whites to be victims of serious crimes of violence but only very slightly more likely to be victims of property crimes. Our figures show that, per 100,000 population, an estimated 748 low-income Negroes per year will be victims of criminal violence and 1,927 victims of property

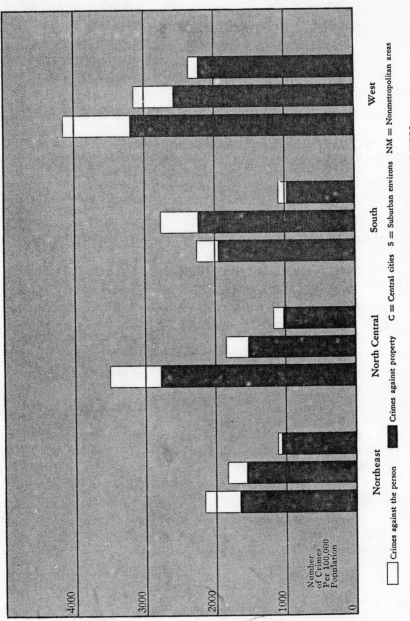

Number of Crimes Per 100,000 Population

4000

3000

2000

1000

0

Northeast   North Central   South   West

☐ Crimes against the person   ■ Crimes against property   C = Central cities   S = Suburban environs   NM = Nonmetropolitan areas

Figure 1. REGIONAL CRIME RATES BY TYPE OF COMMUNITY

offenses, whereas the numbers for whites in the same income bracket are 402 and 1,829. The situation is exactly reversed for upper income groups. The wealthier Negro is not much more likely than the white to be a victim of a violent crime, but he is considerably more likely to have property stolen. His chances of losing property are 3,024 in 100,000, whereas the figure is only 1,765 for whites in the same income bracket. Burglary is the most common property crime against more affluent Negroes. The implication is that ghetto neighborhoods in which poor and richer Negroes live side by side make the latter more vulnerable to property losses than are higher income whites, who can live in more economically homogeneous areas.

Despite the fact, then, that per capita offense rates are generally acknowledged to be higher among Negroes than among whites, the incidence of whites being victimized by Negroes—an image frequently conjured up by the specter of "crime in the streets"—is relatively infrequent. Negroes tend instead to commit offenses against members of their own race. The same is true of whites. Further, to the extent that crime is interracial at all, Negroes are more likely to be victims of white offenders than vice versa. Our figures show that only 12 per cent of the offenses against whites in our sample were committed by nonwhites, whereas 19 per cent of the nonwhite victims reported that the persons who committed offenses against them were white.

WHO CALLS THE POLICE?

What happens when a person is victimized? How often are law enforcement and judicial authorities involved? What changes occur in the victim's attitude and behavior as a result of the incident?

If the "right thing" to do is to call the police when you have been a victim of a crime, and there is considerable pressure to do just that, why is it that half the victimizations were not reported to the police?

The more serious the crime, the more likely it is to be reported: 65 per cent of the aggravated assaults in our sample were reported to the police, but only 46 per cent of the simple assaults; 60 per cent of the grand larcenies, but only 37 per cent of the petty larcenies. Insurance recovery also appears to play a role in the very high rate of reported auto thefts (89 per cent) and reported victimizations that are the result of automobile negligence (71 per cent). Victims of offenses at the border of the criminal law apparently do not think the police should be involved. Only 10 per cent of the consumer fraud victims called the police, whereas 26 per cent of the ordinary fraud victims (mainly those of bad checks) did so.

Those victims who said they did not notify the police were asked why. Their reasons fell into four fairly distinct categories. The first was the belief that the incident was not a police matter. These victims (34 per cent) did not want the offender to be harmed by the police or thought that the incident was a private, not a criminal, affair. Two per cent of the nonreporting victims feared reprisal, either physically from the offender's friends or economically from cancellation of or increases in rates of insurance. Nine per cent did not want to take the time or trouble to get involved with the police, did not know whether they should call the police, or were too confused to do so. Finally, a substantial 55 per cent of the nonreporting victims failed to notify the authorities because of their attitudes toward police effectiveness. These people believed the police could not do anything about the incident, would not catch the offenders, or would not want to be bothered.

The distribution of these four types of reasons for failure to notify police varies by type of crime and by the social characteristics of the victim, but two points are clear. First, there is strong resistance to invoking the law enforcement process even in matters that are clearly criminal. Second, there is considerable skepticism as to the effectiveness of police action.

THE ATTRITION OF JUSTICE

A clue to this skepticism lies in the events which follow a call to the police. All the victims who reported an offense were asked how the police reacted and how far the case proceeded up the judicial ladder—arrest, trial, sentencing, and so forth. We have simplified the process into six stages:

- Given a "real" victimization, the police were or were not notified
- Once notified, the police either came to the scene of the vic-

timization (or in some other way acknowledged the event) or failed to do so
• Once they arrived, the police did or did not regard the incident as a crime
• Regarding the matter as a crime, the police did or did not make an arrest
• Once an arrest was made, there was or was not a trial (including plea of guilty)
• The outcome of the trial was to free the suspect (or punish him "too leniently") or to find him guilty and give him the "proper" punishment

Figure 2 shows the tremendous attrition as the cases proceed from the bottom of the "iceberg," the initial victimization, to the top, the trial and sentencing. Failure of the police to heed a call and their rejection of the incident as a crime account for a large proportion of this attrition. Also noteworthy are the low arrest and trial rates. Once the offender is brought to trial, however, the outcome appears more balanced. About half the offenders were treated too leniently in the victim's view, but the other half were convicted and given "proper" punishment.

SATISFACTION AND REVENGE

How do the victims feel about this truncated legal process? Do they feel that the situation is their own fault and accept it, or are they dissatisfied with the relatively frequent failure of the police to apprehend the offender? When the victims were asked their feelings about the outcome of the incident, only 18 per cent said they were very satisfied; another 19 per cent were somewhat satisfied; 24 per cent were somewhat dissatisfied; and 35 per cent were very dissatisfied (4 per cent gave no answer).

The level of satisfaction was closely related to how far the case went judicially (see Table II). People who did not call the police at all were the most dissatisfied. If they called and the police did not come, about the same percentage were very dissatisfied; but peculiarly, there were more who reported that they were satisfied. An arrest lowered the dissatisfaction level, but the dramatic differences appeared when the offender was brought to trial. If he was

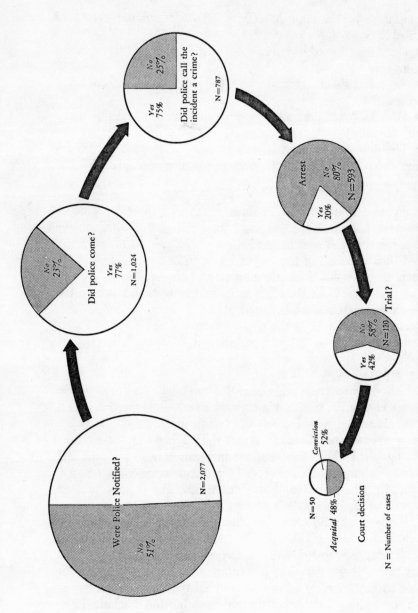

Figure 2 ATTRITION IN THE LEGAL PROCESS

Were Police Notified?
No 51%
N=2,077

Did police come?
No 23%
Yes 77%
N=1,024

Did police call the incident a crime?
No 25%
Yes 75%
N=787

Arrest
No 80%
Yes 20%
N=593

Trial?
No 58%
Yes 42%
N=120

Court decision
Conviction 52%
Acquital 48%
N=50

N = Number of cases

TABLE II   DEGREE OF SATISFACTION WITH OUTCOME OF OFFENSE

Disposition of case	Very satisfied	Somewhat satisfied	Somewhat dissatisfied	Very dissatisfied
No notification of police	13%	18%	28%	41%
Police did not respond to notification	22	22	18	38
Police did not consider incident a crime	24	26	24	26
Crime, but no arrest	20	23	27	30
Arrest, but no trial	33	21	22	24
Acquittal or too lenient penalty	17	13	26	44
Conviction and "proper" penalty	60	16	12	12

acquitted or given too lenient a penalty (in the victim's view), dissatisfaction ran high; if he was convicted and given the "proper" penalty, the victim was generally quite pleased. This suggests that the ordinary citizen's sense of justice includes a vengeful element —a desire for punishment over and above monetary compensation for loss. Advocates of rehabilitation rather than retribution for criminals might well take such public sentiments into account.

Quite independent of the judicial outcome of the case is its impact on the daily life and feelings of the victim and his family. Slightly more than 40 per cent of the victims reported increased suspicion and distrustfulness along with intensified personal and household security measures. It appears that it is the unpredictability of the event and the sense of invasion by strangers rather than the seriousness of the crime that engenders this mistrust. With these strong feelings and the frequent lack of knowledge about the identity of the offender, victimization may well exacerbate existing prejudice against the groups typically blamed for social disorder and crime.

POLICE POPULARITY POLL

How does the public feel about the police? The survey asked all the crime victims and a comparably large sample of nonvictims a series of questions probing their attitudes on how well the local police do their job, how respectful they are toward the citizenry, and how honest they are. Items concerning the limits of police authority and exploring the functions of the police were also included.

Several conclusions emerged. Upper income groups are consistently more favorable in their evaluation of the police and are more in favor of augmenting their power than those with lower incomes. Negroes at all income levels show strong negative attitudes toward the police (see Tables III and IV).

Table III shows rather clearly that Negroes, regardless of income, estimate police effectiveness lower than whites do, with Negro women even more critical than Negro men of the job the police are doing. Furthermore, Negroes show a smaller shift in attitude with increasing income than do whites, who are more favorable in their opinion of police effectiveness as their income rises.

TABLE III   POSITIVE OPINIONS ON LOCAL POLICE EFFECTIVENESS
(Percentage who think police do an excellent or good job in enforcing the law)

Sex	White		Nonwhite	
	Less than $6,000	$6,000 or more	Less than $6,000	$6,000 or more
Male	67%	72%	54%	56%
Female	66	74	39	43

Table IV shows that Negroes are also sharply more critical than whites are of police honesty. Here there are no income differences in attitude among white males. Women at higher income levels, both white and Negro, appear to be relatively less suspicious of police honesty. It is difficult to say how much these attitude differences are attributable to actual experience with police corruption and how much they express degrees of general hostility to the police. In either case the results indicate a more negative attitude toward the police among Negroes than among whites.

The next question probed a more personal attitude toward the police—their respectfulness toward "people like yourself." Almost 14 per cent of the Negroes answered that it was "not so good." Less than 3 per cent of the whites chose this response. This represents a much more critical attitude by Negroes than by whites, with hardly any differences by sex or income. There is some tendency, however, for very low income people of both races and sexes to feel that the police are not sufficiently respectful to them.

One further conclusion is more tentative. It appears that there is no one underlying attitude toward the police. The police have

TABLE IV Opinions on the Honesty of Neighborhood Police

| | Males | | | | Females | | | |
| | White | | Nonwhite | | White | | Nonwhite | |
Police are	Less than $6,000	$6,000 or more	Less than $6,000	$6,000 or more	Less than $6,000	$6,000 or more	Less than $6,000	$6,000 or more
Almost all honest	65%	67%	33%	33%	57%	65%	24%	35%
Most honest, few corrupt	24	26	47	41	27	29	54	49
Almost all corrupt	3	1	9	19	2	0	10	4
Don't know	8	6	11	7	14	6	12	12

many and sometimes only slightly related jobs to do in society. For example, they have a role both in suppressing organized gambling and in maintaining civil order. Most people (73 per cent) feel the police should stop gambling even though it brings a good deal of money into the community. A significant minority (21 per cent) feel the police should act only on complaints, and only 2 per cent said the police should not interfere with gambling at all. With respect to police control of demonstrations for civil and political rights, on the other hand, a slight majority (54 per cent) say police should not interfere if the protests are peaceful; 40 per cent say police should stop all demonstrations; and 3 per cent feel demonstrations should be allowed under any and all circumstances. Negroes are much more permissive about demonstrations than whites, and somewhat more permissive about gambling. Among lower income Negroes there is a significant relation between permissiveness on gambling and a strong prodemonstration attitude. But whites show no such consistent attitudes on the two issues. They tend to favor police intervention in gambling but not in rights demonstrations.

A more dramatic example of discontinuities in attitudes toward police has to do with limitations on their power. A national cross-section of citizens was asked:

• "Recently some cities have added civilian review boards to their police departments. Some people say such boards offer the public needed protection against the police, and others say these boards are unnecessary and would interfere with good police work and morale. In general, would you be in favor of civilian review boards or opposed to them?"

> In favor—45%
> Opposed—35%
> Don't know—20%

• "Do you favor giving the police more power to question people, do you think they have enough power already, or would you like to see some of their power to question people curtailed?"

> Police should have more power—52%
> Have enough power already—43%
> Should curtail power—5%

• "The police sometimes have a hard time deciding if there is enough evidence to arrest a suspect. In general, do you think it is better for them to risk arresting an innocent person rather than letting the criminal get away, or is it better for them to be really sure they are getting the right person before they make an arrest?"

Risk arresting innocent—42%
Be really sure—58%

• "The Supreme Court has recently ruled that in criminal cases the police may not question a suspect without his lawyer being present, unless the suspect agrees to be questioned without a lawyer. Are you in favor of this Supreme Court decision or opposed to it?"

In favor—65%
Opposed—35%

The significance of these results is their lack of consensus. On none of the questions is there overwhelming agreement or disagreement. Opinions are split almost in half, with the exception that hardly anyone is in favor of curtailing present police powers. The advocates of extending police authority in questioning suspects are almost balanced by those who think the police have enough power to do their job. Further, there is lack of internal agreement on the specific facets of the question. Being in favor of a civilian review board does not necessarily make a person support the Supreme Court decision on interrogation of suspects. Nor does a preference for having the police risk arresting the innocent rather than letting a criminal go free strongly predict being in favor of granting more power to the police in questioning people.

It is not clear why attitudes toward the police are so scattered. Perhaps police power is too new an issue on the national scene to have its components hammered into a clear and cohesive whole. Local variations in police practices may also blur the situation. It appears we are only at the beginning of a long process of relocating the police in the political spectrum.

As the federal presence in local law enforcement enlarges, both the shape of crime and the nature of law enforcement itself will change. Accurate crime statistics will be essential in monitoring these changes and in evaluating the worth of new programs designed to protect the public from the growing threat of invasion and victimization by criminal acts.

APPENDIX

The study reported here is one of the major research efforts to provide hard figures for the President's Crime Commission report. Its survey approach originated from well-known difficulties with police statistics. Those difficulties included the lack of comparability of criminal statistics in different cities; the fact that "crime waves" could be made to appear and disappear with changes in the system of reporting; the failure to include some kinds of criminal activities in statistical reports or to differentially report certain types of crimes; and, perhaps most important, the impossibility of estimating how much crime was not being reported to the police.

The excellent work of the FBI's Uniform Crime Reports, upon which the UCR index of major crime is based, repaired only some of these difficulties because these reports still drew on local police records. Was there another way to measure crime that did not rely on the police? Could a survey method do the job? These were the questions that D. Gale Johnson, dean of the social sciences at The University of Chicago, asked Peter H. Rossi, director of the National Opinion Research Center (NORC), in 1962.

The inquiry was of more than academic interest, for Chicago's crime statistics had just been jogged upward by the new police superintendent, Orlando Wilson, pointing out in dramatic fashion all the difficulties just outlined. In Chicago, as well as nationally, important policy questions—what resources had to be given to the police and how they were to be allocated—depended upon accurate social bookkeeping on the amount and distribution of crime.

After considerable experimentation NORC concluded that a survey of individual *victims* of crime could feasibly supply national estimates. Moreover, such estimates were now imperative. The crime problem was becoming more serious daily, and the President's commission had already begun its investigation.

The study's focus on individual victims meant that some crimes could not be measured. People were simply not going to report their participation in illegal activities such as violation of gambling, game, or liquor laws, abortion, or the use of narcotics. Crimes against corporations or other large institutions were also excluded.

Crimes of violence and property crimes against the individual were the main targets. Defining such crimes turned out to be a problem. For example, many people said they had been "robbed" (personally held up) when in fact they had been "burglarized" (had had property stolen from their homes, cars, etc.). Was a fist fight in the schoolyard really an assault? Was being given a bad check by a friend a fraud, a basis for a civil law suit, or just a private matter? Was the man's coat really taken, or did he leave it in the bar? A "stolen" pocketbook may simply have been lost, and a "consumer fraud" have been no more than sharp dealing.

A variety of tactics were used to identify and reduce these potential errors. First, interviewers were instructed to allow the respondents plenty of time to recollect about each type of crime. Then, when an incident was recalled, the special questionnaire form probed intensively into the matter—what had happened, when and where, whether there were witnesses, whether the police were called, the extent of injuries, loss, and damage, and the direct and indirect costs. Was there an arrest, a trial? If not, what was the outcome?

The 3,400 "crimes" reported in the interviews were then reviewed by two different staff members, evaluating each case independently. To check this evaluation procedure, a team of lawyers from the American Bar Foundation and two detectives from the Chicago police department were asked to make independent evaluations of NORC's interviews. The results were most encouraging, with substantial agreement in between 75 and 80 per cent of the cases.

The evaluation outcome reduced the initial 3,400 reported victimizations to about 2,100. These 2,100 offenses—ranging all the way from murder to victimizing incidents typically treated as private matters—were felt to realistically represent the experience of the American people with crime.

EXERCISES

The exercises here are designed to give the student practical experience in drawing samples, constructing questionnaires, and other tasks faced by the survey researcher using a questionnaire. Exercise 4 is a full-scale research project requiring the student to employ all the various techniques of questionnaire surveys; it is suggested that this be done as a class undertaking. It would probably be a good idea to warm up for this final project by completing the other exercises first.

EXERCISE 1

In order to draw a random sample of a universe to be researched, it is generally necessary to begin by having some sort of listing of all the units in the universe. This exercise is designed to give you some practice in locating such listings.

Some universes are familiar and the names of the members readily available, such as the universe of telephone users, which can be found in the telephone directory. Other listings, however, are not so well known or so easily available, such as a list of registered motor-vehicle owners or a list of owners of thoroughbred race horses.

How would you go about finding the universe of students attending your school? Write down everything you must do and everyone you must contact to obtain such a list. Now you should be able to write a set of instructions for locating and obtaining the units for such a universe. Do the same thing for the universe of registered voters, welfare services (not welfare recipients), and local service clubs. Some of these universes contain people as the units; and, in others, organizations or agencies are the universe units. Once you have the lists, draw a simple random sample from each and make up a list of the sample.

EXERCISE 2

For this exercise, you will need a detailed map of your community and a city directory. Your library will have a copy of a city directory, and either the library or your city or county clerk will have a detailed map. (The map should show at least every block in the community and preferably every household.

Once you have the map and the directory, draw an area sample of your community. First, divide the map into sections based on either political or social boundaries (for example, ethnic, socio-economic, age groups, etc.), or simply make a grid and impose it on the map. Number each of the general sections and randomly choose a 50 per cent sample. Next, from this general sample, draw a 25 per cent sample based on blocks. That is, randomly select 25 per cent of the blocks from each of the sections in your general sample. If you have a map showing individual households, select 20 per cent of the households in each block in the sample. If individual households are not represented on your map or there are several apartment buildings on your sample blocks, simply select every fifth household in each of the sample blocks to be in the sample, and write down the address.

Now you have an area sample of your community based on addresses. To find who lives in each household, use the city directory. This will give you the names and telephone numbers of those in your sample in case you want to use a mail questionnaire or conduct a telephone survey.

EXERCISE 3

Develop a questionnaire that would provide the information necessary to test the following hypothesis:

The older people are, the more conservative they are.

In developing the questionnaire, consider the following problems: What kinds of items indicate conservatism? What dimensions of conservatism are there (for example, political, sexual, and so on)? What kinds of items should be included to see whether something other than age is the independent variable (for example, social status, ethnic background)? Have other studies been done on this that might be useful in developing the questionnaire? How could such studies be located? How should the questions be worded so that people of different ages understand them in the same way? How should the questions be constructed so that they can be coded? How long should the questionnaire be? Should the questions be open-ended, closed-ended, or both?

EXERCISE 4

This exercise is intended to test the hypothesis that sex roles influence the career plans of college students. Traditionally, women's role has been domestic and noncareer in orientation, while men's role has been nondomestic and career-oriented. For women, college has been seen largely as an opportunity to meet a prospective husband; while for men, it is seen as a training ground for a future career. Recently, however, more and more women are actively seeking careers and have come to believe that four years of college should prepare them for jobs outside the kitchen and nursery.

To find out the extent to which the traditional sex roles influence women's career plans, develop and administer a questionnaire survey. Take a sample of men and women from different college majors at your school and analyze their responses to determine whether women's career plans are similar to, or different from, men's. If women are less likely to have plans other than for marriage, then the hypothesis will be accepted; but, if there are no differences or very slight differences, the hypothesis will be rejected. Finally, find out which occupations are chosen predominately by women and which by men as well as those that are chosen about equally by both. Then classify the occupations in terms of "women," "men," and "general."

ADDITIONAL READING SUGGESTIONS

HYMAN, HERBERT. 1955. *Survey Design and Analysis*. Glencoe, Ill.: The Free Press. A detailed discussion of how to design surveys in order to test various types of hypotheses and solve different kinds of problems. Also, it shows how to set up the survey so that the data can be readily analyzed, and explains how the analysis should be done.

LAZARSFELD, PAUL F. 1954. "The Art of Asking Why: Three Principles Underlying the Formulation of Questionnaires." In Daniel Katz et al. (eds.), *Public Opinion and Propaganda*, pp. 675–86. New York: Holt, Rinehart and Winston. Lazarsfeld's chapter is extremely helpful for constructing a wide variety of questionnaires. He explains that the purpose of questionnaires is to gather information for testing hypotheses, and outlines the principles for doing so.

SIMMONS, ROBERTA G., and MORRIS ROSENBERG. 1971. "Functions of Children's Perceptions of the Stratification System," *American Sociological Review*, 36 (April), pp. 235–49. A good example of the various steps in survey research. Also, it is useful in showing how survey data are laid out in tables. The analysis is relatively simple, but it is done in such a way as to give the researchers the information they need; therefore, it is both understandable and useful.

5. Observation Survey

DRUNK COURT— THE ADULT PARALLEL TO JUVENILE COURT
—Jacqueline P. Wiseman

THE DISTINCTION THAT PETERSON and Matza (1963:107) draw between two basic types of court procedures—the legalistic court and the so-called socialized court—is especially pertinent to the operation of the drunk court, as will be seen from the following brief outline.

Legalistic courts operate under an adversary system, by which a state attorney and a defense counsel plead a case before a judge and/or jury. The purpose of the trial is to determine whether the defendant in fact committed the crime with which he is charged. Great stress is placed on formal proceedings and rules of evidence, very little on information regarding the defendant's character and background. If he is convicted, the defendant is subject to fine, imprisonment, or execution. The punishment fits the crime, not the particular individual.

Socialized courts usually exercise jurisdiction either over juveniles, both neglected or dependent and delinquent or criminal; or over family law or in some jurisdictions, over both juvenile and domestic problems in one omnibus court. Its methods and procedures have made greatest inroads in the juvenile court. Here, the adversary system is replaced by one or more social workers' reports, which emphasize information regarding the character and background of all

From Jacqueline P. Wiseman, *Stations of the Lost: The Treatment of Skid Row Alcoholics*. © 1970. Reprinted by permission of Prentice-Hall, Inc., Englewood Cliffs, N.J. and the Author.

parties. Judicial procedure is informal; rules of evidence do not apply. The purpose of the hearing is to determine whether a serious problem exists—whether, for example, a child requires help—and to provide the means to meet the needs of the individuals involved.

Although not officially designated as a socialized court in the statutes, drunk court sessions are almost always operated along the latter lines. However, the drunk court judge faces unusual administrative and decisional problems that have a gross distorting effect on its more informal and humanized ideology.

Unlike other cases in other courts, where guilt or innocence of the defendant is the issue, the judge's decision in drunk court is almost always the sentence alone. . . . With but rare exceptions, the men plead guilty. The judge, therefore, has no official reason to assume the men are other than guilty.

Sentencing men who plead guilty to a public drunkenness charge, however, presents a real conflict to a judge who wishes to see himself as compassionate, wise, and just. Because of the widespread discussion of alcoholism as a social problem and a physical illness, a judge must take cognizance of both the need for efficient administration of sentences for public drunks and the theoretical causes of alcoholism. As a collateral matter, he is also aware that ordinary male citizens sometimes "tie one on," perhaps do damage to themselves or others, and are arrested by police. Such men usually have jobs and a family. A jail sentence for public drunkenness would be a severe blow, both socially and economically.

In other words, with each man who appears before him the judge must ask himself whether he should view the defendant as merely an "overindulgent social drinker," or as a "chronic drunken bum," or as a "sick alcoholic."

In the first of these possible definitions, the judge must make a decision about whether the defendant is a wayward, but basically solid, citizen. If this is the case, the sentence can be suspended and the person let off with a warning. On the other hand, if the defendant is the type the judge tends to mentally characterize as a "childlike, hedonistic, willful, chronic drunk," he must be dried out for his own good, since he is a menace to himself and society. All the while, the third possible definition creates great decisional pressures, because the judge is aware that he must consider the prevailing public opinion that alcoholism *per se* is an illness, even if some of the acts of the person who drinks too much may legally be defined as a crime. (See Stem, 1967.) If the judge accepts this latter view, he is forced to consider the possibility he is sentencing a man who may be ill to jail. The implied inhumanity of this act must be explained and justified, even if only self-justification is involved.

This decisional picture is further confused by the fact that the judge must consider not one but two types of illness. The first type is the temporary, acute *physical distress* caused by repeated over-indulgence in alcohol which, in cases of continuous heavy drink-ing, is serious enough to cause death if left unattended. The second type is based on the assumption that some mysterious psychologi-cal compulsion forces a man to drink and, like the plea "not guilty by reason of insanity," the chronic alcoholic is not responsible for his excessive drinking. Each type of illness demands a different kind of concern and treatment, although in judicial discussions these are often blurred together.

If a judge were to think aloud, he might explain the chronic drunk sentence dilemma and his solution to it something like this:

> Alcoholism may be an illness or it may be a weakness. Whatever it is, all alcoholics need help to quit drinking. One of the surest ways to help an alcoholic quit drinking is to separate him forcibly from any supply of liquor. However, jail is a drastic penalty for being found drunk and therefore should be used only after other methods fail. This is because if a man is sent to jail, he may suffer unde-sirable social consequences, such as jeopardizing his job or causing his wife and children great embarrassment. Some men are so upset about being arrested, that is all the punishment they need. It serves as adequate warning. Others should be educated about the dangers of overindulgence through forced attendance at Alcoholism School. Others need a short sentence, but suspended, to scare them a bit; still others need a short sentence to see what jail is like so they don't want ever to go back; and some repeaters need aid in getting off the bottle which can be supplied by a longer separation from it —say 30, 60 or 90 days. The jail is set up to give these men both medical and psychological therapy through the Jail Branch Clinic of the Out-Patient Therapy Center, so they are well taken care of. Transients can be handled by telling them to leave town.

Matching sentences with men who plead guilty is thus the

judge's true concern. This task must be handled within the pressures created by restricting drunk court to a morning session in one courtroom, regardless of the number of men scheduled to be seen that day.

Up until last year (when drunk arrests were temporarily reduced because of the large number of hippies and civil rights demonstrators in jail), 50 to 250 men were often sentenced within a few hours. Appearance before the judge was handled in platoons of five to 50. This meant the judge decided the fate of each defendant within a few short minutes. Thus judicial compassion attained assembly-line organization and speed.

As a court observer noted:

> The Court generally disposes of between 50 and 100 cases per day, but on any Monday there are 200 to 250 and on Monday mornings after holiday weekends the Court may handle as many as 350 cases. I would estimate that, on the average, cases take between 45 seconds and one minute to dispose of (LeClercq, 1966:1).

Later, with drunk arrests drastically curtailed, the court handled no more than 50 cases in an average morning, and perhaps 125 on the weekends, according to the observer. Right after a civil rights demonstration that resulted in many arrests, only 33 persons were observed in drunk court. This reduction in the quantity of defendants, however, did not appear to increase the length of time spent on each person. Rather, it seemed to reduce it. The observer noted the average length of time per person was 30 seconds, although the size of platoons was reduced from 50 to 15 or 20.

SENTENCING CRITERIA

How is the judge able to classify and sentence a large, unwieldy group of defendants so quickly? The answer is he utilizes social characteristics as indicators to signify drinking status—just as in an arrest situation the policeman looked for socal characteristics to identify alcoholic troublemaking potential, combined with the arrestee's legal impotence. The effect is essentially the same: the men are objectified into social types for easy classification. In the case of the judge, the legal decision process must be more refined than for a policeman's arrest, no-arrest decision. Therefore, the judge's sentencing criteria are more complex, as they must include all possible decision combinations.

From court observations, plus interviews with court officers and judges, three primary criteria for typing defendants in drunk court emerge:

The General Physical Appearance of the Man. Is he shaky and obviously in need of drying out? Here, some of the judges ask the men to extend their hands before sentencing and decide the sentence on the degree of trembling.

Physical appearance may actually be the most potent deciding factor. As one court officer put it, when asked how the judges decide on a sentence:

> Primarily by appearance. You can tell what kind of shape they're in. If they're shaking and obviously need drying out, you know some are on the verge of the DT's so these get 10 or 15 days [in jail] to dry out.

One of the seasoned judges said that his criteria were as follows:

> I rely on his record and also his "looks." Their "looks" are very important. I make them put their hands out—see if they are dirty and bloody in appearance (LeClercq, 1966:12).

Past Performance. How many times have they been up before the court on a drunk charge before? A record of past arrests is considered to be indicative of the defendant's general attitude toward drinking. The longer and more recent the record, the greater the need for a sentence to aid the defendant to improve his outlook on excessive liquor consumption. (This is in some contradiction to the presumed greater need the man must have for drying out, since previous recent jailings mean that he could not have been drinking for long.)

The previous comment, plus the answer by a court officer to the question "Who gets dismissed?", illustrates this criterion for sentencing:

> A person with no previous arrests [gets dismissed]. If they have had no arrests, then the judge hates for them to have a conviction on their record. *The more arrests they've had and the more recently they've had them, the more likely they are to get another sentence.* (Emphasis mine.)

The Man's Social Position. Does he have a job he could go to? Is he married? Does he have a permanent address, or will he literally be on the streets if he receives a dismissal?

For these data, dress is an all-important clue, age a secondary one. A man who looks down-and-out is more likely to receive a sentence than the well-dressed man. According to a court officer:

> If they look pretty beat—clothes dirty and in rags, then you figure that they need some help to stop drinking before they kill themselves.

> If they're under 21 we usually give them a kick-out. If they are a business man or a lawyer we have them sign a civil release so they can't sue and let them go.

An observer reports that a judge freed a young man with the following remarks:

> I am going to give you a suspended sentence and hope that this experience will be a warning to you. I don't want you to get caught up in this cycle.

Transients form a category of their own and get a special package deal—if they will promise to leave town, they draw a suspended sentence or probation. The parallel between this practice and the police policy of telling some Skid Row drunks to "take a walk" need only be mentioned. The following interchanges are illustrative:

> *Judge:* I thought you told me the last time you were in here that you were going to leave Pacific City.
> *Defendant:* I was supposed to have left town yesterday. I just got through doing time.
> *Judge:* Go back to Woodland. Don't let me see you in here again or we are going to put you away. Thirty days suspended.
> *Defendant:* I am supposed to leave with the circus tomorrow. If I don't go, I will be out of work for the whole season.
> *Judge:* You promised to leave three times before. Thirty days in the County Jail.

By combining the variables of physical appearance, past performance, and social position, a rough description of the social types expected in drunk court and matching sentences for each type are shown in Table I.

These first two categories in Table I, and sometimes the third, have not been, in Garfinkel's terms, "made strange" (1967). They are treated as though they are full-fledged persons who may have

TABLE I   PARADIGM OF SOCIAL TYPES AND SENTENCES IN DRUNK COURT

Social Type	Probable Sentence
A young man who drank too much: a man under 40, with a job, and perhaps a wife, who has not appeared in court before	A kick-out or a suspended sentence
The young repeater: same as above, but has been before judge several times (may be on way to being an alcoholic)	Suspended sentence or short sentence (5-10 days) to scare him, or possible attendance at Alcoholism School
The repeater who still looks fairly respectable. (Image vacillating between an alcoholic and a drunk)	30-day suspended sentence, with possible attendance at Alcoholism School
Out-of-towner (social characteristics not important as they have nonlocal roots). Therefore not important whether overindulged, a chronic drunk, or an alcoholic	Suspended sentence on condition he leave town. Purpose is to discourage him from getting on local loop and adding to taxpayer's load
The middle-aged repeater who has not been up for some time. (May be an alcoholic who has relapsed)	Suspended sentence with required attendance at Alcholism School or given to custody of Christian missionaries
The derelict-drunk who looks "rough," i.e., suffering withdrawal, a hangover, has cuts and bruises, may have malnutrition or some diseases connected with heavy drinking and little eating; a chronic drunk; seedy clothing, stubble beard, etc.	30–60–90-day sentence depending on number of prior arrests and physical condition at time of arrest. (Has probably attended Alcoholism School already)
The man who looks gravely ill (probably a chronic alcoholic)	County hospital under suspended sentence

over-indulged. The remaining types are stripped-down persons, on the "other side," so far as they are perceived by the judge.

A total of 180 men were observed in drunk court and tabulated according to the social types outlined in the table. Observations were spread over three days. Two different judges presided. The results are shown in Table II.

Of the total tabulated, the Skid Row alcoholics category would include the derelict (38 per cent), the middle-aged repeater who has not been arrested for some time, probably having been in the loop (11 per cent), the out-of-towner (8 per cent), and the man who looks gravely ill (2 per cent), for a total of 59 per cent. This

TABLE II   DISTRIBUTION OF DRUNK ORDINANCE SOCIAL TYPES IN COURT

Social Types	Per cent (N=180)
Derelict who looks "rough"	38
Young repeater	15
Recent repeater who looks respectable	15
Middle-aged repeater who has not been arrested for some time	11
Young man with wife, job, first offense	11
Out-of-towner	8
Man who looks gravely ill	2
Total	100

TABLE III   DISTRIBUTION OF SENTENCES IN DRUNK COURT

Sentences	Per cent of defendants (N=180)	
Kick-out (no sentence, warned only)	2	
County hospital		
With hold	—	
No hold	2	
		74 (non-jail sentence)
Suspended sentence		
10 days or less	—	
11 to 30 days	23	
31 to 60 days	28	
61 to 90 days	19	
Over 90 days	—	
Sentence to County Jail		
10 days or less	1	
11 to 30 days	23	
31 to 60 days	2	26 (jail sentence)
61 to 90 days	—	
Over 90 days	—	
Total	100	

is quite near the usual 40 to 45 per cent of Skid Row men represented in the total arrests for drunkenness in Pacific City.

The detailed pattern of sentencing was also tabulated and is illustrated in Table III. As can be seen in the table, only 26 per cent of the men received sentences to be served in County Jail. This is quite close to the yearly average of 20 to 25 per cent.

Most pertinent to this study, however, is the distribution of sentences among social types of defendants. From Table IV, it

TABLE IV   Distribution of Sentences Among Social Types of Defendants in Drunk Court

Sentences	Per cent of defendants by social types						
	Young man with job, wife, 1st offense (N=19)	Young repeater (N=27)	Middle-aged respectable repeater (N=26)	Out-of-towner (N=15)	Middle-aged repeater, not recent (N=20)	Derelict who looks rough (N=69)	Man looking gravely ill (N=4)
Kick-out (no sentence, warned only)	21	—	—	—	—	—	—
County hospital							
With hold	—	—	—	—	—	—	—
No hold	—	—	—	—	—	—	75
Suspended sentence							
10 days or less	59	22	11	60	15	13	25
11 to 30 days	10	22	35	—	60	30	—
31 to 60 days	10	37	35	33	25	3	—
61 to 90 days	—	—	—	—	—	—	—
Over 90 days	—	—	—	—	—	—	—
Sentenced to County Jail							
10 days or less	—	4	4	7	—	—	—
11 to 30 days	—	15	15	—	—	54	—
31 to 60 days	—	—	—	—	—	—	—
61 to 90 days	—	—	—	—	—	—	—
Over 90 days	—	—	—	—	—	—	—
Totals	100	100	100	100	100	100	100

can be seen that the derelicts who look rough or men who are repeaters (regardless of age or appearance), are most likely to serve time and get the longest sentences. Furthermore, the derelict who looks rough is the least likely of any social type to escape jail.

A word should be said about the suspended sentence. Judges sometimes give exceedingly long suspended sentences to drunk ordinance defendants—often 90 days or more to repeaters. This places a weapon in the hands of the court that is greatly feared. If at any time within the following 90 days (or whatever the length of the sentence), the man is picked up on a drunk charge, he may be sent directly to jail without trial for the entire length of the suspended sentence. Many men, upon receiving a long suspended sentence, and realizing their vulnerability to arrest, will "take out insurance" against being incarcerated for that length of time by seeking admission to another "more desirable" station on the loop. Favorite "hideouts" while waiting for the suspended sentence to run out are (in approximate rank order): Welfare Home for Homeless Men, State Mental Hospital, and the Christian Missionaries.

OTHER SENTENCING ASSISTANCE

Even with the aid of a simplified mental guide, the judge cannot be expected to assemble and assimilate sufficient material on each man, review it, mentally type the man, and then make a sentencing decision in less than a minute. Thus, it is not surprising that almost all drunk court judges employ the aid of one assistant and sometimes two court attachés who are familiar with the Row and its inhabitants. These men are known as court liaison officers. Because of personal familiarity with chronic drunkenness offenders, the liaison officers are able to answer questions about each accused person quickly and to recommend a case disposition. Such persons obviously operate as an informal screening board.

The most important court helper in Pacific City is a man who knows most of the Row men by sight and claims also to know their general outlook on alcohol and life. Known to the defendants as "the Rapper," this man often sits behind the judge and suggests informally who would benefit most from probation and assignment to Alcoholism School, who might need the "shaking-up" that jail provides, and who ought to be sent to alcoholic screening at City Hospital and perhaps on to State Mental Hospital. As each man is named, the Rapper whispers to the judge, who then passes sentence. (See Bogue, 1963:414.)

In Pacific City, the man who was the Rapper for a period of time was an ex-alcoholic who could claim intimate knowledge of the chronic drunkenness offender because he had drunk with them. A relative of the Rapper was highly placed in city politics, and the Rapper made no secret of the fact that his appointment was politically engineered. During the course of the study (several times in fact), the Rapper himself "fell off the wagon" and underwent treatment at Northern State Mental Hospital, one of the stations on the loop. While there, the Rapper told about his recent job with the court and how he helped the judge:

> Each man arrested has a card with the whole record on it. We would go over the cards before the case came up. We see how many times he's been arrested. I could advise the judge to give them probation or a sentence. Many times, the family would call and request a sentence. I would often arrange for them to get probation plus clothes and a place to stay at one of the halfway houses. Oh, I'll help and help, but when they keep falling off—I get disgusted.

The Christian Missionaries also send a liaison man to the drunk court sessions. He acts as Rapper at special times and thereby also serves in an informal screening capacity. Sponsorship by this organization appears to guarantee that the defendant will get a suspended sentence. For instance, this interchange was observed in court several times:

> *Judge*, turning to Missionary representative: "Do you want him [this defendant]?" (Meaning, "Will you take him at one of your facilities?")
> *Missionary*: (Nods "Yes.")
> *Judge*: "Suspended sentence."

Another observer discussed this arrangement with a veteran judge:

> *Interviewer: Isn't there any attempt made to consider the men for rehabilitation?*
> The men are screened by the Christian Missionaries usually. The Christian Missionaries send someone down to the jail who tries to help them. They talk with the men and screen them. Nobody does the job that the Christian Missionaries do in the jails.

Interviewer: The Court abdicates the screening of defendants to the Christian Missionaries, then?

Not completely. We try to keep a record. Some of these men we can help, but most we can't. I know by heart all of their alibis and stories [LeClercq, 1966:11].

Another important informal court post is filled by an employee who is known to some of the men as "the Knocker." The job of the Knocker is to maintain the personal records of the men who appear before drunk court and to supply the judge with this information. A court observer reported the following:

The Knocker spoke to the judge in just about every case. However, I do not know what he said. He may just be reading to the judge the official records, or he may be giving his personal judgment about the possibility of the defendant being picked up again in the near future. One thing seems clear: the judge receives his information from the Knocker just before he hands out the sentence.

Sometimes it is difficult to distinguish the Knocker (who merely gives information to the judge) from the Rapper (who "suggests" the proper sentence.) In 1963, two of these court liaison officers worked together. An interview with one partner is quoted below:

Interviewer: What do you do?

Up here we act as a *combination district attorney and public defender* [emphasis mine]. We are more familiar with these guys than the judges are. The judges alternate. We have the previous arrest records. A lot of times, guys will give phony names. It may take us a while to catch up with them. We try to remember if we have seen a guy before.

Interviewer: How does a judge decide whether to sentence the men and if so, for how long?

We help him out on that. If a guy has been in three times in four weeks, they should get a minimum of 30 days. They need to dry out. You know, if a man has been arrested three times in four weeks, you ask yourself the question: "How many times has he been drunk that he wasn't arrested?" Also, you look at the condition of a man—he may even need hospitalization.

Interviewer: You mean you can tell whether a man ought to be sent to jail by looking at him?

Some of them look a lot more rough looking than others. You can tell they have been on a drunk for more than one day. They are heavily bearded. They have probably been sleeping in doorways or on the street. You can tell they have been on a long drunk [LeClercq, 1966:6–7].

Thus perhaps the most revealing aspect of the sentencing procedure is the virtual absence of interest in the *charge* and the judge's role as spokesman for the court officer's decision. This may account for the fact the judge seldom discusses the case with the defendant, except in a jocular, disparaging way. The following interchanges, which illustrate this attitude, were witnessed by observers:

Defendant: I was sleeping in a basement when a man attacked me with a can opener.
Judge: Did you also see elephants?

Judge: What is your story this time?
Defendant: (As he begins to speak, Judge interrupts.)
Judge: You gave me that line yesterday; 30 days in the County Jail.

COURT ATMOSPHERE

The above exchanges between the judge and the defendant would seem to suggest the atmosphere of drunk court is more informal than most courts of law. From the reports obtained from all observers, this is true. Drunk court is not taken as seriously as other sessions of the municipal court, or other departments, and a great deal of levity and antic behavior is tolerated (in full view of defendants), an attitude not allowed in other Pacific City courts. Excerpts from observers' notes illustrate this unserious aspect of drunk court:

Bailiff came in today and asked other court officers in voice audible to all, "When does the parade [of defendants] begin?"
There is open flirting between a police matron and police before court starts.
The Knocker and bailiff put a sign, "The Flying Nun," over the judge's name before court started. Removed it when judge appeared.
Judge comes in the front door of the court, walks very casually, often presides without robe. Unlike other courts, bailiff asks everyone to remain seated when judge appears. Judge is always five to ten minutes late.

Just as the judge was about ready to start, there was a gasp and a thud. (This didn't seem to shake anyone except me.) One of the defendants had fallen over near the front of the line, and the other defendants stood there like this wasn't anything to get upset about.

The judge asked, "What was his number?" and the Knocker told him. Then one of the court policemen said that he thought the guy was dead. "This man has had an alcoholic seizure. We're going to take him to the hospital," the judge said.

The bailiff asked what should be done about the man's case. The judge dismissed it. It was the only kick-out that day.

From this it can be seen that the operational ideology of the judge in drunk court, although much like that of juvenile court, is lacking in the compassion often shown for juveniles. An attempt is made to sentence the man in terms of his characteristics and not the criminal act he is accused of. Extenuating circumstances of all types are used in arriving at decisions. There is no lawyer or advocacy system in operation. The defendant may be discharged to "responsible" persons in the community (this means some member of his family if he has one, or the Christian Missionaries if they exhibit an interest in him).

Far from freeing the judge to make idiosyncratic personalized decisions, the result of the drunk court system is to standardize drunks on the basis of social types and then with the assistance of court aides objectify them in such a way as to fit the predetermined types. Thus the decision of the patrolman in typification of the Skid Row drinker is not only accepted in the court without question—it is reinforced and embellished.

Justifying the Sentencing Process

How does the municipal court judge, serving in drunk court sessions, allow himself to be a party to such extra-legal activities as platoon sentencing, the heavy reliance on advice from "friends of the court," and the utilization of extraneous social characteristics in setting the sentence? Why is there not a conflict with his self-image of judicial compassion for the individual and scrupulous attention to legal niceties?

For some judges, the conflict is resolved by falling back on the alcoholism-as-an-illness view of drunkenness, and by redefining many of the men who appear before him as *patients* rather than defendants. Thus, when asked to describe their duties, drunk court judges often sound like physicians dealing with troublesome patients for whom they must prescribe unpleasant but necessary medicine, rather than judges punishing men for being a public annoyance. As an example of this:

> I know that jail isn't the best place for these men, but we have to do something for them. We need to put them someplace where they can dry out. You can't just let a man go out and kill himself.

> This is a grave and almost hopeless problem. But you have to try some kind of treatment. Often they are better off in jail than out on the street.

The drunk court judges sometimes add the wish that the city provided a more palatable alternative to the County Jail, but then reiterate the view that it is better than no help at all.

Court attachés have essentially the same attitude:

> Some of these guys are so loaded that they will fall and break their skull if you don't lock them up. Half of these guys have no place to stay anyway except a dingy heap. They are better off in jail.

> The whole purpose of the law is to try to help them. It's for the protection of themselves and for others, that's the way the law reads. For example, say you're driving through here [Skid Row] and you hit a drunk. He could get killed and if you don't stop and render aid, you could become a criminal.

> Giving them 30 days in County Jail is sometimes a kindness. *You are doing them a favor, like a diabetic who won't take his insulin.* Sometimes you must hurt him to help him. (Emphasis mine.)

Like the Skid Row police, the officers, the judge and his coterie are reinforced in their definition of the situation as clinical, and of themselves as diagnosticians and social internists, by the fact that relatives often call the court and ask that a man be given time in jail for his own good. The judge usually complies. Furthermore, as has been mentioned, there is at the jail a branch of the Out-Patient Therapy Center that was originally established to work for the rehabilitation of alcoholics. Having this jail clinic allows the drunk court judge to say:

I sentence you to 30 days and I will get in touch with the social worker at the County Jail and she will help you.

I sentence you to therapy with the psychologists at the County Jail (Also reported by court observers.)

Creation of the Pacific City Alcoholism School also allows the judge to feel that he is fulfilling both judicial and therapeutic duties, giving the defendant a suspended sentence on the condition that he will attend the lecture sessions.

Where the name of the social worker or psychologist of Alcoholism School is not invoked as part of the sentence, an awareness of alcoholism as an illness is frequently used as an introductory statement to indicate the reasoning of the courts for giving a jail sentence.

We realize that you men are sick and need help. Any action I might take, therefore, should not in any sense be construed as punishment. Jail in this case is not a punitive measure, but to help you with your alcoholism problem.

However, the uneasiness of the judge with the jailing of alcoholics has other indicators. The captain of the County Jail, for instance, reports that inmates serving time for public drunkenness have only to write a letter requesting modification and it is almost automatically forthcoming, something not true for modification requests of prisoners convicted of other misdemeanors.

That drunk court's methods and procedures of handling the Row men go against the judicial grain also seems to be indicated by the fact court officers claims a new judge must be "broken in" to drunk court before he operates efficiently. When the judge first arrives, he will sentence differently from an experienced judge and in the direction of greater leniency. This upsets the established pattern.

The result is he is taken in hand and guided to do "the right thing" by the veteran court aides. As one court aide put it:

Most of the judges are pretty good—they rely on us. Sometimes you get a new judge who wants to do things his way. We have to break them in, train them. This court is very different. We have to break new judges in. It takes some of them some time to get adjusted to the way we do things.

The high rate of recidivism of chronic drunkenness offenders leads some experts to question the value of jail as a cure for alcoholism or chronic drunkenness. Publicly, at least, the judges appear to hold to the view that the current arrest and incarceration process can be helpful, but that often the alcoholic simply does not respond to "treatment" permanently and needs periodic "doses" of jail-therapy. As one judge put it:

> Some men have simply gone so far that you can't do anything for them. They are hopeless. All we can do is send them to jail to dry out from time to time.

SENTENCING AS AN ASSEMBLY-LINE OUTRAGE

Although the chronic drunkenness offender makes many trips through drunk court, it is not too surprising that he never becomes completely accustomed to the way he is treated there. The mass sentencing, the arbitrariness of the judge, the extraneous factors that seem to go into sentencing decisions, all these shock and embitter him.

Of the group-sentencing procedures, the Row men have this to say:

> It's law on the assembly line. That's how it really is. No judge would admit it, though. He's got a nice, soft, plush $15,000 or $18,000 job which hinges on this.
>
> I mean there's no concept on the part of anybody that goes into drunk court, that this is a court of law, that the judge is going to weigh the pros and cons. . . .
>
> Let me tell you, he's handling 50 guys in a period of an hour or less. Do you think he has time to, uh, to say, "Well now, why do you drink?" and like that?
>
> The situation here [in jail] could stand a lot of improvement, but the court situation is much worse. When you go down there to court each individual in the courts of the United States is entitled to individual and separate trial. You go down there and they run you into these courts, 30 or 40 at a time, and they sentence you accordingly. The front row first.
>
> I was in there one time, I don't remember who the judge was, when we got in he ran off about seven or eight names, "You people have 30 days in the County Jail." Then he says, "The rest of you in the front row can plead guilty, not guilty, trial by court, trial by jury."

Here is how they describe the seemingly unrelated factors that appear to go into the judge's decision:

If you haven't been picked up for a long time and you've been in town all that time, you'll get a kick-out; but if you've been out of town, you get a sentence, because they figure you were probably drinking all the time.

. . . If you've been [picked up], say, a couple of times in a week or more, why you're subject to be sent to County Jail.

On Monday before court, we all 15 of us shaved on one razor after being picked up on Friday because we knew that if we were whiskery we'd go to County Jail for sure.

Of those arrested before Christmas, everyone who had an address other than Skid Row—even a Beatnik area—got a kick-out. Others like us went to County Jail.

Judge Darlington is a no good son-of-a-bitch. He says to us, "Hold your hands out." They have been holding you in the drunk tank for about eight hours, no beds there, just concrete. After that you go to a holding cell. They line them up ten at a time in front and ten in back. After three days in there, worrying what's going to happen to you, you shake a bit. If you do, Judge Darlington says, "Sixty days."

The fact the judge acts on advice from an ex-alcoholic, a non-professional who clearly is drawing his views from personal (and possibly petty) recollections of the men, further confirms the picture of totally arbitrary power with little concern for justice.

There's this guy they call "the Rapper" and he has the ear of the judge. He actually sets the sentence whenever he's there. I'd like to get my hands on him sometime.

We call him "the Rapper." He has the power of life and death for the men. He sat up next to the judge and would say, "probation," "30 days," "90 days," and that's what you'd get. Is that legal? I don't think anyone should be allowed to play God like that.

We were all glad when he slipped. He looked for the worst of himself in others. (Comment on the fact that the Rapper had recently fallen off the wagon himself and was at State Mental Hospital.)

The Christian Missionary Rapper was no more popular with the men:

Jim Brown, a reformed alcoholic who has no use for another alcoholic, is the Rapper. He will hang a man if he doesn't like him. I was at Barabas Abode and Beacon in the Darkness. We speak to each other, but he's a double-crossing, no-good son-of-a-bitch. Absolutely no good! At 6 a.m. he and the court liaison officer go through the records and *they* decide what each man shall get. They see my name and say, "Give that bastard 60 days!"

The Row men are also aware that there are sometimes drastic differences between the sentences received one day in court and those received another. Empirical evidence of this can be seen in Table V, where sentences received during a time when County Jail was normally full, and during a time when it was beyond normal capacity because of a recent demonstration, are compared. (Arrests were also below average for that day, as well.)

TABLE V   Comparison of Sentences Given in Drunk Court When Jail Was Full and When It Was Beyond Capacity

	State of County Jail			
Sentences	Full (N=180) Per cent		Beyond capacity (N=36) Per cent	
Kick-out (no sentence, warned only)	2		8	
County Hospital				
With hold	—		—	
No hold	2		—	
		74		91
Suspended sentence				
10 days or less	—		5	
11 to 30 days	23		70	
31 to 60 days	28		8	
61 to 90 days	19		—	
Over 90 days	—		—	
Sentenced to County Jail				
10 days or less	1		3	
11 to 30 days	23		6	
31 to 60 days	2	26	—	9
61 to 90 days	—		—	
Over 90 days	—		—	
Total	100		100	

As shown in Table V, only 9 per cent of the men received a County Jail sentence when the jail was beyond capacity (as compared to 26 per cent when it was merely very full).

Skid Row drunks explain such disparity not as a function of jail capacity but as evidence of graft among agents of social control. Collusion is assumed to exist among the police, City Hospital, the Christian Missionaries, the jailers, and the judges in the Municipal Court, and among the judges, the police, the jailers, and the social workers in the Superior Courts. This reinforces the idea of a power ful system beyond the control of a penniless individual. The Row men cite the following evidence (so far as they are concerned) as proof of this.

Sometimes, if you get smart with the policeman, he tells the judge and you get a bigger sentence.

When I was arrested for drunk, they took me first to the hospital. A social worker came around, and she had a folder, and she said, "Let's see now, uh, you won't have any way to pay for your stay here." I'd only been there [in the hospital] a day and a half, and I says, "Well, how do you know?" And she said, "Well, where you're going, you won't be able to pay anyway." So I says, "Well, how do you know where I'm goin'?" She says, "Well, you're goin' to County Jail for 60 days." I says, "Well, how do you know? I haven't even been before the judge yet!" She said, "Oh, it's right here in your folder." I hadn't been to court yet, see, and sure enough, as soon as I went before the judge—60 days at County Jail. I told the judge about it after he sentenced me and he said, "You're being irrelevant," or something like that. In other words you're going for 60 days, and you just don't argue. He said also, "Well, sometimes that's court procedure."

This cooperation is oftentimes suspected by embittered Row men to serve the purpose of enriching unscrupulous agents of social control or at the very least maintain them in their jobs by keeping the jail population at an assigned level:

The key to the whole situation is the cut on the food taken by Sheriff Smith and Captain Jackson and the judges. They are all getting their cut by stealing from the food appropriations to the jail They make $1.50 a day on each one of us. I think they have a quota at County Jail. If they are down 50 men, you can bet that 50 will go out on the next bus.

What a lot of people don't realize is that this institution and most jails need labor and the alcoholic furnishes that. When I was a trusty in Minneapolis, I'd hear the superintendent call the judge and say, "We are short 150 men here"—and in three days the courts would send us our 150 men (Bittner, 1967).

Maneuvers to Escape County Jail

Lacking the power to fight a drunk charge legally or by means of forfeiting bail, the Skid Row alcoholic has developed other ways of avoiding the County Jail, which is hated more than any other locale on the loop. It should be emphasized that if such avoidance tactics are successful the Row man is still incarcerated, but in another (and more desirable) area.

For instance, a "regular" (i.e., chronic drunkenness offender) may get a job at the City Jail as trusty if he is known to be a good worker and is popular with guards.

> After you're sentenced, then you go see the head man there [at City Jail], and if you've been there before, which most of 'em have, then he'll say, "Yeah, you can stay here and work for me." It's who you know that counts.

A second means of avoiding County Jail is for a man to act psychotic so that he is referred to the City Screening Facility at the hospital, and perhaps even to the psychiatric ward there. Often this results in a five-day hospitalization or a sojourn in the Northern State Mental Hospital rather than a jail sentence. As one man put it:

> One good way is to act or talk suicidal. That scares them sometimes. Do a lot of yelling and pretend to hear voices. This will often break them [the jailers] down and you'll get to go to City Hospital.

The Feeling of Unfairness

The judge may feel righteous because he is saving a man from drinking himself to death by sending him to jail to dry out, but the Skid Row alcoholic is neither convinced this alleged judicial "good will" exists, nor is he grateful even if it does. With the exception of those Row men who have settled on the jail as a second home, most believe there is great inequity in the way Pacific City courts are operated. They point to other state jurisdictions that deal with the drunk far less harshly:

> You take Alabama, Georgia, any place, they'll give you a ten dollar fine. Texas, you get two days in jail. You can get in jail ten times and you'll still only get two days and more chance the judge'll let you go.

Chicago doesn't treat its alcoholics like this city, neither does New York. Most of the time they keep you overnight or a couple of days. They don't send you to jail for a month or more.

The alcoholics' opinion of being sent to jail for drunkenness is perhaps best summed up in this quote:

As far as the jail goes, all jails are the same. Nobody likes to be in 'em regardless of whether they give you steak or, uh, filet mignons, or whatever it is, nobody likes to be in jail. They don't beat you or nothin' like that. Like any place, it's a place of detention; that's their job, that's what the judge said; we're just taken away from the public. As far as gettin' here, it's for drunk, and as far as the sentence goes I believe that's quite a price to pay. Even if it's ten days, I think it's too much myself—even ten days, takin' ten days away from your life for gettin' drunk.

REFERENCES

BITTNER, EGON. 1967. "The Police on Skid Row: A Study of Peace-Keeping," *American Sociological Review*, 32 (October).

BOGUE, DONALD J. 1963. *Skid Row in American Cities*. Chicago: University of Chicago.

GARFINKEL, HAROLD. 1956. "Conditions of a Successful Degradation Ceremony," *American Journal of Sociology*, 61 (March), pp. 420–22.

LECLERCQ, FREDERIC S. 1966. "Field Observations in Drunk Court of the Pacific Municipal Court," unpublished memorandum, p. 1.

PETERSEN, WILLIAM, and DAVID MATZA. 1963. "Does the Juvenile Court Exercise Justice?" In Petersen and Matza (eds.), *Social Controversy*. Belmont, Calif.: Wadsworth.

STEM, GERALD. 1967. "Public Drunkenness: Crime or Health Problem?" *Annals of American Academy of Political and Social Science*, 374 (November), pp. 147–56.

EXERCISES

Like the observation survey, the questionnaire survey requires the researcher to draw a sample and analyze quantitative data. However, some of the issues and problems are different, and this set of exercises is designed to give the student some experience in the tasks of observation survey. Exercise 4, however, is a research project, and most of the analysis it requires is similar to that in questionnaire surveys.

EXERCISE 1

This exercise is designed to give the student a feel for recording observations and finding a spot from which to observe. The purpose is to identify windowshoppers in terms of easily observable features—sex, age, and race.

Make a simple observation schedule by establishing categories of sex, age, and race. Find a display window where there is frequent pedestrian traffic, preferably near a place where you can sit down and take notes, such as a bus stop. Record the characteristics of those who stop and look at the display. It is not important that you guess the exact age of a person. Rather, this exercise is intended to give you some experience in observing different categories of people.

EXERCISE 2

In observational surveys on the police, some researchers have found that the decision to make an arrest is based on the demeanor of the subject under suspicion. Other studies have found that a more important causal variable is the complaining party's attitude toward having the police make an arrest. Is the suspect's demeanor more important in a potential arrest situation, or is it the complainant's desire to have the police take the suspect to jail? Design an observation schedule that would resolve this argument. Remember, though, that the schedule is based on what can be seen and heard by the observer without asking questions.

EXERCISE 3

The samples considered in questionnaire surveys generally involve such units as individuals and households; while in observation surveys, time samples and situation samples are more important. The purpose of this exercise is to demonstrate the importance of sampling at different times of the day and days of the week.

Choose a public place frequented by different groups at all times of the day, such as a public park, a bowling alley, or a downtown street. On slips of paper write all the hours of day. Put the slips in a box and draw a 25 per cent sample. Observe the setting you have chosen during the sample hours to see whether there are different groups or forms of activities during the different times. Also, compare weekdays and weekends.

Exercise 4

The purpose of this exercise is to determine, using an observation survey, whether there is a relationship between the way in which a person presents himself in traffic court and what the judge decides to do with the case. This exercise is very much like Wiseman's study, which found a relationship between social type and sentencing, except that a traffic court, instead of a drunk court, is the observational setting.

The observation schedules should be typed on duplication masters and several copies made, so that there is a sheet for each case to be observed. Below is an example of what the observation sheet might look like; but, since state and local traffic laws differ depending on where you live, be sure that the observation schedule reflects your particular court.

Traffic Court Observation Schedule

Date _____ Judge _____ Violation _____

Researcher _____ Case # _____

1. Appearance
   a. Dressed up   _____
   b. Casual   _____
   c. Sloppy   _____
2. Sex
   a. Female   _____
   b. Male   _____
3. Ethnic Background
   a. White   _____

b. Black _____
c. Other _____
   (specify)
4. Demeanor
   a. Antagonistic _____
   b. Polite _____
   c. Humble _____
5. Age
   a. Juvenile (under 18) _____
   b. Young adult (18–25) _____
   c. Adult (26–40) _____
   d. Middle age (40–60) _____
   e. Senior citizen (60 +) _____
6. Plea
   a. Guilty _____
   b. Not guilty _____
7. Type of Explanation
   a. Apology _____
   b. Police officer's
      fault _____
   c. Accident _____
   d. Road or traffic
      conditions _____
   e. Ignorance _____
   f. Other (specify) _____
8. Outcome (what the judge decided)

_____

_____

_____

Once the data have been collected, categorize the open-ended observations—the offences and the outcomes. For example, violations can be grouped into "speeding," "illegal maneuver," and other such categories. Outcomes should be dichotimized into relative "win" and "lose" categories. A small fine, for example, might be seen as a "win" in a case where the possible fine is high. Then code the data and analyze the results, using multivariate analysis.

Treat the "outcome" as the dependent variable and each of the other items as the independent variable. Keep the analysis simple by taking only a single item at a time, as the independent variable to be compared to the dependent variable. Finally, see which item has the highest relationship with the courtroom outcome.

ADDITIONAL READING SUGGESTIONS

CUMMING, ELAINE, IAN CUMMING, and LAURA EDELL. 1965. "Policeman as Philosopher, Guide and Friend," *Social Problems,* 12, pp. 276–86. This observation survey provides a useful model for the student. Instead of using an observation sheet or note pad, the researchers recorded their observations of incoming police calls on tape. The analysis of these data was then done in the same way as any other survey.

REISS, ALBERT J., JR. 1968. "Stuff and Nonsense about Social Surveys and Observation," in Howard S. Becker et al. (eds.), *Institutions and the Person,* Chicago: Aldine, pp. 351–67. In this discussion of a large-scale study of the police, Reiss explains how many of the elements of survey research can be accomplished with observers in the place of questionnaires. He also discusses the problems that observers have in overidentifying with their subjects—a problem not found when questionnaire surveys are used.

III: THE EXPERIMENT

IN ORDER TO SHOW THAT A CRIME COULD HAVE HAPPENED IN A GIVEN manner, detectives often use demonstrations and experiments. In the investigation of President Kennedy's assassination, for example, several experiments were performed with the suspect's rifle in order to show that it was the murder weapon (Osterburg, 1967:82–83). In scientific terminology, the rifle was the experimental variable, and it was demonstrated that it could have produced certain consequences under specific conditions—which is the purpose of all experiments.

Like surveys, which are sometimes used to find causal relationships between variables, experiments are also intended to find such relationships. Unlike surveys, however, experiments are designs in which the researcher manipulates variables intentionally in order to locate causal relationships (Simon, 1969:228). Specifically, the researcher manipulates an independent variable to find what effect it has on a dependent variable. In the Middleton experiment (Chapter 6), the independent variable was a film denouncing anti-Semitism, and the dependent variable consisted of anti-Semitic attitudes.

The basic logic behind experiments is that if, in the presence of a given variable, certain changes are seen to occur in another variable, and if these changes do not occur in the absence of the given variable, then the changes, all other elements being equal, must have been due to the given variable. In other words, if the dependent variable changes when the independent variable is present but does not when it is absent, then the independent variable caused the change in the dependent variable. For example, if a class of students talks noisily while the instructor is out of the class but becomes quiet when he enters the room, the change in the level of classroom noise (dependent variable) is caused by the instructor's presence (independent variable).

In order to create a situation in which the effect of an independent variable can be tested, two similar groups are observed or tested at two different times. The first test is intended to establish their similarity. Then one group is exposed to the independent variable and the other is not. The results of a post-test of the two groups indicate the effect of the independent variable. This design is the *classical experiment* (Phillips, 1971:113–115). The elements of the classical experiment include a *pretest* and a *post-test*, a *control group* and an *experimental group*, and an *experimental variable*.

The sequence of operation for the classical experiment begins with a hypothesis. For example, an educator might hypothesize that, if students are given positive encouragement, they will perform better in a learning task—say, mastering a list of spelling words. In order to test this hypothesis experimentally, the researcher would take a group of students who were equal in academic ability and divide them into a control group and an experimental group. Next, the researcher would test each group to make sure they were equal. This is the pretest. In this case, the researcher might use a spelling test as a pretest. Next, the researcher introduces the experimental variable, positive encouragement—for instance, saying a kind word—but only to the experimental group. He would not give the control group positive encouragement of any sort. Both groups would be treated the same in every other way, with the sole exception that only members of the experimental group would receive encouragement. Finally, the two groups would be tested a second time on the list of spelling words to find whether there were any performance differences between them. If there is a difference, and all other aspects of the composition of the group and the experimental procedure were held constant, the difference can be attributed to the experimental variable—that is, the experimental variable can be said to have *caused* the difference.

The classical experimental design has been highly successful in the natural sciences, and it has therefore been widely used in social research as well. Unlike natural scientists, however, sociologists deal with a subject matter that has a mind of its own, and they have therefore encountered problems not found in the natural sciences. For example, when people enter an experimental setting or situation, they are generally aware that the experimenter is attempting to find experimentally induced change, and they often attempt to "help" the experimenter by responding "properly" (Webb et al., 1966:12–21). Awareness that they are subjects in an experiment, in other words, becomes the causal factor in their behavior, instead of the experimental variable. Sometimes, the pretest itself will raise questions in the subjects' minds that themselves cause the subjects later to change their minds on the post-test. Middleton, in his experiment, found, for example, that anti-Semitic attitudes for both the experimental and the control group was less on the post-test than on the pretest. Apparently, once the subjects realized that they were anti-Semitic, they re-evaluated their attitudes; and the realization was prompted by the pretest, not by the experimental variable.

In order to determine the effect of the pretest on subjects, the Solomon four-group design was developed (Solomon, 1949). Besides having all the elements of a classical experiment, the Solomon four-group design has an additional control group and experimental group that are not given pretests. All four groups are randomly selected and are therefore equal. If there are any differences in the post-tests of the two control groups or the two experimental groups, these differences are attributed to the effect of the pretest. If, however, both control groups are the same in the post-test but different from the experimental groups, the difference can be attributed solely to the experimental variable. Diagrammatically, the Solomon four-group appears as follows:

	Pretest	Experimental variable	Post-test
Control Group 1	Yes	No	Yes
Control Group 2	No	No	Yes
Experimental Group 1	Yes	Yes	Yes
Experimental Group 2	No	Yes	Yes

An attempt to offset the artificiality of a laboratory setting is the natural or field experiment (Swingle, 1973). Basically, a field experiment is one in which the researcher introduces the experimental variable into a natural setting to see what effect it has on behavior in the setting. In such experiments, the researcher lacks the control he has in experiments that take place in a small group laboratory or in other settings he arranges; but they have greater external validity, because they take place in naturally occurring social life. For example, to find whether there is a relationship between having a Black Panther bumper sticker and being cited for traffic violations, a researcher selected 15 subjects who had no traffic violations in twelve months and had them affix Black Panther bumper stickers to their cars (Heussenstamm, 1971). The subjects began receiving so many tickets that the experiment had to be discontinued. The results thus confirmed the causal relationship hypothesized (Heussenstamm, 1971). The "pretest" in this experiment, as in many other field experiments, consisted of the events preceding the introduction of the experimental variable— the absence of traffic violations—and the "post-test" consisted of the events subsequent to the introduction of the experimental variable.

The two selections that follow represent a classical experiment and a field experiment. Middleton's study contains all the elements of a classical experiment. The study by Russo and Sommer, on the other hand, is a creative example of a field experiment, introducing "sitting too close" as an experimental variable to test the maintenance of personal space.

REFERENCES

HEUSSENSTAMM, F. K. 1971. "Bumper Stickers and the Cops," *Trans-action* 8, pp. 32–33.

OSTERBURG, J. W. 1967. *The Crime Laboratory.* Bloomington: Indiana University Press.

PHILLIPS, B. S. 1971. *Social Research: Strategy and Tactics.* New York: Macmillan.

SIMON, J. L. 1969. *Basic Research Methods in Social Science.* New York: Random House.

SOLOMON, R. L. 1949. "Extension of Control Group Design," *Psychological Bulletin,* 46, pp. 137–50.

SWINGLE, P. G. 1973. *Social Psychology in Natural Settings.* Chicago: Aldine.

WEBB, EUGENE, D. T. CAMPBELL, R. D. SCHWARTZ, and L. SECHREST. 1966. *Unobtrusive Measures: Nonreactive Research in the Social Sciences.* Chicago: Rand McNally.

6. Laboratory Experiment

ETHNIC PREJUDICE AND SUSCEPTIBILITY TO PERSUASION
—Russell Middleton

AS MOTION PICTURES AND TELEVISION have come increasingly to dominate recreational life in this country, the potentialities for mass influence have been greatly broadened. Of the several studies concerned with the possible influence of motion pictures upon ethnic prejudice, most of them have found that motion pictures which urge tolerance toward minority groups and foreign nationalities do reduce the expression of ethnic prejudice among those exposed to them. (See, for example, Goldberg, 1956; Raths and Trager, 1948; Rosen, 1948; and Wiese and Colt, 1946). Motion pictures may also increase prejudice, as two investigations have demonstrated. In their pioneer study, Peterson and Thurstone (1933) found that schoolchildren who saw Birth of a Nation, a classic film which presents a southern view of Reconstruction, tended to produce a slight increase in prejudice toward Negroes. A training film shown to American soldiers during World War II also tended to generate greater feelings of hostility toward Germans (Hovland et al., 1949). Pressures on the motion picture and television industries are such today, however, that minority groups are very rarely portrayed in an unfavorable light. For example, in a recent television

From The American Sociological Review, Vol. 25 (October, 1960), pp. 679–86.

production of Oliver Twist, Fagin lost all Jewish identification. In the last fifteen years several motion pictures and television programs have been produced which have made pleas for tolerance toward Jews, Negroes, and other minority groups. Research interest has consequently centered on the problem of whether or not motion pictures of this type are effective means of reducing ethnic prejudice.

In spite of the positive results reported by many of these studies, several students of the subject remain skeptical regarding the effectiveness of mass media in bringing about changes in attitudes —especially ethnic prejudice. (See, for example, Cooper and Dinerman, 1951; Cooper and Jahoda, 1947; Flowerman, 1947; Hyman and Sheatsley, 1947; Hulett, 1949; and Zeisel, 1949.) One common criticism is that the exposure of the public to a particular motion picture is usually highly limited, and those who do see it are likely to be people who already agree with the film's theme. This type of selectivity would seem to be less important in the case of television, however, than in that of motion pictures. Another type of criticism involves the interpretation of the motion picture by the audience. It is argued that people do not attribute accuracy or seriousness of purpose to commercial films which are meant to entertain. Or people may evade propaganda with which they disagree: rather than accepting or refusing the message, they may fail to understand it or they may twist and misinterpret it. Finally, the point is sometimes made that because ethnic prejudices are deeply ingrained, brief exposure through the mass media to a message of tolerance is hardly sufficient to bring about changes in attitudes deriving from the personality systems of individuals. There may even be a "boomerang effect," with prejudices being strengthened in the face of attack.

The validity of these criticisms can be established or rejected only on the basis of empirical investigation, and the present study is addressed toward this end. To what extent may a motion picture advocating tolerance for a minority group have an effective impact? Is the impact limited in scope, or is it more general, extending to other minority groups as well as the one dealt with specifically in the film? Is there any boomerang effect and, if so, how extensive is it? To what extent do persons who see the film perceive the theme correctly?

In addition to these questions, some attention is given here to the correlates of persuasibility. Several investigations of differential persuasibility have been conducted, but they have usually concentrated on personality factors such as neurotic anxiety and aggression needs or on general persuasibility as a personality factor. (See for example, Mussen, 1950; Janis, 1954; and Hovland and Janis, 1959.) This study investigates relations not previously explored between social factors and attitude constellations, on the one hand, and, on the other, susceptibility to persuasion in the area of ethnic prejudice.

METHOD

The skill with which motion pictures pleading for ethnic brotherhood and tolerance are produced varies greatly, and it is not possible to generalize about the effectiveness of this type of film from a study of only one. One film may be highly effective, another may actually antagonize its audience. For purposes of this study optimum conditions for influence were sought. Therefore a film which received wide praise by critics was selected for showing to the experimental group. *Gentleman's Agreement** has an additional virtue in that it was first released in 1947, when most of the subjects were small children, and is only now beginning to be shown on television. Consequently, only about five per cent of the subjects had to be eliminated because they had previously seen the motion picture.

An experimental group and a control group of students were selected from required and semi-required introductory social science classes at a southern state-supported university. Those students in the experimental group were assigned by their instructors to attend a showing of *Gentleman's Agreement*, whereas the students in the control group were not given information about the showing. A questionnaire dealing with social characteristics, attitudes toward Jews and Negroes, and certain other attitudes was administered to students in both the experimental and the control groups before the showing of the film on the campus. After the

* *Gentleman's Agreement* was released by Twentieth Century-Fox, produced by Darryl Zanuck, and directed by Elia Kazan. It starred Gregory Peck, Dorothy McGuire, John Garfield, and Celeste Holm. The film won the Academy Award for the year 1947, and it was highly praised by many film critics.

showing a second questionnaire, which included the original ethnic prejudice scales as well as questions about reactions to the motion picture, was administered to both groups. The elimination of all Jewish subjects, persons who had previously seen the film, and those in the experimental group who failed to see the film as instructed left a total of 329 students in the experimental group and 116 in the control group. In order to minimize the effect of extraneous factors the film was shown and both questionnaires were administered within one week in early October, 1959. Anonymity was maintained by having students sign the questionnaires with their mothers' maiden names. This made it possible to match the two questionnaires for each individual without identifying the respondent.

Anti-Semitic prejudice was measured by means of the ten-item Berkeley AS scale (Adorno *et al.*, 1950). To measure anti-Negro prejudice a special scale was constructed for this study. Like the Berkeley AS scale, the anti-Negro scale is of the Likert type and has a seven-point response scale for each item, ranging from strongly agree to strongly disagree. Items from the Berkeley E scale pertaining to Negroes together with a large number of other items selected on theoretical grounds were tested for internal consistency in a pretest administered to approximately 100 university students. Ten items very high in discriminatory power were selected for the final scale.* Both the anti-Semitism and anti-Negro scales suffer from the fact that all items are unidirectional and thus may be distorted

---

* ANTI-NEGRO SENTIMENTS SCALE:

1. It would be a mistake ever to have Negroes for foremen and leaders over whites.
2. Manual labor and unskilled jobs seem to fit the Negro mentality and ability better than more skilled or responsible work.
3. Most Negroes would become overbearing and disagreeable if not kept in their place.
4. Even if Negroes had the same living conditions as white people, most Negroes would have lower morals than whites.
5. Negroes and whites should never dance together.
6. Negroes and whites should not be roommates in a college dormitory.
7. Negroes and whites should not live in houses next door to one another.
8. Negro girls should not be hired as secretaries or typists to work in the office of a business managed by whites.
9. Negroes and whites should not sit together on buses and trains.
10. Negro and white children should not attend the same elementary and high schools.

by an "acquiescent response set."* Since the same scales were administered before and after the showing of the film, however, the response set factor should have remained fairly constant.

Social characteristics such as sex, community of residence, and principal state of residence since the age of six were ascertained by direct questions, and scales were used to measure socio-economic status (Vaughan, 1958), anomia (Meier and Bell, 1959), status concern (Kaufman, 1957), conservatism (McClosky, 1958), authoritarianism, † and religious orthodoxy.‡

The attitudinal data on anti-Semitism constitute an ordinal, not an interval scale; therefore, the comparison of the scores of an individual before and after the showing of the motion picture cannot properly be made by subtraction. For example, it should not be assumed that a change from a score of 70 to a score of 60 is of the same magnitude as a change from 50 to 40. Thus it is difficult to generalize about the magnitude of changes. For statistical analysis, then, the subjects were dichotomized into those who showed some reduction in scores on the AS or AN scales and those with no reduction or an increase in scores. Statistical significance of the findings was determined by the computation of chi square values corrected for continuity from two-by-two, two-by-three, or two-by-five tables. In a few instances, which are specified below, the AS scale was treated as if it were an interval scale in order to give some rough estimates of the magnitudes of changes.

FINDINGS

A measure of the impact of *Gentleman's Agreement* is presented in Table I. The proportion of subjects in the experimental group who showed a reduction in scores on the anti-Semitism scale after exposure to the motion picture is significantly greater than the proportion in the control group. Of those in the experimental

* For a discussion of this problem in connection with the F-scale and the anomia scale, see Bass (1955); Christie, Havel, and Seidenberg (1958); and Lenski and Leggett (1960).

† The five-item version of the F-scale developed by the Department of Scientific Research of the American Jewish Committee was utilized. See Srole (1956).

‡ Snell Putney and Russel Middleton, "Dimensions and Correlates of Religious Ideologies," read at the annual meeting of the Southern Sociological Society, April, 1960.

TABLE I   CHANGES IN EXPRESSED ANTI-SEMITISM FOLLOWING THE
SHOWING OF *Gentleman's Agreement*

Changes in expressed anti-Semitism	Experimental group		Control group	
	Number	Per cent	Number	Per cent
Reduction in anti-Semitism	228	69.3	49	42.2
No change or increase in anti-Semitism	101	30.7	67	57.8
Total	329	100.0	116	100.0

$\chi^2 = 25.58$ 1 d.f. P<.001.

group, who did see the film, 69.3 per cent had lower scores on anti-Semitism on the second questionnaire than on the first, as compared with 42.2 per cent of those in the control group, who did not see the film. The figure for the control group is surprisingly high, but most of the reductions were quite small and probably are primarily due to the lack of complete reliability of the scale. Few persons scored exactly the same on the scale both times, and most individuals varied from their original scores by at least a few points.* The difference between the experimental and control group nevertheless is highly significant statistically.

Some indication, perhaps, on the magnitude of changes in scores is presented in Table II, derived by subtracting the AS scores on the second questionnaires from the AS scores on the first. (Recall, however, that these are ordinal data which may not properly be manipulated arithmetically; the figures serve only as a very rough indication of magnitudes.) The findings are similar to those presented in Table I. Subjects in the experimental group were five times more likely to show a reduction of 11 or more scale points than those in the control group. Reductions of four to ten scale points were also much more common among those in the experimental group. These data strongly suggest that the showing of *Gentleman's Agreement* had a very considerable impact on the expression of anti-Semitic prejudice.

* The relatively small number of persons who made identical scores both times may be the result of their sensitization to the instrument. In future research, it would seem advisable to adopt two experimental groups and two control groups. If the attitudes of one experimental group and one control group were measured only after the experimental stimulus were introduced, comparisons with the groups measured both before and after would give some indication of the operation of the sensitization factor.

TABLE II   Degree of Change in Expressed Anti-Semitism Following the Showing of *Gentleman's Agreement*

Degree of change in anti-Semitism scale scores	Experimental group		Control group	
	Number	Per cent	Number	Per cent
−11 or more	52	15.8	4	3.4
−4 through −10	112	34.0	27	23.3
No change or change of 3 points or less	112	34.0	49	42.3
+4 through +10	39	11.9	28	24.1
+11 or more	14	4.3	8	6.9
Total	329	100.0	116	100.0

To determine whether or not the film had a boomerang effect the experimental and control groups were also compared with regard to the proportion showing an increase in AS scores on the second questionnaire. Twice as large a proportion of those in the control group as in the experimental group had greater scores on anti-Semitism following the showing of the film. Thus it appears that the film itself probably had no significant boomerang effect on the experimental group. In a few individual cases, however, the

TABLE III   Changes in Expressed Anti-Negro Sentiments Following the Showing of *Gentleman's Agreement*

Changes in expressed anti-Negro sentiments	Experimental group		Control group	
	Number	Per cent	Number	Per cent
Reduction in anti-Negro sentiments	184	55.9	50	43.1
No change or increase in anti-Negro sentiments	145	44.1	66	56.9
Total	329	100.0	116	100.0

$\chi^2 = 5.15$ 1 d.f. $P < .05$.

motion picture probably did antagonize the subjects. For example, one male from the Miami area scored 53 on the AS scale in the first questionnaire, but the score increased to 69, one point below the possible maximum, on the second. This subject disliked the motion picture intensely and made the following comment about its theme: "The movie was put out by Paramount [actually Twentieth Century-Fox] which is own [sic] or operated primarily by Jewish people. I think the movie is typical of the action a Jew might take. The main point was for everyone to all of a sudden get rid of the prejudices and love Jewes [sic]. The movie didn't touch my heart." Another male from Miami, who described the film as the "shallowest movie I ever saw," showed an increase in AS scale scores from 34 to 39.

Although Gentleman's Agreement is devoted primarily to the problem of anti-Semitic prejudice, the message of brotherhood, equality and democracy has implications for other minority groups as well. As one subject expressed it, the purpose of the film is "to make you aware of prejudice against the Jews and to make you evaluate your attitudes and feelings toward any minority group." The effect of the film on attitudes toward Negroes is presented in Table III. Once again those in the experimental group were more likely than those in the control group to show a reduction in scores on the anti-Negro scale, although the difference is not as great as in the case of anti-Semitism. Almost 56 per cent of those in the experimental group showed a reduction, as compared with 43 per cent of those in the control group. The difference is significant at the .05 level. In the experimental group there was also a highly significant tendency for reductions in AS scores to be associated with reductions in AN scores. Of those who showed a reduction in expressed anti-Semitism, 62 per cent also showed a reduction in the expression of anti-Negro sentiments.

The principal theme of the film Gentleman's Agreement and of the novel upon which it is based (Hobson, 1947) is that the people who are chiefly to blame for the persistence and growth of anti-Semitism are the decent, intelligent individuals who are not anti-Semitic but who remain passive and take no militant steps to stamp out prejudice. On the second questionnaire members of the experimental group were asked to indicate in a sentence or two what they thought to be the principal theme of the motion picture. Only 15 per cent of the subjects correctly identified the specific theme, but another 82 per cent identified the general theme— the injustice which Jews suffer as a result of anti-Semitic prejudice. A meager 3 per cent failed to identify either the specific or the general theme. It appears then that, although many subjects may have practiced evasion to avoid the specific message, such evasion did not extend to the general theme. Indeed, one wonders how the three per cent could have remained oblivious to the theme, for in the motion picture there are frequent pauses in the action while one of the characters delivers an earnest speech for tolerance and brotherhood.

The data on the experimental group were subjected to further analysis in an effort to determine the characteristics of those who were influenced and those who were not influenced by the film. Two major types of factors appear to have been related to persuasibility. First, those who correctly perceived the theme, who agreed with the theme, and who rated the film highly were more likely to show a reduction in the expression of anti-Semitism than those who did not. Of those who correctly perceived the specific theme, 81.6 per cent showed a reduction in AS scores, as compared with 67.5 per cent of those who perceived only the general theme, and 42.8 per cent of those who failed to identify either the specific or general theme. (See Table IV.) Table V indicates a direct relationship between agreement with the perceived theme and reductions in AS scores, and Table VI a direct relationship between ratings of the motion picture and reductions in AS scores. All of these differences are significant beyond the .05 level.

Why did some persons more than others perceive the theme correctly and react favorably to the film? No data were available on

TABLE IV   CHANGES IN EXPRESSED ANTI-SEMITISM BY PERCEPTION
OF THEME

Perception of theme	Number of subjects	Per cent of subjects showing reduction in expressed anti-Semitism
Correct perception of specific theme	49	81.6
Perception of general theme only	271	67.5
Failure to identify specific or general theme	7	42.8

$\chi^2 = 6.18$ 2 d.f. P<.05.

TABLE V   CHANGES IN EXPRESSED ANTI-SEMITISM BY AGREEMENT
WITH PERCEIVED THEME

Agreement with perceived theme	Number of subjects	Per cent of subjects showing reduction in expressed anti-Semitism
Strongly agree	157	76.4
Moderately or slightly agree	127	68.5
Don't know or disagree	43	46.5

$\chi^2 = 14.31$ 2 d.f. P<.001.

TABLE VI CHANGES IN EXPRESSED ANTI-SEMITISM BY RATING
OF MOTION PICTURE

Rating of motion picture	Number of subjects	Per cent of subjects showing reduction in expressed anti-Semitism
Excellent	43	76.7
Good	162	73.5
Average	89	68.5
Fair	21	47.6
Poor	13	38.5

$\chi^2 = 12.98$ 4 d.f. P<.02.

the intelligence of the subjects, but it seems plausible that the more intelligent would be more likely to perceive the theme correctly. The major factor in this connection discovered in this study, however, is the degree of initial anti-Semitism. The lower the degree of expressed anti-Semitism, the greater was the tendency toward correct identification of the specific theme, agreement with the perceived theme, and rating of the film as good or excellent.

These findings might lead one to be pessimistic about the possibility of influencing the highly prejudiced through the mass media. But there is a second factor, which at first glance appears to be contradictory to the set of factors cited above. As indicated in Table VII, a direct relationship was found between the initial expression of anti-Semitism and the tendency to show a reduction in AS scores after viewing the film. It is precisely the individuals with the highest AS scores who were most likely, after this exposure, to have lower scores, and those with the lowest AS scores who were least likely to show such a change.

To some extent, of course, this relationship may be an artifact of an unreliable testing instrument. Persons with low original AS scores have less chance of showing a score reduction than those who originally score high if unreliability is the only factor at work. However, the distribution of reductions and increases presented in Table II makes it clear that unreliability is not the sole cause of the variations. Whereas the distribution is symmetrical for the control group, it is skewed heavily toward reductions in the experimental group. In order to decrease the effect of unreliability, small reductions of fewer than four AS scale points were discounted in further computations, presented also in Table VII. This proce-

TABLE VII   CHANGES IN EXPRESSED ANTI-SEMITISM
BY INITIAL ANTI-SEMITISM

Initial anti-Semitism	Number of subjects	Per cent showing reduction in AS scores[a]	Per cent showing reduction of four or more AS scale points[b]
Low (10–19)	39	43.6	7.7
Moderate (20–39)	195	67.7	49.0
High (40 and over)	95	83.2	68.4

[a] $\chi^2 = 20.92$ 2 d.f. $P < .001$.
[b] Since these data are ordinal, the figures should be taken only as a very rough indication of magnitudes.

dure resulted in even greater differences among those with low, moderate, and high initial scores on anti-Semitism. Thus it seems unlikely that unreliability is a major factor responsible for the differences in persuasibility related to initial anti-Semitism.

The data in Table VII refer only to absolute, not to relative, changes in AS scale scores. A person with an initial score of 20 cannot show a reduction of more than 10 points, whereas there is a maximum possible reduction of 50 points for a person originally scoring 60. So as to examine further the relationship between initial anti-Semitism and persuasibility, reductions in AS scores relative to the maximum possible reduction for each individual are presented in Table VIII. The relationship of initial anti-Semitism

TABLE VIII   CHANGES IN ANTI-SEMITISM SCORES BY PER CENT
OF MAXIMUM POSSIBLE REDUCTION AND BY INITIAL ANTI-SEMITISM*

Per cent of maximum possible reduction in anti-Semitism scale scores	Initial anti-Semitism		
	Low (10–19)	Moderate (20–39)	High (40 and over)
80–100	7.7	3.6	0
60–79	7.7	7.7	2.1
40–59	2.5	18.0	12.6
20–39	15.4	20.5	31.6
1–19	10.3	17.9	36.8
No change	7.7	4.1	3.2
Increase	48.7	28.2	13.7
Total	100.0	100.0	100.0
Number of subjects	39	195	95

* Since these data are ordinal, the figures should be taken only as a very rough indication of magnitude.

to relative reductions is exactly the reverse of that which holds for absolute reductions: those who originally scored low on anti-Semitism were the most likely to show a 60 per cent or greater reduction of the maximum reduction possible; and each of the four subjects with 100 per cent relative reductions had low AS scores originally.

In drawing conclusions concerning initial prejudice and persuasibility, then, we must distinguish between absolute reductions and reductions relative to the maximum reduction possible for an individual. In evaluating any program for the reduction of ethnic prejudice, probably the absolute measure is more meaningful than the relative measure for it enables one to estimate more clearly the effectiveness of the program in lessening prejudice.

In this study, those persons who initially had favorable attitudes toward Jews were less likely to show a reduction in prejudice in absolute terms than those who were more anti-Semitic—there is obviously no possibility of persuading an individual to accept views he already holds. These persons, however, tended to show greater reductions relative to the maximum possible reduction because of the reinforcement by the motion picture of their favorable predispositions. They were more likely to perceive the theme and the implications of the film, and they tended to react more favorably toward it.

Those individuals who were initially highly prejudiced toward Jews were more vulnerable to attack by the motion picture and consequently more often showed an absolute reduction in AS scale scores. In many cases they held views specifically condemned by *Gentleman's Agreement*, and hence there was a wider area in which influence could be brought to bear. Although the highly prejudiced individual may not see the full implications of the motion picture and may not react to it in a particularly favorable manner, still his extreme views may be moderated somewhat by the impact of the general theme. The more anti-Semitic the subject, the greater is his vulnerability to persuasive appeals, but the greater also is the tendency for the impact to perceive the theme and by his negative reaction to the theme.

Since in this study initial anti-Semitism appears to be a major factor related to persuasibility, an attempt was made to keep this factor constant while examining the relationship of other variables to persuasibility. In the experimental group there were originally 228 subjects who showed reductions in AS scores and 101 subjects who showed no reductions. Cases were randomly discarded until the proportions falling to each of six categories of initial anti-Semitism were matched between the group which showed reductions in AS scores and the group which did not. The total number of cases thereby was reduced to 261, with approximately the same distribution of initial anti-Semitism scores in each group.

With the factor of initial anti-Semitism controlled, only one of the other variables investigated proved to be significantly related to persuasibility. Of those who scored relatively low on the status-concern scale, 78.8 per cent showed reductions in AS scores after seeing *Gentleman's Agreement*, whereas only 61.3 per cent of those who scored relatively high on status concern showed reductions. The difference is statistically significant at the .01 level. Of sex, socio-economic status, year in college, region of residence, size of community, proportion of Jews in the community, anomia, authoritarianism, conservatism, and religious orthodoxy, none is significantly related to persuasibility at the .05 level. In fact, sex difference is the only one of these variables which reaches significance at the .20 level, with females proving to be slightly more persuasible than males.*

Two final cautions are in order. First, although *Gentleman's Agreement* did appear to have a considerable impact on these students, the second questionnaire was administered within a few days of the showing of the film and it is by no means certain that the influence was a lasting one. Second, there is a possibility that the motion picture merely exerted pressure toward surface conformity to the theme. Rather than a real change in the attitudes and sentiments of the subjects toward Jews, they may have been simply manifesting embarrassment in admitting to anti-Semitic attitudes. The maintenance of anonymity on all the questionnaires, however, was designed to keep this tendency at a minimum.

---

* This is consistent with the finding that females show a greater tendency toward general persuasibility than males. See Janis and Field (1959).

References

ADORNO, T. W., et al. 1950. *The Authoritarian Personality.* New York: Harper.

BASS, BERNARD M. 1955. "Authoritarianism or Acquiescence?" *Journal of Abnormal and Social Psychology,* 51 (July), pp. 616–23.

CHRISTIE, RICHARD, JOAN HAVEL, and BERNARD SEIDENBERG. 1958. "Is the F-Scale Irreversible?" *Journal of Abnormal and Social Psychology,* 56 (March), pp. 143–49.

COOPER, EUNICE, and HELEN DINERMAN. 1951. "Analysis of the Film 'Don't Be a Sucker': A Study in Communication," *Public Opinion Quarterly,* 15 (Summer), pp. 243–64.

COOPER, EUNICE, and MARIE JAHODA. 1947. "The Evasion of Propaganda: How Prejudiced People Respond to Anti-Prejudice Propaganda," *Journal of Psychology,* 23 (January), pp. 15–25.

FLOWERMAN, S. H. 1947. "Mass Propaganda in the War Against Bigotry," *Journal of Abnormal and Social Psychology,* 42 (October), pp. 429–39.

GOLDBERG, ALBERT L. 1956. "The Effects of Two Types of Sound Motion Pictures on the Attitudes of Adults Toward Minorities," *Journal of Educational Sociology,* 29 (May), pp. 386–91.

HOBSON, LAURA K. 1947. *Gentleman's Agreement.* New York: Simon and Schuster.

HOVLAND, C. I. and I. L. JANIS (eds.). 1959. *Personality and Persuasibility.* New Haven: Yale University Press.

HOVLAND, C. I., et al. 1949. *Experiments on Mass Communication.* Princeton: Princeton University Press.

HULETT, J. E., JR. 1949. "Estimating the Net Effect of a Commercial Motion Picture Upon the Trend of Local Public Opinion," *American Sociological Review,* 14 (April), pp. 263–75.

HYMAN, HERBERT H., and PAUL B. SHEATSLEY. 1947. "Some Reasons Why Information Campaigns Fail," *Public Opinion Quarterly,* 11 (Fall), pp. 413–23.

JANIS, IRVING L. 1954. "Personality Correlates of Susceptibility to Persuasion," *Journal of Personality,* 22 (June), pp. 504–18.

JANIS, IRVING L., and PETER B. FIELD. 1959. "Sex Differences and Personality Factors Related to Persuasibility." In C. I. Hovland and I. L. Janis (eds.), *Personality and Persuasibility,* p. 59. New Haven: Yale University Press.

KAUFMAN, WALTER C. 1957. "Status, Authoritarianism, and Anti-Semitism," *American Journal of Sociology,* 62 (January), pp. 379–82.

LENSKI, GERHARD E., and JOHN C. LEGGETT. 1960. "Caste, Class, and Deference in the Research Interview," *American Journal of Sociology,* 65 (March), pp. 463–67.

McCLOSKY, HERBERT. 1958. "Conservatism and Personality," *American Political Science Review,* 52 (March), pp. 27–45.

MEIER, DOROTHY L., and WENDELL BELL. 1959. "Anomia and Differential Access to the Achievement of Life Goals," *American Sociological Review,* 24 (April), pp. 189–202.

MUSSEN, P. H. 1950. "Some Personality and Social Factors Related to Changes in Children's Attitudes Toward Negroes," *Journal of Abnormal and Social Psychology,* 45 (July), pp. 423–41.

PETERSON, RUTH C., and L. L. THURSTONE. 1933. *Motion Pictures and the Social Attitudes of Children*. New York: Macmillan.

RATHS, L. E., and F. N. TRAGER. 1948. "Public Opinion and Crossfire," *Journal of Educational Sociology*, 21 (February), pp. 345–68.

ROSEN, IRWIN C. 1948. "The Effects of the Motion Picture 'Gentleman's Agreement' on Attitudes Toward Jews," *Journal of Psychology*, 26 (October), pp. 525–36.

SROLE, LEO. 1956. "Social Integration and Certain Corollaries: An Exploratory Study," *American Sociological Review*, 21 (December), pp. 709–16.

VAUGHAN, CHARLES L. 1958. "A Scale for Assessing Socio-economic Status in Survey Research," *Public Opinion Quarterly*, 22 (Spring), pp. 19–34.

WIESE, MILDRED J., and STEWART G. COLT. 1946. "A Study of Children's Attitudes and the Influence of a Commercial Motion Picture," *Journal of Psychology*, 21 (January), pp. 151–71.

ZEISEL, HANS. 1949. "A Note on the Effect of a Motion Picture on Public Opinion." *American Sociological Review*, 14 (August), pp. 550–51.

EXERCISES

Many laboratory experiments are conducted in elaborate settings with two-way mirrors, special rooms for control and experimental groups, and a vast array of hardware to ensure total environmental control. While such facilities are desirable for experiments, they are not mandatory. The following exercises are designed to require minimal laboratory facilities. The first two exercises deal with problems in experimental design and require no facilities of any sort; the second two require only a room in which the experiments can be conducted. A small room or even an office will suffice for Exercise 3, and a larger room where a group presentation can be made is necessary for Exercise 4. These facilities should be available at your school.

EXERCISE 1

In the introduction to this section, we described an experiment in which the researcher introduced as the experimental variable "positive encouragement", defined, in this case, as a "kind word." In fact, a great many other things could be regarded as positive encouragement. The purpose of this exercise is to develop experimental variables in terms of concrete actions to be introduced in experiments. Consider the following as experimental variables:

1. Positive Encouragement
2. Threat
3. Authority
4. Disorganization

Now take each one of these variables and write a set of actions that will be introduced in an experiment. It will help to consider each variable in terms of a hypothesis stating its causal effect on social behavior. For example, you might think of the variable "authority" (such as a police officer, a dean, or a boss) as causing more or less group interaction. The important thing is not what the experimental variable will cause but, rather, what concrete actions can be introduced as representing the variable.

EXERCISE 2

The purpose of this exercise is much like that of Exercise 1, except that, rather than develop a set of actions that can be introduced as an experimental variable, here you are to develop a measurement for a dependent variable. The task should be done in groups of three or four, each of which will attempt to develop an observable or testable measure of "group cohesiveness." Group cohesiveness, or group solidarity, refers to the strength of the relationships in a group and of ties to the group. For example, during prolonged periods of combat, fighting units develop very strong ties and have a high amount of solidarity. The problem is to measure such cohesiveness. If a researcher has the hypothesis that group solidarity increases as threat to the group increases, he needs some measure to find whether the group's cohesiveness increases or decreases. By working with a group, the student will discuss what might be observed or tested. Each member of the group is to write a set of observations or questions that would serve as such a measure. He will then compare his list with the list of other members in an effort to develop a measurement that the group agrees on. Each group will present its measurement to the other groups for discussion. (The purpose of working in groups is so that the measurement that is developed can be tested in the group.)

EXERCISE 3

This exercise is a simple experiment to test whether there is a relationship between negative images and presentations of self. Using an experimental group and a control group and a one-time observation, present the following set of symbols to both groups:

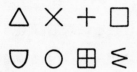

The experimental group will be told that two of these symbols have a high preference among mental patients (negative image); the control group will simply be shown the drawings and told nothing. Each group will be told to rank the drawings on a continuum from most intuitively pleasing to least pleasing. If the hypothesis is correct, the experimental group will have a lower ranking of preference for the two symbols (presentation of self) that were said to have a high preference among mental patients than will the control group.

If there is no difference between experimental and control groups in preferences, take the two figures most preferred by the two groups combined and do the experiment again with different subjects, telling the experimental group that the two new figures were highly preferred by mental patients. If there is still no difference, reject the hypothesis.

Exercise 4

This exercise is designed to test whether there is a relationship between antismoking propaganda and smoking behavior. Design the experiment along the lines used by Middleton, using some form of antismoking propaganda as the experimental variable. (It is suggested that a film be used, since there is less control with written material; but a presentation by a physician or someone from the local health department would serve the same function.) Pretest the control and experimental groups for similarity in smoking behavior; all subjects in both groups must be smokers. After the introduction of the experimental variable, use several post-tests over a period of time to determine whether the propaganda has had any effect on smoking behavior. You might find that there is an immediate effect, or there may be no effect for some time, if at all; by administering post-tests over a period of time, any delayed effects can be found.

ADDITIONAL READING SUGGESTIONS

Asch, Solomon E. 1956. "Studies of Independence and Conformity: A Minority of One Against a Unanimous Majority," *Psychological Monographs*, Vol. 70, No. 9. Describes a now-famous experiment. In a unique design, Asch showed how group pressure affected decision-making. A good example of an innovative experiment.

Milgram, S. 1963. "Behavioral Study of Obedience," *Journal of Abnormal Social Psychology*, 67 (October), pp. 371–78. Another example of innovation in experimental design. Milgram found that experimental subjects were quite obedient when told to give another subject an electric shock. Among other things, this experiment suggests that researchers have a good deal of influence in defining the experimental situation.

Ross, JOHN, and PERRY SMITH. 1968. "Orthodox Experimental Designs." In Hubert M. Blalock and Ann B. Blalock (eds.), *Methodology in Social Research*, Chapter 9. New York: McGraw-Hill. A brief discussion of designs, variables, and analyses used in experiments in sociology and other disciplines. Points out many of the problems and pitfalls awaiting the experimental researcher in the collection and analysis of data.

7. Field Experiment

INVASIONS OF PERSONAL SPACE
—Nancy Jo Felipe Russo and Robert Sommer

THE LAST DECADE HAS BROUGHT an increase in empirical studies of deviance. One line of investigation has used the case study approach with individuals whom society has classified as deviants—prostitutes, drug addicts, homosexuals, mental patients, etc. The other approach, practiced less frequently, has involved staged situations in which one individual, usually the investigator or one of his students, violates the norm or "routine ground" in a given situation and observes the results. (See, for example, Garfinkel, 1964.) The latter approach is in the category of an experiment in that it is the investigator himself who creates the situation he observes and therefore has the possibility of systematically varying the parameters of social intercourse singly or in combinations. From this standpoint these studies have great promise for the development of an experimental sociology following the model set down by Greenwood (1945). With topics such as human migration, collective disturbance, social class, the investigator observes events and phenomena already in existence. Control of conditions refers to modes of observations and is largely on an *ex post facto* statistical or correlational basis. On the other hand, few staged studies of deviance have realized

From *Social Problems*, Vol. 14, No. 2 (Fall, 1966), pp. 206–14. Reprinted by permission of the authors and The Society for the Study of Social Problems.

their promise as experimental investigations. Generally they are more in the category of demonstrations, involving single gross variations of one parameter and crude and impressionistic measurement of effect without control data from a matched sample not subject to the norm violation. Of more theoretical importance is the lack of systematic variation in degree and kind of the many facets of norm violation. The reader is left with the impression that deviancy is an all-or-none phenomenon caused by improper dress, impertinent answers, naive questions, etc. It cannot be denied that a graduate student washing her clothes in the town swimming pool is breaking certain norms. But we cannot be sure of the norms that are violated or the sanctions attached to each violation without some attempt at isolating and varying single elements in the situation.

The present paper describes a series of studies of one norm violation, sitting too close to another individual. Conversational distance is affected by many things including room density, the acquaintance of the individuals, the personal relevance of the topic discussed, the cultural backgrounds of the individuals, the personalities of the individuals, etc. (Hall, 1959). There are a dozen studies of conversational distance which have shown that people from Latin countries stand closer together than North Americans (Hall, 1960), eye contact has important effect on conversational distance (Argyle and Dean, 1965), introverts stand farther apart than extroverts (Williams, 1963), friends place themselves closer together than strangers (Little, 1960), and so on, but there is still, under any set of conditions, a range of conversational distance which is considered normal for that situation. Several of these investigators, notably Birdwhistell (1952), Garfinkel (1964), Goffman (1963), and Sommer (1959) have described the effects of intruding into this distance or personal space that surrounds each individual. The interest shown in the human spacing mechanisms as well as the possibilities of objective measurement of both norm violation and defensive postures suggests that this is an excellent area in which to systematically study norm violations.

The present paper describes several studies of invasions of personal space that took place over a two-year period. The first was done during the summer of 1963 in a mental hospital. At the time it seemed that systematic studies of spatial invasions could only take place in a "crazy place" where norm violation would escape some of the usual sanctions applied in the outside world. Though there is a strong normative control system that regulates the conduct of mental patients toward one another and toward staff, the rules governing staff conduct toward patients (except cases of brutality, rape, or murder), and particularly higher status staff, such as psychiatrists, physicians, and psychologists, are much less clear. At times, it seems that almost anything can be done in a mental hospital provided it is called research, and one can cite such examples as psychosurgery, various drug experiments, and recent investigations of operant conditioning as instances where unusual and sometimes unproven or even harmful procedures were employed with the blessings of hospital officialdom. To call a procedure "research" is a way of "bracketing" it in time and space and thus excluding it from the usual rules and mores. This is one reason why we supposed that spatial invasions would be more feasible inside a mental hospital than outside. We had visions of a spatial invasion on a Central Park bench resulting in bodily assault or arrest on a sex deviant or "suspicious character" charge. It seemed that some studies of norm violation were deliberately on a one-shot basis to avoid such difficulties. After the first study of spatial invasions in a mental hospital had been completed, however, it became apparent that the method could be adapted for use in more typical settings. We were then able to undertake similar intrusions on a systematic basis in a university library without any untoward consequences, though the possibilities of such problems arising were never far beyond the reaches of consciousness in any of the experimental sessions.

METHOD

The first study took place on the grounds of Mendocino State Hospital, a 1,500-bed mental institution situated in parklike surroundings. Most wards were unlocked and many patients spent considerable time outdoors. In wooded areas it was common to see patients seated beneath trees, one to a bench. Because of the easy access to the outside as well as the number of patients involved in hospital industry, the ward areas were relatively empty during the day. This made it possible for the patients to isolate themselves from other people by finding a deserted area on the grounds or remaining in the almost empty wards. The invasions of personal space took place both indoors and outdoors. The victims were chosen on the basis of these criteria: the victim would be a male, sitting alone, and not engaged in any clearly defined activities such as reading, card playing, etc. All sessions took place near the long-stay wards, which meant that newly admitted patients were largely omitted from the study. When a patient meeting these criteria was located, E walked over and sat beside the patient without saying a word. If the victim moved his chair or moved farther down the bench, E would move a like distance to keep the space between them about six inches. There were two experimental conditions. In one, E sat alongside a patient and took complete notes of what ensued. He also jiggled his keys occasionally and looked at the patient in order to assert his dominance. In the second experimental condition, E simply sat down next to the victim and three or four times during the twenty-minute session, jiggled his keys. Control subjects were selected from other patients seated at some distance from E but still within E's visual field. To be eligible for the control group, a patient had to be sitting by himself and not reading or otherwise engaged in an activity as well as be visible to E.

Each session took a maximum of twenty minutes. There were 64 individual sessions with different patients; 39 involved the procedure in which E took notes, and 25 involved no writing.* One ward dayroom was chosen for additional, more intensive observations. During the daylight hours this large room was sparsely populated and the same five patients occupied the same chairs. These patients would meet Esser's (Esser *et al.*, 1965) criteria of territoriality in that each spent more than 75 per cent of his time in one particular area.

RESULTS

The major data of the study consist of records of how long each patient remained seated in his chair following the invasion. This

---

* Four incomplete sessions are omitted from this total. On two occasions, a patient was called away by a nurse, and, on two other occasions, the session was terminated when the patient showed signs of acute stress. The intruder in Study One was the junior author, a thirty-five-year-old male of slight build. It is likely that invasions by a husky six-footer would have produced more immediate flight reactions.

can be compared with the length of time the control patients remained seated. Figure 1 shows the cumulative number of patients who had departed at each one-minute interval of the twenty-minute session. Within two minutes, all of the controls were still seated but 36 per cent of the experimental subjects had been driven away. Within nine minutes fully half of the victims had departed compared with only 8 per cent of the controls. At the end of the twenty-minute session, 64 per cent of the experimental subjects had departed, compared with 33 per cent of the controls. Further analysis showed that the writing condition was more potent than the no-writing condition but that this difference was significant only at the .10 level ($x^2 = 4.61$, df $= 2$). The patient's actual departure from his chair was the most obvious reaction to the intrusion. Many more subtle indications of the patient's discomfort were evident. Typically the victim would immediately face away from E, pull in his shoulders, and place his elbows at his sides. Mumbling, irrelevant laughter, and delusional talk also seemed to be used by the victim to keep E at a distance.

Repeated observation of the same patients took place on one particular ward where the patients were extremely territorial in their behavior. Five patients generally inhabited this large room and sat in the same chairs day after day. There were gross differences in the way these particular territorial patients reacted to the writer's presence. In only one case (S_3) was E clearly dominant. At the other extreme with S_1 and S_2, it was like trying to move the Rock of Gibraltar. E invariably left these sessions defeated, with his tail between his legs, often feeling the need to return to his colleagues and drink a cup of coffee before attempting another experimental session. S_5 is a peculiar case in that sometimes he was budged but other times he wasn't.

Study Two

These sessions took place in the study hall of a university library, a large room with high ceilings and book-lined walls. The room contains fourteen large tables in two equal rows. Each table is 4 x 16 feet, and accommodates six chairs on each long side. Because of its use as a study area, students typically try to space themselves as far as possible from others. Each victim was the first female sitting alone in a pre-determined part of the room with at least one

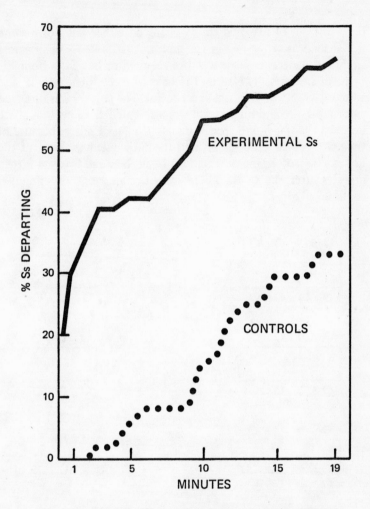

Figure 1. CUMULATIVE PERCENTAGE OF PATIENTS
HAVING DEPARTED AT ONE-MINUTE INTERVALS

book in front of her, two empty chairs on either side (or on one side if she was at the end of the table), and an empty chair across from her. An empty chair was also required to be across from E's point of invasion. The second female to meet these criteria and who was visible to E served as a control. The control was observed from a distance and no invasion was attempted. Sessions took place between the hours of 8-5 on Mondays through Fridays; because of time changes between classes and the subsequent turnover of the library population, the observations began between five and fifteen minutes after the hour. There were five different experimental conditions (Fig. 2).

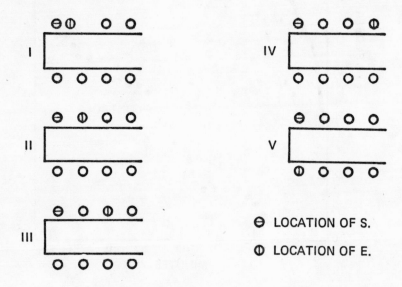

Figure 2. SEATING OF INTRUDER VIS-À-VIS
VICTIM IN EACH EXPERIMENTAL CONDITION

Condition I: E walked up to an empty chair beside an S, pulling the chair out at an angle, and sat down, completely ignoring S's presence. As E sat down, she unobtrusively moved the chair close to the table and to S, so that the chairs were approximately within three inches from one another. Then E would lean over her book, in which she surreptitiously took notes, and tried to maintain constant shoulder distance of about 12 inches between E and S. To use Crook's (1961:125–49) terms, E tried to maintain the arrival distance, and to keep the S from adjusting to a settled distance. This was sometimes difficult to do because the chairs were 18½ inches wide and an S would sometimes sit on the other half of her chair, utilizing its width as an effective barrier. However, E tried to get as close to the Ss as possible without actually having any physical contact. If the S moved her chair away, E would follow by pushing her chair backward at an angle and then forward again, under the pretense of adjusting her skirt. At no time did she consciously acknowledge S's presence. In this condition E took detailed notes of the S's behavior, as well as noting time of departure.

Condition II: E went through the same procedure, except instead of moving the adjacent chair closer to S, E sat in the adjacent chair at the expected distance, which left about 15 inches between the chairs or about two feet between the shoulders of E and S.

Condition III: One empty seat was left between E and S, with a resulting shoulder distance of approximately three and a half feet.

Condition IV: Two empty seats were left between E and S with a resulting shoulder distance of about five feet.

Condition V: E sat directly across from S, a distance of about four feet.

In all conditions E noted the time of initial invasion, the time of the S's departure (or the end of the thirty-minute session, depending on which came first), and any observable accommodation to E's presence such as moving books or the chair. For the controls E noted the time the session began and the time of the C's departure if it occurred within thirty minutes after the start of the session.

Results

Figure 3 shows the number of subjects remaining after successive five minute periods. Since there was no significant difference between the scores in Conditions II–V, these were combined in the analysis. At the end of the thirty minute session, 87 per cent of the controls, 73 per cent of the Ss in the combined conditions

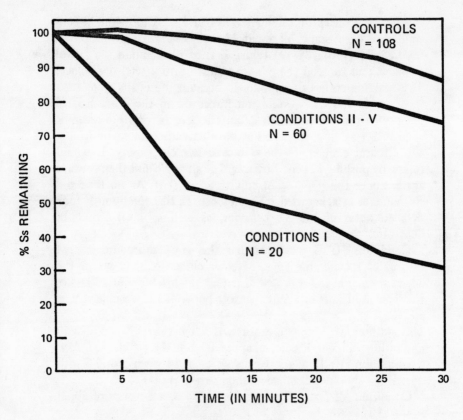

Figure 3. PER CENT OF VICTIMS REMAINING AT
FIVE MINUTE INTERVALS AFTER THE INVASION

remained, compared to only 30 per cent of the experimental Ss
in Condition I. Statistical analysis shows that Condition I produced significantly more flight than any of the other conditions,
while there was a slight but also significant difference between the
combined conditions (II–V) and the control condition. Although
flight was the most clearly defined reaction to the invasion, many
more subtle signs of the victim's discomfort were evident. Frequently an S drew in her arm and head, turned away from E
exposing her shoulder and back, with her elbow on the table, her
face resting on her hand. The victims used objects including

books, notebooks, purses, and coats as barriers, and some made the
wide chair into a barrier.

DISCUSSION

These results show clearly that spatial invasions have a disruptive
effect and can produce reactions ranging from flight at one extreme
to agonistic display at the other. The individual differences in
reacting to the invasion are evident; there was no single reaction
among our subjects to someone "sitting too close." The victim
can attempt to accommodate himself to the invasion in numerous
ways, including a shift in position, interposing a barrier between
himself and the invader, or moving farther away. If these are pre-
cluded by the situation or fail because the invader shifts positions
too, the victim may eventually take to flight. The methods we
used did not permit the victim to achieve a comfortable *settled
distance.* Crook (1961:125–49) studied the spacing mechanisms
in birds, and found three component factors that maintain individual distance, which he defined as the area around an individual
within which the approach of a neighboring bird is reacted to with
either avoidance or attack. A number of measurements may be
taken when studying individual distance—the arrival distance (how
far away from settled birds a newcomer will land), settled distance
(the resultant distance after adjustments have occurred), and the
distance after departure. The conditions in Study One and in Condition I of the second study called for E to maintain the arrival
distance, and to keep the victim from adjusting to a settled distance. In these conditions, the victim was unable to increase the
arrival distance by moving away (since the invader followed him
down the bench in Study One and moved her chair closer in
Study Two), and the greatest number of flight reactions was produced by these conditions. McBride (1964; also McBride *et al.*,
1963), who has studied the spatial behaviors of animals in confine-
ment, has found that avoidance movements and turning aside are
common reactions to crowding, particularly when a submissive
animal is close to a dominant animal. Literally the dominant bird
in a flock has more space and the other birds will move aside and
look away when the dominant bird approaches. Looking away to
avoid extensive eye contact was also a common reaction in the

present studies. This probably would not have occurred if a subordinate or lower status individual had invaded the personal space of a dominant or higher status individual. There was also a dearth of direct verbal responses to the invasions. Only two of the mental patients spoke directly to E although he sat right beside them, and only one of the 80 student victims asked E to move over. This is some support for Hall's (1959) view that "we treat space somewhat as we treat sex. It is there but we don't talk about it."

We see then that a violation of expected conversational distance produces, first of all, various accommodations on the part of the victim. The intensity of his reaction is influenced by many factors including territoriality, the dominance-submission relationship between invader and victim, the locus of the invasion, the victim's attribution of sexual motives to the intruder (in this case all victims and intruders were like-sex individuals), etc. All of these factors influence the victim's definition of the situation and consequently his reaction to it. In the present situation the first reaction to the invasion was accommodation or adaptation: the individual attempted to "live with" the invasion by turning aside, interposing a notebook between himself and the stranger, and pulling in his elbows. When this failed to relieve the tension produced by the norm violation, flight reactions occurred.

There are other elements in the invasion sequence that can be varied systematically. We have not yet attempted heterosexual invasion sequences, or used invaders of lower social standing, or explored more than two unusual and contrasting environments. We are making a start toward using visual rather than spatial invasions, in this case staring at a person rather than moving too close to him. Preliminary data indicate that visual invasions are relatively ineffective in a library where the victims can easily retreat into their books and avoid a direct visual confrontation. There are many other types of intrusions, including tactile and olfactory, that have intriguing research potentialities. It is important to realize that the use of staged norm violations permits these elements to be varied singly and in combination, and in this sense to go beyond the methods of ex post facto or "natural experiments" or single-point demonstrations. It is noteworthy that the area of norm violation provides one of the most fruitful applications for the experimental method.

REFERENCES

ARGYLE, MICHAEL, and JANET DEAN. 1965. "Eye-Contact, Distance, and Affiliation," *Sociometry*, 28 (September), pp. 289–304.

BIRDWHISTELL, R. L. 1952. *Introduction to Kinesics*. Washington, D.C.: Foreign Service Institute.

CROOK, J. H. 1961. "The Basis of Flock Organization in Birds." In W. H. Thorpe and O. L. Zangwill (eds.), *Current Problems in Animal Behaviour*. Cambridge: Cambridge University Press.

ESSER, ARISTIDE H., et al. 1965. "Territoriality of Patients on a Research Ward." In Joseph Wortis (ed.), *Recent Advances in Biological Psychiatry*. Vol. 8. New York: Plenum Press.

GARFINKEL, HAROLD. 1964. "Studies of the Routine Grounds of Everyday Activities," *Social Problems*, 11 (Winter), pp. 225–50.

GOFFMAN, ERVING. 1963. *Behavior in Public Places*. Glencoe, Ill.: The Free Press.

GREENWOOD, ERNEST. 1945. *Experimental Sociology*. New York: Kings Crown Press.

HALL, EDWARD T. 1959. *The Silent Language*. Garden City, N.Y.: Doubleday.

————. 1960. "The Language of Space," *Landscape*, 10 (Autumn), pp. 41–44.

LITTLE, KENNETH B. 1960. "Personal Space," *Journal of Experimental Social Psychology*, 1 (August), pp. 237–47.

McBRIDE, GLEN. 1964. *A General Theory of Social Organization and Behaviour*. St. Lucia, Australia: University of Queensland Press.

McBRIDE, GLEN, et al. 1963. "Social Forces Determining Spacing and Head Orientation in a Flock of Domestic Hens," *Nature*, 197, pp. 1272–73.

SOMMER, ROBERT. 1959. "Studies in Personal Space," *Sociometry*, 22 (September), pp. 247–60.

WILLIAMS, JOHN L. 1963. "Personal Space and Its Relation to Extraversion-Introversion," unpublished M.A. thesis. Edmonton, Alberta, Canada: University of Alberta.

EXERCISES

The essential difference between field and laboratory experiments is control. In the latter, the researcher can control the situation, while, in the former, all the researcher controls is the experimental variable. Both experiments, however, use the introduction of an experimental variable to test a hypothesis. The following exercises will provide experience in working with field experiments. While the student should understand the differences in the administration of laboratory and field experiments, it is important to look for the similarities as well.

Exercise 1

The purpose of this exercise is to sensitize the student to indicators that the experimental variable has caused change in the observed situation. Indicators in field experiments are generally inferred from the differences in patterned behavior before and after the introduction of the experimental variable. For example, in the television program "Candid Camera," the producers wondered what would happen if they had people face the back instead of the front of elevators. They found that the more people there were facing the back, the more likely other riders on the elevator would be to conform and do likewise. The indicator of change here was the degree of variation from the norm that people face the front of elevators. In a situation when a social norm has been violated, people may laugh, become angry, demand explanations, or make snide comments about the violator. For this exercise, simply become cognizant of such reactions in everyday interactions. Whenever you observe someone reacting to another's behavior, write down what caused the reaction and what the content of the reaction was. Actually, what you will be doing is observing naturally occurring field experiments. This will not only give you several ideas for your own experiments, it will also provide you with a set of indicators for norm violations.

Exercise 2

For this exercise, you are to design some simple field experiments to test the following hypothesis:

Individuals will conform to the group in situations where a substantial number of people behave in a manner contrary to normal behavior in that situation.

In the "Candid Camera" situation, for example, when several people faced the back of the elevator, individuals who entered the elevator did the same even though people normally face the front. What other situations could be designed to show the same thing? Make up four and discuss them with the class.

EXERCISE 3

Some social norms are matters of etiquette, some matters of law, and some matters of special group behavior. Such norms are easily seen and understood, but other norms are so ingrained that we do not think of them as norms but as "natural" ways of doing things. One such norm is the rule of pace. As children, we learn not to do things too slowly or too quickly, and, as we develop and mature, we take on a certain pace—a "normal" pace—in everything we do. To see this, and to see the reactions to one who breaks normal pace, conduct the following field experiment.

Go through some motion you normally engage in, but do it in slow motion. For example, eat dinner in slow motion. Do not act as though it is a joke or anything out of the ordinary. After you have sufficient reactions from others (and yourself!), explain the action in terms of the experiment. Record both the reactions of others and how you felt while engaging in the action. This will give you insight into the force of social control, as both an external and an internal phenomenon.

EXERCISE 4

This exercise is designed to find, using a field experiment, whether there is a relationship between how people present themselves and how they are treated. In the observation survey (Chapter 5), it was seen that the way a drunk presented himself in court may have affected his sentence. Here, you will discover whether the way you present yourself has any effect on your treatment as a customer.

Using a new- or used-car dealer as the experimental setting, different students will present themselves in different dress, demeanor, and style to see whether they are treated with the same attention. Students should conduct the experiment both singly and in pairs. The continuum for appearances and types of pairs should be broad enough to ensure that they are seen by the car dealers as clearly different types. On one end of the continuum, the presentation should be that of the socially unconventional and irresponsible, while, on the other end, it should be that of the well-to-do. Different groups in the class can be used to find whether there is a difference between dealers in inexpensive cars and those in luxury cars.

ADDITIONAL READING SUGGESTIONS

CAMPBELL, D. T., and J. C. STANLEY. 1963. "Experimental and Quasi-experimental Designs for Research on Teaching." In N. L. Gage (ed.), *Handbook of Research on Teaching*, pp. 171–246. Chicago: Rand McNally. Discusses "quasi-experimental" designs, offering a solid grounding in "field experiments."

ROSS, H. L., and D. T. CAMPBELL. 1968. "The Connecticut Speed Crackdown: A Study of the Effects of Legal Change." In H. Laurence Ross (ed.), *Perspectives on the Social Order*, pp. 30–35. 2d ed. New York: McGraw Hill. A good example of experimental design.

SWINGLE, PAUL G. (ED.). 1973. *Social Psychology in Natural Settings*. Chicago: Aldine. This collection provides numerous examples of field experiments. The role and importance of field experiments are discussed in the Introduction. A valuable resource.

IV: THE ETHNOGRAPHY

IN CHAPTER 3, SACKS EXPLAINED HOW POLICE COME TO KNOW normal activities on their beats, so that they are able to recognize incongruous behavior or unusual events. Detectives also come to know and understand the character of various neighborhoods, and they realize that they must approach people in different neighborhoods in terms of what is considered proper for the people who live there. The methods used in "getting to know" a group of people include observing and participating in their activities, talking with them, and noting various signs and artifacts typically associated with one group or another. The methods employed in obtaining such understanding are called *ethnographies*.

The purpose of ethnographic methods is to uncover social, cultural, or normative patterns of a group of people. Generally, this involves an analytic description of a cohort's behavior in terms of a social setting, organization, or culture. For example, Cavan (1966) studied the patterns of behavior in bar settings, showing that there were standardized forms of sanctioned behavior for people who entered various types of bars. Sudnow (1967) described and explained the organization of hospitals in terms of how death was routinely handled, and Zimmerman and Wieder (1974) studied a drug subculture in terms of the group's beliefs and values pertaining to drug use. All these studies incorporated participant observation, intensive interviewing, and qualitative analysis in order to arrive at an understanding of the observed patterns of behavior engaged in by those being studied.

Of the numerous methods used by ethnographers, three will be discussed here. While each will be discussed separately, it is not uncommon that they are used in conjunction with one another. For example, in the study described in Chapter 8, participant observation was the primary method employed, but intensive interviewing was also used in gathering data.

PARTICIPANT OBSERVATION

Participant observation can be defined as a method in which the researcher spends time in the normal flow of social life in a setting, organization, or culture. Thus, William Foote Whyte (1943) lived in a lower-class Italian neighborhood, participating in the daily life of a street-corner gang. He boarded with a neighborhood family; spent his time with a gang, engaging in most of their activities; and made notes of what he observed and experienced. In this way, he developed an understanding of the way of life of the people who lived in the neighborhood.

The greatest problem encountered in participant-observation research is deciding what to observe. In any observational setting, innumerable activities are taking place; unlike a researcher doing an observation survey, who has a list of items to look for, the participant observer has a much less specific guide. He is attempting to come to terms with a complex set of relationships, norms, and beliefs, all of which are being acted out in front of his nose. Until he develops a sense of what meanings the swirl of activities has for the subjects, it is difficult to distinguish between significant and insignificant behavior.

To guide his observations, the researcher uses his conceptual framework. For instance, if a sociologist is using a normative framework, he assumes that behavior is regulated by a set of sanctioned rules. If a rule is broken, it is expected that those who observe the rule violation will become upset and will impose sanctions. With such a framework, the participant observer may begin to look for behavior that upsets those around him. For instance, at the race track there are rules regulating sitting and standing in the audience (Scott, 1968). If someone stands up at the beginning of the race, members of the audience may tell him to sit down or even swat him with a racing program. However, the same sanctions against standing are not imposed as the horses come down the home stretch.

In this way, the observer can begin to hypothesize about normative patterns of behavior and start looking for behavior in terms of these patterns. The researcher at the race track found that there were definite, observable patterns regarding standing and sitting, depending on where the horses were. From the beginning of the race to the first turn, the audience remained seated; as the horses entered the back stretch, the crowd began standing; and, as the horses came down the home stretch, they began standing on their seats.

Not all patterns, however, are social patterns. Some may be idiosyncratic or individual forms of behavior and are not reflective of the social milieu. In order to determine social patterns, the participant observer attempts to find behavior that is (1) typical, (2) persistent, (3) trans-situational, and (4) transpersonal. A behavior is *typical* if it occurs in a standardized, regular fashion. For example, in their study of a drug culture, Zimmerman and Wieder (1974) found that "passing the joint" (passing a marijuana cigarette from one person to another) characteristically occurred whenever marijuana smokers came together to smoke marijuana. Similarly, the pattern of passing a joint was *persistent* in that it was observed repeatedly over a period of time. Third, the act was *trans-situational* in that it was distributed in several different situations. Finally, the act was *transpersonal* in that various groups engaged in the same behavior.

Before the researcher can begin his research, he must gain access. On the one hand, there is an ethical problem involved in whether the researcher should tell his subjects of the study. (As was pointed out in Chapter 1, such announcements depend on the situation.) On the other hand, there is an interpersonal problem in gaining access to the subjects. If the owner of a factory gives a researcher free reign to research anything he desires but the workers in the factory shun the researcher, very little data can be gathered, even though access to the setting is gained. Winning the trust and confidence of subjects is a matter of rapport, and, in participant observation more than any other method, rapport is essential, for the researcher must spend a great deal of time with his subjects; if the subjects would rather not have the researcher around, the project is doomed to failure (Douglas, 1972). Generally, rapport is a matter of being noncritical, interested in what the subjects do and say, and, most important, genuinely open to an understanding of how they see and experience their social world. There is a danger of overrapport if the researcher becomes so much a part of what he is studying that he ceases to function as a researcher; but, if the participant observer attempts to bear his purpose in mind, this will not be a problem.

A final matter of importance is note-taking. Good notes will later bring back to memory that which was observed. The more detailed the notes, the more will be remembered. Therefore, participant observers attempt to write as much as possible about their observations as soon afterwards as possible. In some situations, very little on-the-scene note-taking is possible, and the researcher must frequently leave the scene to write up his notes. Other situations, especially those where the subjects know that the observer is engaged in research and expect note-taking, provide lulls in activity when notes can be taken. However, any notes taken in the field should be expanded after the researcher leaves the field and should be typed for ease in later reference.

The notes should include the time and date of the observations, for some patterns may take place only at certain times or on certain days. For instance, we have noted that, in observations of public parks, especially in urban areas, different patterns are observed during different times of the day and different days of the week. Children's play patterns are certain to be different during the hours school is in session and after school. After dark, a park setting belongs to such groups as muggers and the police, and their patterned behavior is substantially different from that observed during the day.

Notes not only serve as a record of observations but are also used as a guide to further observations. For instance, if certain activities are found to occur only at certain times of the day or days of the week, these findings can be used to schedule subsequent observations. This is especially important when one group supplants another, or when one behavior pattern begins and another one ends. In order to know when such a shift occurs, the time will have to be in your notes.

INTENSIVE INTERVIEWING

Intensive interviewing is much like a conversation one might have with a friend not seen for a long time. Unlike more structured interview schedules, where the researcher has a list of questions he asks the respondents, the intensive interview begins with a general question, and the interviewer's subsequent questions are developed in terms of the respondent's replies. For example, if a researcher wanted to know why policemen chose their careers, he might begin simply by asking what influenced them to become police officers and then ask further questions in terms of the response. The following interchanges are hypothetical examples of how an interview might go in different directions:

INTERVIEW 1

Q. What made you decide to become a policeman?

A. The pay seemed good, and the department has a good pension program.

Q. Well, a lot of jobs have good pay and pension plans. There are a number of office jobs and factory jobs with the same pay and pension. Why didn't you take one of them?

A. It's not just the pay. I like the work. In a factory or an office, you've gotta stay indoors all day.

INTERVIEW 2

Q. What made you decide to become a policeman?

A. The work is interesting. You get to work with people, and every day is different. Not the same old nine-to-five.

Q. Well, a social worker has a variety of unusual tasks and gets to work with people; and, besides, a social worker's job is a lot safer.

A. Well, you see, that's part of it. If it's safe, it's not as interesting. Look, what's the kind of days you remember and talk about the most? The safe, routine days, or the ones where something dangerous happens? Like the earthquake. I'll bet you can remember everything that happened that morning, but I'll bet that if someone asks you about today next month, you won't remember. Right?

Q. Okay, then you're saying that it's exciting and interesting because of the danger?

A. Right.

INTERVIEW 3

Q. What made you decide to become a policeman?

A. Well, I don't know. Let me think. I guess I felt I'd be doing something important by enforcing the law.

Q. There are a lot of important jobs. Why did you decide that enforcing the law was more important than, say, building houses?

A. I didn't say that building houses wasn't important.

Q. I know. I was just using that as an example of something that was important. Why do you think being a policeman and enforcing the law is the most important?

A. I don't know if it's the most important thing. I think doctors do the most important thing in saving lives.

Q. Okay, but why law enforcement?

A. It's something like doctors in a way. If you prevent somebody from hurting someone else, then it's even better than patching them up after someone has hurt them.

In each of the interviews, the interviewer pressed for specifics in the responses. Instead of merely accepting such general responses as "good pay," "interesting," or "important," he attempted to find concrete answers and the meanings of general responses (Cicourel, 1964:73–104). Moreover, the intereviewer simultaneously built his questions on the responses and, at the same time, pressed for an answer to the original question.

Sometimes in an interview situation, the respondent will not have really thought about the kinds of things the interviewer wants to know. For example, in Interview 3, the respondent was vague and evasive. In such cases, if the interviewer probes enough, he may eventually find that the respondent actually has only the vaguest sense of an answer to his question. If this is the case, rather than attempting to supply a concrete response for the subject, the researcher should simply note that the respondent was unsure or ambiguous. It is important, however, to keep the respondent on the right track if his talk begins to wander or becomes evasive. In Interview 3, it can be seen that the interviewer has to keep returning to questions that the respondent evades.

It is important to remember that intensive interviewing involves a skill in listening. If the respondent does not think you are interested, or if he feels that you disapprove of what he says, he is unlikely to give you the information you need. On the one hand, if the respondent believes that the interviewer is not interested, he is likely to give short, choppy replies; if he believes that the interviewer is interested, he is likely to elaborate his answers so that there is a complete sense of his meaning. On the other hand, if the respondent feels that the interviewer disapproves of his beliefs, the interview data will be invalid, for the respondent may attempt to impress the interviewer with replies manufactured for the situation.

UNOBTRUSIVE MEASURES

Every research method discussed so far has had the problem of controlling the effect of the method on the subjects. In surveys and interviews, the subject's responses may be a reaction to the way a questionnaire was worded or how the interviewer combed his hair; in experiments, the subjects may try to "help" the experimenter prove his hypothesis; in participant observation, the subjects may act in one way when the observer is present and another way when he is not. All such methods have potential reactive capacities, in that the data collected may be tainted by the reaction to the method (Webb et al., 1966). Unobtrusive measures are nonreactive, in that they are taken from signs that are given off by social actors in normal, everyday interaction. For example, to estimate liquor consumption, a researcher simply counted the number of liquor bottles discarded in the trash (Sawyer, 1961). Such measurements avoid researcher-produced reactions, in that those who provide the information do so unintentionally.

In addition to being nonreactive and serving as checks on other measurements, these types of measures serve as legitimate measures in their own right. They can be used to describe characteristics of social phenomena, and they can be used to measure relationships between variables. For example, to measure a community's perception of criminal activity, the number of large locks and alarm systems installed might be used. In looking for a relationship between religious-oriented college education and smoking behavior, the researcher can simply note whether religious-oriented colleges have fewer ashtrays, cigarette-vending machines, or cigarette butts on campus.

QUALITATIVE ANALYSIS

In looking for causal explanations, researchers using ethnographic techniques are more likely to describe social processes and forms of behavior verbally than to show statistical relationships or use statistical description. Some refer to data used in statistical analysis as "hard data" and data used in qualitative analysis as "soft data," but this dichotomy belies the fact that both types of data are equally "hard" or "soft." The difference is simply that one type has been transformed into numbers and the other has not.

Since qualitative data are not transformable into numbers, statistical analysis is impossible. This does not mean, however, that the analysis used is invalid. Rather, the focus of the analysis is different. For example, a survey researcher may show a statistical relationship between voting behavior and ethnic background. He may find that 90 per cent of all blacks in his sample voted for a liberal candidate over a conservative one; but such a finding tells us only that a relationship exists, not necessarily why it exists. An ethnographer, through participant observation or intensive interviewing, can tell us the understandings blacks have of liberalism and conservatism to explain why they vote as they do. Thus, qualitative analysis is more likely to explain relationships in terms of social meanings, social realities, social norms, and definitions of the situation. Such understandings are not readily quantified (transformed into numbers), and, if they were, they might lose their sense and complexity.

Essentially, then, qualitative analysis is a means of locating patterns and forms of social behavior and explaining verbally why people who engage in such behavior do so. Sociological theories provide the qualitative analyst with concepts such as norms, definition of the situation, roles, and so on, which he can use as a direction in explanation. The content of the concepts in terms of meanings and behavior is provided in the data the researcher has gathered.

The following readings represent participant observation, intensive interviewing, and unobtrusive measures. The first is a participant-observation study of a detective division, in which the authors show that detectives investigate cases (pattern) only if they are seen to be particular kinds of cases (social reality). A causal relationship is established between the patterns and the social reality—a good example of qualitative analysis. In Cressey's discussion of how he formulated a sociological conception of embezzlement and developed and redeveloped hypotheses from intensive interviewing, the process of qualitative analysis and the role of intensive-interview data are well illustrated. Finally, Webb and his associates discuss the creative use of exterior physical signs, expressive movements, and physical location as nonreactive measures.

REFERENCES

CAVAN, SHERRI. 1966. *Liquor License: An Ethnography of Bar Behavior*. Chicago: Aldine.

CICOUREL, AARON. 1964. *Method and Measurement in Sociology*. New York: The Free Press.

DOUGLAS, JACK (ED.) 1972. *Research on Deviance*. New York: Random House.

LOFLAND, JOHN. 1971. *Analyzing Social Settings*. Belmont, Calif: Wadsworth.

SAWYER, H. G. 1961. "The Meaning of Numbers," speech before the American Association of Advertising Agencies.

SCOTT, MARVIN B. 1968. *The Racing Game*. Chicago: Aldine.

SUDNOW, DAVID. 1967. *Passing On: The Social Organization of Dying*. Englewood Cliffs, N.J.: Prentice-Hall.

WEBB, EUGENE, D. T. CAMPBELL, R. D. SCHWARTZ, and L. SECHREST. 1966. *Unobtrusive Measures: Nonreactive Research in the Social Sciences*. Chicago: Rand McNally.

WHYTE, WILLIAM F. 1943, 1955. *Street Corner Society*. Chicago: University of Chicago Press.

ZIMMERMAN, D., and D. L. WIEDER. 1974. "The Diary: Diary Interview Method." In Robert Smith (ed.), *Social Science Methods: A New Introduction*. New York: The Free Press.

8. Participant Observation

DETECTIVE WORK:
PATTERNS OF
CRIMINAL
INVESTIGATIONS
—William B. Sanders
and Howard C. Daudistel

SOCIOLOGICAL JURISPRUDENCE IS the study of what actually happens under the auspices of a law (Weber, 1956:11–20). If a law exists along with sanctions for breaking the law, but the law is not generally enforced or obeyed, then from a sociological point of view there is no law in effect. It is moot to argue that a law on the books could be enforced even though it typically is not, for if we are to understand social behavior in relation to the law it is necessary first to understand how the law typically works on a day-to-day basis, not how it conceivably could work given total obedience and enforcement.

To this end, sociologists have focused on various aspects of the criminal justice system. The study of a public defender's office by Sudnow (1965); studies of the police by La Fave (1965), Reiss (1971), Skolnick (1967), Banton (1964), Wilson (1968), and Bittner (1967; 1970); Miller's (1969) study of prosecution, Newman's (1966) study of conviction, and Blumberg's (1967) work on the entire criminal justice system, all point to the day-to-day working of law. These studies have noted to some extent the role of discretion in the application or non-application of the law in legally equivocal and unequivocal situations. At each step in the criminal justice system, from the citizen's decision to lodge a complaint (Reiss, 1971:65–70) or to define the situation as one in which it is necessary to "call the cops" (Bittner, 1970:95), to the judge's decision as to what sentence a convicted criminal should receive, decisions are made that are not prescribed by statutory law.

The role of discretion provides an area of investigation in law that cannot be accounted for in terms of the law. Wilson (1968), for example, showed that police discretion in the United States varied with departmental policy and community political structure. Departments in communities with partisan political structures were more likely to have "watchman" styles of enforcement, with fewer arrests for almost all types of law violation than departments characterized by "legalistic" styles, which were typically found in communities experiencing a "reform" or "good government" political atmosphere. There is nothing in legal jurisprudence that accounts for such variations in the application of the law. True, the law does provide sanctions for non-enforcement by police, district attorneys, and judges as well as other officials sworn to uphold the law (La Fave, 1965), but since these sanctions are not routinely employed for the typical discretionary acts of the police and others, then such mandates are no different from laws that are typically not enforced. They exist only as potentials and, when applied, only as exceptions.

In addition to their interest in the organizational and political elements entering into decisions to invoke the law, sociologists have been interested in the role of custom in interpretations of situations as legal or illegal (cf. Simmel, 1950:99–104). The influence of custom on discretion has been viewed in terms of prejudice, especially racism, and in terms of broader, more general aspects of customs as well. Reiss (1971) and Black and Reiss (1970) found that black citizens were more likely to demand an arrest in potential arrest situations than were whites; thus they account for the differential arrest rates for blacks and whites, in terms of citizen discretion. Other writers (e.g., Skolnick, 1972; Werthman and Piliavin, 1967; and Piliavin and Briar, 1964) have attributed the differential arrests to ethnic prejudice. La Fave (1965), more than anyone else, has shown that custom provides police with an understanding of what is considered proper and improper in deciding whether or not to make an arrest. For example, as religious customs have changed, so too have the instances when police invoke "blue laws" still on the books.

Another largely ignored aspect of discretion concerns the interpretive practices in formulating accounts of a crime. Sudnow (1965:255) treated the sections of criminal law, not as categories for classifying acts as one type of crime or another, but rather as conceptual schemes used by personnel in the criminal justice system for organizing their everyday activities. Reports of crimes were formulated by the public defenders in terms of normal typifications.* Thus, each case, rather than being treated as unique, was treated as an instance of a typical sort of crime consisting of the circumstances, props, and actors normally making up that type of crime. "Normal" crimes, as opposed to "weird" crimes, "unusual" crimes, or "odd instances of an otherwise normal crime," were crimes that were construed as instances of situations consisting of typical characteristics. For example, normal burglaries were seen to involve kinds of criminals, circumstances, and props that were different from those involved in normal robberies, rapes, and other normal crimes.

Crimes tended to be handled by public defenders and prosecutors on the basis of what sort of normal crime was used as an interpretive scheme for understanding how to proceed. Subseqent decisions were based on typifications that served as interpretive schemes for information pertaining to the case. For example, if a crime involved the use of nylon hosiery, the hosiery in a crime seen to be a normal burglary would be interpreted as having been used by the burglar to cover his hands so as not to leave prints. However, if the crime were formulated to be a typical robbery, the hosiery would be interpreted as having been used as a mask. Similarly, other elements of a crime would be differentially formulated depending on what typification of the crime and criminal the public defender incorporated. Since the initial formulation of a crime serves as an interpretive scheme for subsequent action, it is crucial for understanding how the criminal justice process works to study those whose everyday work involves formulating crimes to be of one normal type or another.

NORMAL CRIMES AND NORMAL DETECTIVE WORK

Citizen Response Detectives. A substantive area of the criminal justice system that has not been studied in detail by sociologists

* For a full discussion of the concept of "typification," see Schutz (1971).

involves the role of the police detective in the legal process. Skol-nick (1967) examined vice squad detectives and their organization; however, there has been no in-depth study by sociologists of what might be called "citizen response detectives." Members of the vice squad, narcotics details, and intelligence divisions have to "drum up their own business," and their work involves what have been called crimes without victims (Schur, 1965). On the other hand, citizen response detectives* respond to complaints that someone has been victimized and needs the police to find the criminal and bring him to justice.

Formulating Crimes. In order for a reported crime to be inves-tigated by detectives, it first has to be formulated as a type of crime that is normally investigated. Generally, the detectives will simply treat a crime in terms of the penal code type reported by the patrol. For example, if the patrol reports a 415 PC (disturbing the peace), the detectives will formulate the circumstances in the same way, interpreting the particulars of the report in terms of a 415 PC. Sometimes, however, a patrol report will use a penal code (or any other legal code) that does not provide the proper typifica-tion of the circumstances of the case for the detectives. In one case, for example, the patrol officer used the penal code for attempted murder (217 PC) to characterize a family dispute. The major crimes sergeant looked at it and said it was a "glorified domestic," referring to a kind of dispute generally typified as "415 PC Domestic" (a family fight that disturbs the peace). Typifica-tions of family fights do not include attempts by family members to murder one another; therefore, the charge of attempted murder was seen as an improper characterization of the event.†

In this way, a case will be formulated as either a case-to-be-worked or a case-to-be-ignored. Once a complaint is established as a case-to-be-worked, it is formulated as either a typical-case-of-this-sort-of-crime or an unusual-instance-of-this-sort-of-crime. For exam-ple, a crime in which only stereo components were taken is seen as a typical burglary, whereas one in which only pencils and shoe-

* For the remainder of this paper, we will use the term "detective" to denote "citizen response detective."

† In a purely statistical sense, the typification of family fights as non-mur-derous is inaccurate, for such disputes are more likely to end in murder than any other single situation.

laces were taken while television sets, radios, and other property commonly taken in burglaries were not is seen as an unusual burglary.

The constituted sense of a crime (i.e., what a crime is formulated to be), moreover, is subject to reformulation in the course of the investigation depending on what leads develop and what information is uncovered. If the leads and information substantiate the initial formulation, it will then tend to crystallize as an interpretive scheme for understanding the events in the case. If, on the other hand, the original formulation cannot account for information uncovered in the case and rival formulations can, either the case will take a new direction or it will cease to be seen as a case-to-be-worked. For example, a case was reported by a girl as a robbery-kidnapping. She told the detectives that she had been forced at gunpoint to drive to an isolated location and give up $1,300 belonging to her employer, which she had been taking to the bank. Several aspects of her account, however, were not consistent with various particulars discovered by the investigators. She had said that the robber wedged himself behind the seat of the vehicle and pointed a gun at her, but packages on the floor behind the seat were not crushed, as they would have been if the robber had been where she said he was. If, on the other hand, the events were interpreted in terms of an embezzlement—i.e., as if the girl had taken the money and made up the story about the robber—such particulars could be accounted for consistently.

METHODOLOGY

In order to convey the method and approach of this study, it will be necessary to explain its context in a larger project engaged in by the researchers. The larger project involved three researchers studying various aspects of the paperwork in a county sheriff's office. Two of the researchers conducted observations and interviews with detectives, and the third did the same with patrol deputies.

Data collection involved participant observation and interviews. Each researcher collected field notes and completed "case reports" (standardized observation schedules for each case on which they accompanied a detective). The field notes were typed and duplicated so that the data collected by one researcher were available to the others. The "case reports" were developed for following cases from their inception, usually with the patrol deputies, through the detective office, to final disposition in the courts. The forms included spaces for recording the type of crime listed by the deputies and the detectives in terms of the California Penal Code, the dispatch code, unused sections of the narrative section of the report forms, an estimate of the adequacy of the report, involvement of the identification (ID) bureau, and twelve items that are typically involved in cases and are relevant to how that case is worked. The patrol researcher would give his form, based on the report taken by the patrol unit, to the detective researchers, who would, if possible, follow the case through the detective division. However, since we were seldom fortunate enough to have a case that was observed by the single patrol researcher assigned to the detective whom the detective researchers were accompanying, the patrol reports themselves were usually used as a source of information. Finally, the researchers made and transcribed tape recordings of interviews with detectives, radio transmissions, and interrogations as well as other recordable events.

For this paper the researchers examined their notes and tapes to find typical instances of reported crimes that were normally handled by the detectives. Data were organized around the hypothesis that criminal acts regarded as instances of typical crimes, such as burglary, rape, etc., would initiate a typical investigative pattern linked to that formulation. Conversely, crimes regarded as unusual instances of a type of crime would be handled in a manner unlike the typical investigations.

Two detective units, the burglary detail and the major-crimes detail, were chosen for the study. Both details typically involved citizen-response types of crimes, yet the nature and circumstances of the crimes for each detail were different enough to show different investigative procedures.

Case-Working Patterns

The formal activities of detectives in the law-enforcement agency studied can be seen in terms of a "case-working role." With the exception of detective sergeants and the detective captain, who have administrative duties, detectives are expected to spend their working hours on assigned cases. Normally, the cases are assigned on the basis of a detective's special ability to work a particular type of case, such as arson or bomb threats, a detective's request to work a particular case, or simple caseload availability.

In contrast to patrol officers and special investigation detectives (i.e., narcotics and vice officers), the detectives always received their cases after a victim had made a complaint (except in the case of homicides, of course) and an initial patrol report was filed. Consequently, all the cases received by the burglary and major-crimes details can generally be defined as criminal offenses that have been reported to and officially recorded by patrol officers.

In the organizational context, a case can be seen as an investigation that consists primarily of gathering and processing information, some of which has been assessed and documented by others within the organization. For example, a victim places a call to the sheriff's department and reports that a burglary has taken place. The information provided by the caller is recorded on tape and documented by a watch commander. On the basis of this information, the watch commander requests that a patrol car be sent to the crime scene and contact made with the reporting party. A departmental dispatcher then assigns a patrol officer to the address given by the caller. The patrolman "takes a report" of the burglary to provide the detectives with information on the type of crime, victim's name and address, names and addresses of witnesses or persons who may have knowledge or information, name or description of possible suspects, method of committing crime, and a narrative description of the crime including a list of the items or amount of cash taken if it's a robbery, the extent of harm or nature of act committed upon the victim if it involves attack, and a description of any physical evidence found at the scene.

On occasion, after a call has been made to the department and a patrol unit assigned, the documentation of the crime may not proceed in a chronological fashion from patrol report to detective investigation. Sometimes patrol officers who are dispatched to major burglaries or major crimes such as homicides, robberies, or bombings call on detectives and request them to be present during the initial investigation. On these occasions, even though the detectives may begin their investigation before an official written report has been received from patrol, a formal report is always filed by patrol and eventually reviewed by detectives.

DECISION TO WORK A CASE

At the detective bureau, the detective sergeants take ("pull") those reports that seem to be relevant to their detail. From those pulled, they decide which cases are to be worked and what order of priority they will receive if they are to be worked. If the case is not to be worked, the sergeant decides whether to inactivate it, close it, or "PR" the case.

Working a case means that the sergeant assigns one or more detectives to investigate it in an attempt to find and catch the culprit. In some cases the sergeant was not certain whether a case should be worked and asked one of the detectives to "check it out" so that he could later decide whether time should be spent on investigation. Such cases were treated here as "worked" cases.

Cases thought not to be significant enough to work or in which the victim did not want to prosecute the criminal were *closed*— that is, simply filed away and ignored. Many cases that were worked ended up closed if the investigation showed that the circumstances did not constitute grounds for action, or if the victim changed his mind and did not want prosecution.

A case that was *inactivated* was neither worked nor closed but filed away waiting for information or leads that would give the detectives something concrete to investigate. Minor cases with no investigative leads were inactivated immediately by the sergeant. Many other cases that were worked ended up being inactivated after the investigation failed to uncover a suspect or evidence that could be used to convict a suspect.

When a case was pulled but not investigated, the victim would sometimes demand that someone should do something. The department in such instances felt that it was good public relations to contact the victim and go through the routine questions they would ask were they working the case. If good leads did develop, the case would be worked, but generally this was simply a means of mollifying the victim. (Cf. Goffman, 1952.) The detectives referred to such contacts as "PR's" (public relations), and to work a case in such a way was to "PR" the victim.

Working Burglaries. The decision to work a burglary is based to a great extent on the amount of loss. Since most burglaries have no leads for the detectives to work, very few burglaries would be investigated if the existence of leads were the only criterion. If, however, a number of small burglaries amounting to relatively little loss are seen to have been committed by the same burglar, any burglary that is believed to have been committed by that burglar will be investigated no matter how small the loss.

Once the decision to work a case has been made by the sergeant, depending on whether the detective assigned to the case sees it as an instance of a typical burglary (juvenile, junkie, professional, inside job, etc.), the case will be worked with the expectation that it will eventually be solved or inactivated. In cases involving no leads but substantial loss, the focus of the investigative work is to determine the exact extent of loss for insurance purposes and to get an accurate description of the property taken, so that if found it can be returned to the owner and used to locate the culprit. In such cases, after the initial investigation and logging of the property, the case is typically inactivated pending further leads.

On the other hand, if the detective formulates the crime as a solvable case, much more work and different patterns of work will ensue. If there are witnesses, usable physical evidence, and possible suspects, the detective has something to follow. Witnesses can be contacted and interviewed, physical evidence can be used to estimate how and when the crime was committed, and possibly may reveal something about the criminal. All this gives the detective something to work with, although it may not be enough for him to clear the case.

The following burglary, although atypical of that crime, illustrates elements in a case that can be worked.

Case 35

A girl was burglarized of $80 in cash and her room was set on fire, destroying her bed and some of the room's furnishings. The burglar's point of entry was believed to be a window which had been broken and then opened. Fingerprints were found on either side of a piece of the broken glass. The detective believed these belonged to the burglar since he felt it unlikely that anyone else would have left fingerprints on both sides; someone looking out the window would have left his prints on only one side. The victim was asked whether anyone she knew might have been responsible, and she gave the detective a list of several names. The prints from the window pane were compared with the prints of those people the victim thought might have been involved and were found to match those of one of the people mentioned. The detective arrested the suspect, and he was subsequently convicted of second-degree burglary.

Because of the availability of a list of possible suspects and the fingerprints, the detective had several leads. With only fingerprints, there would have been little to follow in the case since fingerprints are of little value without a limited list of suspects.* Several thousand fingerprints are on file in the sheriff's office, and the department lacks the devices and the personnel necessary to locate a single print out of the huge number on file. Typically, however, burglaries do not hold such investigative leads which can be followed for identifying and locating the burglar.

Working Major Crimes. Working a case in major crimes differs from working a burglary case in several respects. First, the cases referred to the major-crimes detail for the most part involve acts against persons, whereas the burglary detail handles crimes against property. "Crimes against persons" in the sheriff's office include everything from disturbing the peace (415 PC)† by loud parties, fights, domestic quarrels, noisy vehicles, and the like to homicide (187 PC) (Daudistel, 1971:19). Other typical crimes referred to the major crimes detail include battery (242 PC), assault with a deadly weapon (245 PC; ADW's), rape (261 PC), robbery (211 PC), kidnapping (207 PC), arson (447a PC), and annoying phone calls (653m PC).‡ What most of these crimes (except annoying phone calls and arson) have in common is that the victim comes face-to-face with the criminal and, except for homicides, can usually identify the suspect.

---

* Most victims believe that if fingerprints are found a case can automatically be solved. Television dramas are greatly responsible for this myth, and burglary detectives are invariably asked by victims why they have not caught the burglar and recovered their property in cases where prints are found.

† Throughout this paper, reference is made to the California Penal Code statutes in order to demonstrate the way in which detectives refer officially and informally to various crimes. For instance, it would be unusual to hear a detective refer to "disturbing the peace"; rather he would refer to a "415." "PC" simply designates "Penal Code" as opposed to "HS" (Health and Safety Code), "VC" (Vehicle Code), and other legal codes.

‡ Any form of annoying phone call, usually threatening and obscene ones, was reported by patrol and detectives as a 653m PC.

These crimes also differ from burglary in that, with the exception of robbery, there is rarely any property involved. Moreover, in robberies the "property" is usually money, and usually an amount that exceeds what is normally carried by a person. Burglaries most commonly involve non-cash property, such as bicycles, stereo equipment, television sets, and similar items that can easily be converted into cash.

Burglaries and major crimes also differ in the cases worked, the way in which they are worked, and the volume of cases worked. Most cases reported as 459 PC (burglary) are worked to some extent, and the burglary detective has a more or less constant flow of cases he works on a day-to-day basis. On the other hand, cases seen as "workable" come to the attention of the major crimes sergeant only sporadically. This is not to say that the crimes are reported sporadically by patrol and pulled by major crimes; rather, the crimes to be worked are sporadic. For instance, the following list represents a typical set of crimes pulled by the major crimes sergeant, but none of the crimes reported in this particular set were worked:

1. 415 Disturbing the peace
2. 415 Disturbing the peace
3. Possible 653m—Annoying phone call
4. 245 Assault with a deadly weapon/ 459 Burglary
5. 242 Battery
6. Suspicious vehicle
7. Possible 245, assault with a deadly weapon
8. Missing person (mentally retarded)
9. Attempted suicide 5150 W&I* (mental case)

The two 415's and the battery case were not worked, as is typically the case, since generally by the time the detectives get the reports the trouble has been resolved either by the disputing parties or by the patrolman. Likewise, many annoying phone calls, like the one in this case, involve people who know one another, often

---

* "W&I" refers to the Welfare and Institutions Code. All attempted suicides are classified as 5150's.

divorced or separated couples, and they have settled their differences by the time the report reaches the detective detail. On the other hand, in cases where the victim does not know the caller, there is generally no way to find who made the call and nothing to go on unless the caller has developed an identifiable "MO" (method of operation) known to the detectives. In most 653m cases where the caller is not an acquaintance of the victim, the caller is either unidentifiable or ceases his activities before any leads develop.

On the other hand, the two 245's received were not seen as typical assaults. For example, the one reported with the burglary was part of an ongoing altercation between a family and an unknown youth the family said had been bothering them. A burglary detective had been working the case and, because he believed that no actual burglary or assault was involved, the major crimes sergeant preferred not to waste time on it. The other reported assault involved a car being run off the road by a truck. There was nothing in the report to indicate that the incident was intentional, and there was only a vague description of the truck. Thus, it was not seen to be an unequivocal assault, nor was there a way to begin to locate a suspect.

The final two reports in the sample, missing person and attempted suicide, were pulled by the major crimes sergeant only for information since no investigation was necessary. The "missing person" report involved a mentally retarded child who had wandered away but was later found. By pulling such reports, the detectives have information about a particular individual who may turn up missing again; should this occur, the report pulled can serve as a resource for locating him. Missing persons who are able to stay out of sight and successful suicides are always worked by the major crimes detail. Similarly, the suspicious vehicle report represents an incident that need not be worked but may provide useful information.

It may appear from the foregoing that the major crimes detail finds excuses for doing very little work. This is not so, but it is true that detectives prefer to devote their time and resources to transgressions that are seen as "righteous" (i.e., actual, unequivocal) crimes, and in which the victim wants or needs action to be taken by the detectives. Thus, such crimes as disturbing the peace, making annoying phone calls, and batteries are typically not worked, whereas assaults, rapes, robberies, and other serious crimes against persons typically are worked. Because such crimes occur irregularly, the pace of crimes worked is one of frenzied activity and lulls.

Other indicators of activity can be gleaned from borderline cases-to-be-worked. In the previous example, the reported assaults were not worked, but 245 assaults normally are worked. On the other hand, 242 batteries are not typically worked, for, as we explained earlier, the trouble is usually over by the time the report is received by the detectives. As might be expected, battery cases are more likely to be worked during lulls in activities and assault cases are put aside during busy periods. However, the decision to work a case is determined primarily by whether it is seen as "workable" and by the citizen's eagerness to have the case pursued.

In the above example, it was shown that the 245 assaults that were not worked were not seen to be workable. One was regarded as phony and the other was not clearly an intentional assault. On the other hand, it is important to see why 242 batteries are worked. From observations and interviews, it appears that the discretion to work a battery case lies largely with the victim. Two battery cases worked while the researcher was present illustrate this aspect of what Reiss (1971) calls "citizen discretion."

CASE 57

A delivery boy claimed he was shoved by an elementary school teacher when he attempted to deliver some flowers to the school. The delivery boy came down to the detective bureau and filled out a statement as to what occurred. Even though the boy was not harmed, it appeared to be a clear case of battery. The victim had lost his job over the incident and wanted to bring charges against the teacher.

The detective assigned to the case first contacted the florist where the delivery boy had been employed. There he learned the name of the "teacher" and found that he was actually the school principal. He then contacted the principal and interviewed him as the suspect in the case. The principal denied the charges, claiming that the delivery boy had been rude and was asked to leave, but that he, the principal, had not shoved the boy. The principal filled out a statement and gave the detective the name of a witness to the incident.

Before leaving, the detective asked the principal not to contact the witness until he had had a chance to talk with him. The principal agreed.

It later appeared that the principal *had* contacted the witness since he was waiting at the side of the house when we arrived but went around back and reappeared at the front door when the detective rang the bell. In general he backed up the principal's story, but there were some discrepancies. The principal said the delivery boy came from one part of the building, and the witness said he came from another.

From this investigation, the detective said it was the principal's word against the delivery boy's as far as a judge or jury would be concerned, but he felt that the principal may have been lying. He submitted the report of the information he had gathered to the district attorney and let him make the decision whether or not to file charges. (The final decision rests with the district attorney anyway, but in general detectives will give their opinion as to the culpability of suspects involved.)

CASE 63

A man and woman came to the detective bureau to make out a statement. They claimed that the man's former girlfriend had struck his present girlfriend in a bar, where the man worked as a piano player. The detective assigned to work the case said he was not planning to arrest the suspect since the battery appeared to be an "unprosecutable case," but he wanted to talk with the suspect and warn her against any further attacks on her old boyfriend's new girlfriend. He explained that the case appeared to be unprosecutable because the suspect had four children to care for and was on welfare and because the complainants may have fought back, making it a case of mutual combat. He felt that the DA would take into consideration the suspect's circumstances and not take the complaint; therefore, a thorough investigation to prepare the case for trial would be a waste of effort.

In both of these cases, the work done by the detectives was initiated by a citizen's insistence that something be done. Normally, no investigation of such cases would be made without citizen demand.

It is in the cases that are almost always worked and worked extensively that the investigative patterns of the major crimes detail as distinct from those of the burglary detail can be seen most clearly. Most typical of the major crimes worked in some volume during the period of observation were rapes, attempted rapes, and other sex crimes in which a victim complained to the police. (Of course, homicides, robberies, kidnappings, and other serious crimes against persons are always worked by the major crimes detectives, but in the county where the research was conducted such crimes were rare compared to reported rapes.)

In most burglaries, as noted, working the case consists of contacting the victim, getting a list of the property taken, and attempting to find leads that might be useful in identifying the perpetrators. Typically, the burglarized victim has little information, and the crime scene yields no leads. Thus, working a burglary involves comparatively little time. However, a rape case normally involves extensive work and time, for leads are available through the victim. For example, the following case took the investigating detective over a month to clear, and while he was involved with this case he worked no others.

Case 48

A girl was forcibly taken from her apartment and raped by 15 to 20 members of a motorcycle gang. She was forced to perform fellatio on her assailants and anally raped as well. The suspects were charged with 207 PC (kidnapping), 261 PC (rape), 288a PC (oral copulation), and 286 PC (sodomy). In the investigation twenty-eight different forms were used, including eighteen follow-up reports and numerous teletypes used in identifying and locating the suspects. Several of the gang members were arrested, but because of a mistake in the DA's office only the kidnapping charge was filed.

In another rape case, the detective spent sixteen days working on identifying and locating the suspect.

Case 50

A girl walking on a beach was raped at knifepoint by the suspect. The suspect then forced the girl to drive him to another location in a populated area where the girl escaped. The suspect followed the girl and was seen by several witnesses. The detective working the case interviewed the witnesses who were able to describe the suspect. Going through the field interrogation files, the detective was able to get a name for a person who fit the description given by the victim and witnesses. Since the suspect had prior convictions, the detective was able to get a mug shot which was identified by the victim and witnesses. With the suspect identified, the detective was able to locate him through relatives. The suspect was finally arrested when he came to pick up his pay check from his former employer.

This case involved four follow-up reports, a complaint report, and an arrest report by the detectives working the case. A typical burglary, on the other hand, usually involves only a single follow-up report, which explains that the case has been inactivated because of a lack of investigative leads. This is not to say that burglary detectives do not have cases that involve weeks of investigative work and numerous reports, but because of the perceived circumstances of typical burglaries (i.e., how detectives view what is involved in most burglaries), there are no leads to work with or follow up. Given the necessary leads, burglary cases are worked with the same intensity as major crimes, but major crimes are typically worked and involve a good deal of time whereas this is not typical of burglaries.

A final type of major crime that is worked involves a suspect who is caught immediately and with little question as to his guilt. The following case represents this type of situation.

CASE 59

A man entered a girl's apartment claiming that he was looking for someone who lived there. She told him that the person he was looking for did not live there and asked the man to leave. Instead of leaving, the man attacked and raped her. He then fell asleep. When she was sure the suspect was sound asleep, the victim called the sheriff's office. When the deputies arrived at the scene of the crime, the suspect was still asleep in the victim's bed and was arrested there.

Unlike most rapes, this one involved very little investigative work; all the detective needed was a statement by the victim, and all he had to do was to prepare a single follow-up report for the DA. However, even when there is a suspect in custody and there is little doubt concerning his guilt, the case may involve massive investigative and paper work. For example, the following case involved numerous follow-up reports, interviews, interrogations, and examination of physical evidence even though the suspect immediately turned himself over to the sheriff's office.

CASE 68

A man called the sheriff's office claiming he had shot two men. The man had invited two foreign diplomats to Mountainbeach, where he had promised to give them a painting stolen from one of their former monarchs and a bank note signed by famous revolutionaries. In return, they had promised to give him a letter of commendation from their government. When the diplomats arrived, an argument ensued and both diplomats were shot and killed.

The FBI, the U.S. Attorney General, and even the President became interested in the case because of the status of the victims. A nationally known defense lawyer took up the cause of the defendant, and what would otherwise have been a "walkthrough" (i.e., a homicide where the suspect immediately admits his guilt and pleads guilty in court) developed into a *cause célèbre*.

The case was seen to have international implications, and because of this, rather than the objective elements of the case, a great deal of investigative work had to be done.

In conclusion, it appears that whether a case is worked or not depends primarily on its being formulated as "workable" (i.e., the existence of leads, the amount of loss or harm), except in situations where the victim demands that something be done for a case that is not taken to be workable or where the work load of the detectives preclude their working a borderline case they normally would take. Because the cases-to-be-worked by the major crimes detail are more likely to have workable leads, they were more likely than burglaries to be worked further and to be solved. Conversely, because of the lack of investigative leads in typical burglary cases, a greater proportion of inactivated cases and fewer follow-up reports per case are found in the burglary file.

REFERENCES

BANTON, MICHAEL. 1964. *The Policeman in the Community.* New York: Basic Books.
BITTNER, EGON. 1967. "The Police on Skid Row: A Study in Peace-Keeping," *American Sociological Review*, 32, October.
———. 1970. *The Functions of the Police in Modern Society.* Chevy Chase: National Institute of Mental Health.
BLACK, DONALD J., and ALBERT J. REISS, JR. 1970. "Police Control of Juveniles." *American Sociological Review*, 35 (February).

BLUMBERG, ABRAHAM. 1967. *Criminal Justice*. Chicago: Quadrangle Books.
DAUDISTEL, HOWARD. 1971. *Cop Talk: An Investigation of the Police Radio Code*, unpublished M.A. thesis. Santa Barbara: University of California.
GOFFMAN, ERVING. 1951. "On Cooling the Mark Out: Some Aspects of Adaptation to Failure," *Psychiatry*, 15 (November), pp. 451–63.
LA FAVE, WAYNE. 1965. *Arrest: The Decision to Charge a Suspect with a Crime*. Boston: Little, Brown and Company.
MILLER, FRANK W. 1969. *Prosecution: The Decision to Charge a Suspect With a Crime*. Boston: Little, Brown and Company.
NEWMAN, DONALD J. 1966. *Conviction: The Determination of Guilt or Innocence Without Trial*. Boston: Little, Brown and Company.
PILIAVIN, IRVING, and SCOTT BRIAR. 1964. "Police Encounters with Juveniles," *American Sociological Review*, 70 (September).
REISS, ALBERT J., JR. 1971. *The Police and the Public*. New Haven: Yale University Press.
SCHUR, EDWIN M. 1965. *Crimes Without Victims*. Englewood Cliffs, N.J.: Prentice-Hall.
SCHUTZ, ALFRED. 1971. *Collected Papers: The Problem of Social Reality*. Edited and introduced by Maurice Natanson. The Hague: Martinus Nijhoff.
SIMMEL, GEORG. 1950. *The Sociology of Georg Simmel*. Edited by Kurt H. Wolff. New York: The Free Press.
SKOLNICK, JEROME H. 1967. *Justice Without Trial: Law Enforcement in Democratic Society*. New York: John Wiley & Sons.
————. 1972. "The Police and the Urban Ghetto." In Charles E. Reasons and Jack L. Kuykendall, *Race Crime and Justice*, 236–58. Pacific Palisades: Goodyear.
SUDNOW, DAVID. 1965. "Normal Crimes: Sociological Features of the Penal Code in a Public Defender Office," *Social Problems*, 12 (Winter), pp. 255–76.
WEBER, MAX. 1956. *Max Weber Law and Economy*. Edited by Max Rheinstein. Cambridge, Mass.: Harvard University Press.
WERTHMAN, CARL, and IRVING PILIAVIN. 1967. "Gang Members and the Police." In David J. Bordua, *The Police: Six Sociological Essays*. New York: John Wiley & Sons.
WILSON, JAMES Q. 1968. *Varieties of Police Behavior*. Cambridge: Harvard University Press.

EXERCISES

The following set of exercises is designed to introduce the student to some of the practical problems of participant observation. The first exercise offers experience in the initial problems of participant observation research, and the following two are observation projects that cover a spectrum of techniques and problems in this method.

EXERCISE 1

The purpose of this exercise is to develop skills and understanding in gaining access to settings, organizations, and cultures and to find how observations can be recorded under different situations. To do this, take a setting, an organization, and a culture (including subcultures) that you think might be interesting to study and find out what is necessary to gain access. The setting and organization may be public or private domains: for example, a museum would be a public setting, while a living room would be a private setting; your local government would be a public organization, and the IBM corporation would be a private one. The cultures or subcultures may be deviant or nondeviant; heroin users would constitute a deviant subculture, and ski enthusiasts would constitute a nondeviant subculture. Some subcultures, especially nondeviant ones, have formal organizations, and access to the subculture may be through such organizations; therefore, explain how access is gained to the organization, and how this might lead to access to the subculture.

Public, nondeviant situations are generally much easier to gain access to than are private, deviant situations.

Once you have explained how access is gained in each of the three situations, explain how you would collect and record your observations. Could notes be taken while observations are being made, or would the researcher have to make notes later? Would the researcher be known or unknown, and how would he account for his presence if unknown? Would the researcher have access to several different situations or only a few? At what times could the researcher be present? Once these questions are answered, you should be able to give instructions to a researcher on how to gain access and collect all the data he needs.

EXERCISE 2

The purpose of this exercise is to develop skills in recognizing social patterns of behavior. As was pointed out in the introduction, patterns are behaviors that are typical, persistent, trans-situational, and transpersonal. To begin to recognize social patterns, it is helpful to observe situations when there is a dramatic change in behavior patterns. For example, the interaction in a hospital emergency ward changes when an emergency case arrives, or in a firehouse when the firemen mobilize for a fire. There are other situations in settings, organizations, and cultures when one routine behavior pattern changes to another. In these situations, the two different social patterns, seen in juxtaposition, highlight one another and are therefore more easily observed.

To find such situations, it will be necessary to use your imagination and think of where in your own experience such abrupt changes occur. Two questions will be helpful in locating such situations. First, what social behavior is organized to handle changing circumstances routinely? Secondly, what time changes are there that entail changes in behavior? Behavior at bus stops, for example, is organized to prepare for the arrival of the bus; when the bus arrives, the circumstances have changed, and those waiting behave differently from the way they did before. The behavior of spectators at a horse race, mentioned earlier, is another example. On the other hand, time orders changes in behavior. Before a coffee break, office workers engage in one type of behavioral pattern that can be seen to change as the time for the office break arrives.

EXERCISE 3

This exercise has a dual purpose. On the one hand, it is designed to find relationships between behavioral settings and social-behavioral patterns using participant observation. On the other hand, it is intended to demonstrate how more than a single method can be usefully employed in doing research.

For predicting social behavior, few indicators are better than social settings. It is obvious that different behavior will be found in churches from what will be found in bars, and it is not difficult to predict the forms of behavior one will observe. Group prayer in churches, for instance, is setting-specific to churches, temples, and synagogues. On the other hand, some behavior is independent of a particular setting and can be found in numerous settings, such as face-to-face conversations.

For this exercise, observe some social setting and describe a setting-specific behavior. If feasible, students should be divided into groups of five with each student in the group observing a different setting. Once a behavior pattern has been identified as setting-specific, it should be described in detail, so that the description could be used to replicate the behavior. Then, each student should give the description of his setting-specific behavior to another student, to be used as an experimental variable in a field experiment. The students will then introduce the behavior from another setting into the setting they originally observed. If there are negative sanctions for the behavior, this will serve as evidence that the behavior is setting-specific for the setting in which it was originally observed. If not, then the behavior can be taken to be general to more than a single setting.

Some settings you might consider are parks, amusement arcades, restaurants, waiting rooms, and other places where a lot of people gather. Behaviors to look for include smoking, talking, using drugs, laughing, drinking, eating, and the specific absence of these and other activities.

A word of caution is in order, however. Some behavior that is quite normal in one setting can be seen as intolerable in another, and the consequences for such behavior may be quite dramatic. For instance, if one member of a group observed a nudist colony and another member tested the specificity of nudist-colony behavior in a courtroom, the experimenter might land in jail. It is important to use discretion in this exercise. If you believe that a certain behavior would have dangerous consequences in another situation, instead of actually introducing the behavior, interview participants of the setting and ask what their reactions would be.

ADDITIONAL READING SUGGESTIONS

GOFFMAN, ERVING. 1963. *Behavior in Public Places*. New York: The Free Press. Offers a conceptual framework for analyzing public interaction. Useful for analyzing public social settings and organizations.

LOFLAND, JOHN. 1971. *Analyzing Social Settings*. Belmont, Calif.: Wadsworth. An excellent resource for setting up and analyzing participant-observation research as well as research using intensive interviewing. Lofland designed the book to be used while the research is in progress. It serves as a useful guide in doing ethnographies.

ZIMMERMAN, DON H., and D. LAWRENCE WIEDER. 1974. "The Diary: Diary Interview Method." In Robert Smith (ed.), *Social Science Methods: A New Introduction*. New York: The Free Press. Discusses research in a drug subculture, using diaries kept by subjects as a source of data. Besides providing a useful new tool for ethnographic research, it includes an outstanding discussion of how the authors located social patterns.

9. Intensive Interviews

DEVELOPMENT OF
A GENERALIZATION
EXPLAINING
VIOLATION OF
FINANCIAL TRUST
—Donald R. Cressey

ALMOST ALL PUBLISHED MATE-rials pertinent to the current research are studies of "embez-zlement," and this legal con-cept was at first used to define the behavior under scrutiny here.* Upon contact with only a few cases, however, it was discovered that the legal category did not describe a homogeneous class of criminal behavior. Persons whose behavior was not adequately described by the definition of embezzlement were found to have been imprisoned for that offense, and persons whose behavior was adequately described by the definition were confined for some other offense. From the legal viewpoint, the use of the word "embezzlement" to denote the behavior of one who has been convicted of forgery or some other offense is obviously erroneous. Also, generalization about a kind of "embezzlement" different from that described by the legal defini-

* "The fraudulent appropriation to his own use or benefit of property or money entrusted to him by another, on the part of a clerk, agent, trustee, public officer or other person acting in a fiduciary capacity." *Black's Law Dictionary* (1933:633).

From *Other People's Money: A Study in the Social Psychology of Embezzlement*, by Donald R. Cressey, © 1957, 1971 by Wadsworth Publishing Company, Inc., Belmont, California 94002. Reprinted by permission of the publisher.

tion would be of little scientific value, since another investigator would be unable to search for negative cases.*

To avoid these legal and scientific difficulties, the legal concept "embezzlement" was abandoned, and in its place two criteria for inclusion of any particular case in the investigation were established. First, the person must have accepted a position of trust in good faith. This is almost identical with the requirement of the legal definition that the "felonious intent" in embezzlement must be formulated *after* the time of taking possession. All legal definitions are in agreement in this respect. Second, the person must have violated that trust by committing a crime. These criteria permit the inclusion of almost all persons convicted of embezzlement and larceny by bailee and, in addition, a proportion of those convicted of confidence game, forgery, and other offenses. Some of the offenses in each category are violations of positions of trust which were accepted in good faith. The phenomenon under investigation was therefore defined as "criminal violation of financial trust." The use of this new concept had the effect of providing a rigorous definition of the behavior under investigation, so that a generalization about all instances of the behavior could be attempted, but it did not do violence to the legal definition of "embezzlement" or of the other crimes.

To illustrate the inadequacy of the use of legal concepts, as such, in scientific generalization about embezzlement we need only refer

* The literature on "embezzlement" is replete with examples of the vague use of the concept in this way, and as a result there has been practically no progress toward the cumulative development of a theoretical explanation of the type of behavior that embezzlement entails, and even the factual conclusions of empirical studies are not immediately comparable in all aspects. Bonding companies, for instance, ordinarily use the term to denote the behavior of all fidelity and surety bond defaulters (United States Fidelity and Guaranty Company, 1937, 1950; and Peterson, 1947). It also has been used to denote the criminal behavior of all persons employed in banks (Pratt, 1947; 1948). In one instance, the concept has been used in such a way that it included swindlers as well as embezzlers (Riemer, 1941). The varied usage of the term is due to oversight on the part of some investigators, but it is also due in part to the existence of a variety of legal definitions among the states and foreign countries. For example, in Swedish law, "embezzlement" includes some of the offenses that the laws of some of our states define as confidence game or obtaining money under false pretenses, and in some states there is no embezzlement, that type of offense being included in a broad definition of "larceny."

to the varied usage of legal terms by the state of Illinois in sentencing men to its penitentiaries. First, this state uses "obtaining money by means of confidence game" to cover a multitude of offenses including, in order of frequency used for commitment, the issuing of a fraudulent check, obtaining money or property by some other trick in which advantage is taken of the confidence which the offender has established in the victim, and the criminal conversion of money or property accepted in good faith while acting in a fiduciary capacity. The last type of behavior is fundamentally different, sociologically, from that in which a man sells non-existent goods to a victim or issues a check on a non-existent account, and it is obviously much closer to embezzlement than it is to classical confidence game. However, in such cases it frequently is difficult for a defendant to prove that "criminal intent" was absent at the time the money or property was accepted and that instead it was present only after the property had come into his legal possession. Often the defendant is not interested in producing such proof.

Second, the definition of forgery is in Illinois more precise than that of confidence game, but again some forgeries are more closely related to embezzlement than they are to other forgeries. Those forgeries committed in situations where the criminal is trusted (*i.e.*, a forged check is accepted by a victim) are no more homogeneous sociologically than crimes called "confidence game" are homogeneous because the person is similarly trusted. In many instances, one forges as a part of his embezzlement, so that the prosecuting attorney has, in effect, the choice of prosecuting him for either or both crimes. The behavior of a bank teller who, for example, forges a customer's name on a withdrawal slip made out in the amount of $100 and then pockets the money is logically identical, using the concept "criminal violation of financial trust," to embezzlement by a teller who simply indicates that a $100 withdrawal has been made when in fact it has not been made.

Third, larceny by bailee and embezzlement are legally distinguishable in Illinois (this is not true in all states), but the legal distinction is relevant for scientific purposes only in the way that the legal distinction between forgery and embezzlement is relevant. The legal differentiation hinges on the nature of the trust relationship—whether of trustor-trustee or of bailor-bailee—but such differentiation is unnecessary if the trust-violation concept is used instead of the legal categories. Again, the matter of legal proof presents perplexing problems, since it is difficult to prove in court, for example, whether one who rented an automobile and absconded with it actually intended to abscond with it at the time he rented it (confidence game) or whether he rented it in good faith and then later decided to abscond with it (larceny by bailee).

Fourth, not even the relatively precise definition of embezzlement is used consistently in the state. We encountered four different cases in which persons convicted of embezzlement had obviously intended to "beat" their victims at the time they accepted the position of trust. In one such case, which demonstrates the legal importance of proving the presence of criminal intent at different periods, a man was convicted of embezzlement after selling a truckload of merchandise belonging to his employer. He confessed to the interviewer that this was the seventh or eighth time he had obtained a fictitious driver's license and applied for a truck-driving job with the intention of absconding with merchandise. Had the state been able to prove this, it probably would have convicted him of confidence game. The case was not used in the research, since it was not subsumed under the sociological concept.

The main source of direct information in regard to the behavior under scrutiny, now called "the criminal violation of financial trust," was interview material obtained in informal contacts with all prisoners whose behavior met the criteria and who were confined at the Illinois State Penitentiary at Joliet (April–September, 1949), the California Institution for Men at Chino (October–May, 1950–51), and the United States Penitentiary at Terre Haute, Indiana (June–August, 1951). In each institution the names of all inmates confined for offenses such as embezzlement, larceny by bailee, confidence game, forgery, uttering fictitious checks, conspiracy, grand theft (California), theft of government property, falsification of a bill of lading used in interstate shipment, and theft of goods in interstate shipment was obtained. The personal file of each of 503 inmates was examined with the aim of screening out those cases which obviously did not meet the criteria. Official documents such as the "State's Attorney's Report," "The Attorney General's Report," pre-sentence investigation reports, the prosecuting agency's report, and official commitment papers were heavily relied upon, but other documents, such as letters from former employers and from relatives and friends, newspaper clippings, and the prisoner's statement upon admission to the institution also were consulted. These documents revealed, as expected, that many cases did not meet the first criterion—acceptance of a position of trust in good faith—and these cases were not considered further. Whenever there was doubt, however, the case was kept in the list of eligible cases and later the subject was interviewed.

All persons whose cases were not eliminated in this screening process were then interviewed briefly. The main purpose of these interviews was to introduce the subjects to the investigator. They were assured that he was in no way connected with a law-enforcement agency or with the security of the institution. These interviews were of from one-half hour to one and one-half hours duration, depending entirely upon the subject's willingness to talk without being questioned and with a minimum of encouragement and prompting. If analysis of the official and personal documents had established doubt as to whether a subject's case met the criteria, his history in the position of trust was reviewed in regard to the circumstances under which the position was accepted, the term of incumbency before violation, and the circumstances of the violation. Thus, if one answers a "blind" newspaper advertisement for an employee and through it obtains a position, or if he more or less "falls" into a position, it usually may be presumed that he accepted the position of trust in good faith. On the other hand, if he accepts a position of trust under an assumed name there is reason to be suspicious of his intentions. Similarly, one who worked honestly as an accountant for a firm for ten years before he embezzled usually can be presumed to have accepted the position in good faith, and one who absconded with the available funds on the first day of his employment ordinarily can be presumed not to have accepted the position in good faith. Finally, there is a high probability that one who reports his dishonest behavior to his employer or to law enforcement officers accepted the position in good faith. Statements concerning the circumstances surrounding the trust violation could ordinarily be found in official documents, and the subject could be interviewed in respect to the other two aspects of his history without much direct reference to his offense.

In the interviews the subjects were never asked the question, "Did you accept your position of trust in good faith?" Instead, the interviewer prompted each subject to talk about the circumstances surrounding acceptance of the position of trust and the term of incumbency before violation, then waited for the subject to give the desired information spontaneously. The subjects did not know what the criteria were, and it was not until later that they learned that trust violators were the subject of the study. When he reported for the initial interview one subject believed that only Jewish prisoners were being studied. Thus, it was impossible for an inmate to construct logical lies in order to deceive the investigator about whether or not his case met the criteria. Ordinarily, evidence of acceptance in good faith came out in the first interview in the form of statements such as the following: "I had no idea I was going to do this until the day it happened." "For two years I have been trying to understand why I did this after being honest all my life." "I never at any time had any intentions of beating that man." "He wouldn't give me what he'd promised so I just decided to pay myself." Evidence of acceptance in bad faith was presented as follows: "I'm the biggest Con Man in Chicago." "I thought this looked like a pretty good score, so I took it." "My case wasn't like embezzlement because I knew when I took their money that I was going to use it for myself."

The 73 inmates at Joliet, the 21 at Chino and the 39 at Terre Haute whose cases met the criteria were interviewed frequently and at length. Not all were seen the same number of times, and in general the interviews with those seen a small number of times were longer than those with the men interviewed more frequently. Most of the interviews were conducted in a special interviewing room, but a few were conducted at the inmate's place of employment in the institution. In some cases verbatim notes could be written during the interviews without disturbing the subject, but in other cases it seemed appropriate to make only outline notes, and in some cases no notes could be taken at all. In the last two instances the content of the interview was written down in the subject's own words as soon as he left the room. At Chino a few cases were recorded on tape.

The length and frequency of interviews with individual subjects depended to a large extent upon the subject himself. Those subjects who seemed reluctant to talk freely were seen more frequently than those with whom a friendly and confidential relationship was established early in the process, but those who were unable to talk freely and spontaneously about the details of their cases and backgrounds, even if they so desired, were not interviewed as frequently as those who were able to do so. That is, "good" subjects were interviewed more often and more extensively than "poor" subjects —those whose intelligence, educational background, or vocabulary restricted the communication of their experiences. Those who described their behavior fluently became crucial cases, their testimony causing the abandonment of the hypothesis which had guided the research up to the time they were encountered. In sessions in which the interviewer asked indirect questions and the subject gave short, restricted answers, the new hypotheses were then checked against the less fluent cases.

Hypotheses in regard to the problem of systematic causation were formulated progressively in much the same way that the behavior being studied was clarified and redefined to include more than is denoted by the legal term "embezzlement." When a hypothesis was formulated, a search for negative cases was conducted, and when such cases were found the hypothesis was reformulated in the light of them. Consequently, after the final generalization was formulated much of the interview material became obsolete. . . . An average of about fifteen hours was spent with each subject. . . .

The first hypothesis about which information was sought in the interviews was that positions of financial trust are violated when the incumbent has learned in connection with the business or profession in which he is employed that some forms of trust violation are merely technical violations and are not really "illegal" or "wrong," and, on the negative side, that they are not violated if this kind of definition of behavior has not been learned. This hypothesis was suggested by Sutherland in his writings on white collar crime (Sutherland, 1949), but it was abandoned almost immediately. Some of the first violators interviewed expressed the idea that they knew the behavior to be illegal and wrong at all times and that they had merely "kidded themselves" into thinking that it was not illegal. Others reported that they knew of no one in their business or profession who was carrying on practices similar to theirs and some of them defined their offenses as theft, rather than trust violation.

In view of these negative cases, a second hypothesis, which included some of the popular notions regarding the importance to trust violation of gambling and family emergencies, as well as the potential trust violators' attitudes toward them, was formulated. This hypothesis was in part based on Riemer's observation that the "opportunities" inherent in trust positions form "temptations" if the incumbents develop anti-social attitudes which make possible an abandonment of the folkways of business behavior (Riemer, 1941). The formulation was that positions of trust are violated when the incumbent defines a need for extra funds or extended use of property as an "emergency" which cannot be met by legal means, and that if such an emergency does not take place trust violation will not occur. This hypothesis proved fruitful, but like the first one it had to be revised when persons were found who claimed that while an emergency had been present at the time they violated the trust, other, perhaps even more extreme emergencies, had been present in earlier periods when they did not violate it. Others reported that there had been no financial "emergency" in their cases, and a few "explained" their behavior in terms of antagonistic attitudes toward the employer, feelings of being abused, underpaid, or discriminated against in some other way.

The next revision was based on the second hypothesis but it shifted the emphasis from emergency to psychological isolation, stating that persons become trust violators when they conceive of themselves as having incurred financial obligations which are considered as non-socially sanctionable and which, consequently, must be satisfied by a private or secret means. Negatively, if such non-shareable obligations are not present, trust violation will not occur. A similar hypothesis has been suggested by LaPiere and Farnsworth who cite Sutherland as having shown that in cases of white collar crime the person is frequently confronted "with the alternative of committing a crime or losing something he values above his integrity" (LaPiere and Farnsworth, 1949:344). But the specific hypothesis here was unknowingly suggested by a prisoner who stated that he believed that no embezzlement would ever occur if the trusted person always told his wife and family about his financial problems, no matter what the consequences. It directed attention to the fact that not all emergencies, even if they are created by prior "immoral" behavior on the part of the trusted person, are important to trust violation. However, when the cases were re-examined to determine whether the behavior in question could be explained by this hypothesis it was found that in a few of them there was nothing which could be considered as financial *obligation*, that is, as a debt which had been incurred in the past and for which the person at the present time felt responsible. Also, in some cases there had been non-sanctionable obligations at a prior time, and these obligations had not been alleviated by means of trust violation. It became increasingly apparent at this point that the origin of trust violation could not be attributed to a single event, but that its explanation could be made only in terms of a series or conjuncture of events, a process.

Again the hypothesis was re-formulated, emphasizing this time not financial *obligations* which were considered as non-socially sanctionable, and hence as non-sharable, but non-sharable *problems* of that nature. That is, by using the more general "problem" concept it was emphasized that the subject could be in financial difficulty not only because of an acknowledged responsibility for past debts, but because of present discordance between his income and expenditures as well. This hypothesis also pointed up the idea that not only was a non-sharable problem necessary, but also that the person had to, first, be aware of the fact that the problem could to some extent be solved by means of trust violation and, second, possess the technical skill necessary for such violation. Negative cases appeared, however, in instances where men reported that what they considered a non-sharable problem had been present for some period of time and that they had known for some time before the trust violation took place that the problem could be solved by violating their position of trust by using a particular skill. Some stated that they did not violate the trust at the earlier period because the situation was not in sharp enough focus to "break down their ideas of right and wrong."

Such statements suggested the final revision, which took the following form: Trusted persons become trust violators when they conceive of themselves as having a financial problem which is non-sharable, are aware that this problem can be secretly resolved by violation of the position of financial trust, and are able to apply to their own conduct in that situation verbalizations which enable them to adjust their conceptions of themselves as trusted persons with their conceptions of themselves as users of the entrusted funds or property.

This hypothesis proved to be far superior to the others, and no evidence necessitating its rejection has been found as yet. It was developed in the initial phase of the study, at the Illinois State Penitentiary, and was, consequently, based on all cases of trust violation confined in one state institution. A search of the cases reported in the literature, and examination of about two hundred cases collected by E. H. Sutherland in the 1930's likewise showed no negative cases. While many of the reports in the literature and in the Sutherland materials did not contain crucial information which would either affirm or contradict the hypothesis, those which did contain pertinent information affirmed it.

Similarly, in the second phase of the study at the state institution at Chino, California, no negative cases were found, and the final phase, at the United States Penitentiary at Terre Haute, Indiana, was explicitly undertaken so that a search for negative cases could be made among Federal bank embezzlement and post office embezzlement cases. In all of the cases interviewed the process was found to be present, and when cases were examined with a view to answering the question: "Why did these men not violate their trust in an earlier period?" it was seen that in earlier periods one or more of the events in the process had not been present. None of the interviewees were informed about the hypothesis, and the fact that any of the cases might have contradicted it but that none did so may be considered as evidence of validity. In a sense, a prediction for unknown cases of trust violation at Chino and Terre Haute was made on the basis of experience with trust violation in Illinois, and this prediction was borne out in all instances.

The presence of a non-sharable financial problem will not in itself guarantee that the behavior in question will follow. The entire process must be present. While most socialized persons have problems which they consider non-sharable, private, and personal, not all of those persons violate positions of trust which they might hold. A trusted person, for example, who feels that the investment which has resulted in his insolvency was so stupid that he must keep it secret in order to avoid ridicule and disgrace could conceivably commit suicide, become a philosopher of the sort that renounces all worldly things, or use one of countless means to conceal or relieve his distress (cf. Hall, 1947:403). Similarly, one in somewhat the same position could conceivably be sharply aware of the fact that his disgrace could be avoided if he violated his trust position, yet he would not necessarily violate that position. He must first apply to the situation a verbalization which enables him to violate the trust and, at the same time, to look upon himself as a non-violator.

The final hypothesis in its complete form made it possible to account for some of the features of trust violation and for some individual cases of that behavior which could not be accounted for by other hypotheses. However, the fact that it was revised several times probably means that future revision will be necessary, if negative cases are found. The location by another investigator of persons who have violated positions of trust which were accepted in good faith, but in whose behavior the process was not present, will call for either a new revision of the hypothesis or a re-definition of the behavior included in the scope of the present hypothesis.

REFERENCES

Black's Law Dictionary. 1933. St. Paul: West.

HALL, JEROME. 1947. Principles of Criminal Law. Indianapolis: Bobbs-Merrill.

LA PIERE, R. T., and P. R. FARNSWORTH. 1949. Social Psychology. New York: McGraw-Hill.

PETERSON, VIRGIL. 1947. "Why Honest People Steal," Journal of Criminal Law and Criminology, 38 (July–August), pp. 94–103.

PRATT, L. A. 1947. Bank Frauds: Their Detection and Prevention. New York: Ronald Press.

———. 1948. "I Catch Bank Embezzlers," Collier's, 122 (November 20), pp. 51 ff.

RIEMER, SVEND. 1941. "Embezzlement: Pathological Basis," Journal of Criminal Law and Criminology, 32 (November–December), pp. 411–23.

SUTHERLAND, E. H. 1949. White Collar Crime. New York: Dryden.

United States Fidelity and Guaranty Company. 1937. 1001 Embezzlers. Baltimore: Author.

———. 1950. 1001 Embezzlers: Post War. Baltimore: Author.

EXERCISES

This set of exercises explores the many uses of the interview. Without language, society would not exist as we now know it. More than anything else, language sets man apart from the lower animals. The interview uses language as the medium for discovering not only another's experiences, attitudes, and values but also his perception of reality. Moreover, the interview can be used with just about every other method in one fashion or another. Skills in interviewing are therefore the most important of those the sociologist must learn.

Exercise 1

One of the uses of the interview is in combination with participant observation. Often a researcher will observe behavior that he does not understand and will simply inquire why the actors do what they do. In this way, he is able to find the subjective meaning or the social meaning of the act. Take, for example, the observable action of people stopping at stoplights when no cars are approaching the intersection. To an uninformed observer, such behavior may seem strange; the act is observable, but its social meaning is not, and unless he asks why people behave that way, he may draw incorrect conclusions. The informal interview is very useful for finding the meanings of such behavior.

For this exercise, attend a sports event that is foreign to you. While you're watching the event, ask the people around you why the players are doing what they do. As soon as you understand why the game is played in the manner it is, you will have enough data. If you are familiar with all sports, both foreign and domestic, then find a setting where the people act in a way you do not fully understand and, using the informal interview, find out what meaning their acts have for them.

Exercise 2

A form of interviewing called "snowballing" entails asking one person a question that will lead to another person and so on until the researcher has the answer to his question. For example, a group of students in a large city wanted the city to repair a road leading to their school, where there had been several accidents. They began by calling one agency, which referred them to another agency, which in turn referred them to still another agency. This went on for days until they finally found out who could do the necessary work. By recording each call, they were able to create a "map" of the city bureaucracy and the process of the "runaround." Thus, the snowball interview was used successfully to solve a social problem as well as to describe an all too typical bureaucratic process. By doing the same thing, you will be able to find how your city government responds to citizens' legitimate complaints as well as gain skill in interviewing.

Exercise 3

One problem in interviewing is knowing what the respondent is talking about. Many groups use a special language or jargon to communicate with other members. The language might be informal, such as that employed by drug users, surfers, or jazz musicians; or it may be a formal language, such as the code used by the police in their communications. Simply choose a group of interest and interview one or more members concerning the language peculiar to that group. From these interviews, construct a glossary of terms and phrases. In this way, you will not only build up a valuable resource for interviewing the group in later research, but you will also have a set of indicators that a person is or is not a member of this group.

Exercise 4

The purpose of this exercise is to find why people join the organizations they do. It would probably expedite the data gathering and avoid redundancy if this exercise were carried out as a class project, since the various groups and organizations in your school will be used as the source of data.

Design an interview schedule that will allow you to find under what conditions an individual came into contact with a given group (for example, was he recruited by a group member or did he seek out the group on his own?), whether the individual joined the group for sociability or because of special properties of the group or both, and whether his reasons for remaining in the group are the same as those he had for joining it. Once the data are collected from a sample of groups and organizations in your school, analyze them in terms of the type of group and type of reason for joining. For example, if the organization's function is a service one, you might find that members joined expecting little sociability; however, they may have met people they enjoyed doing things with in the group and remained in it for sociability. Below is an outline of a form that can be used in such an analysis:

	Reason for Joining			Reason for Remaining		
Group	Group Function	Sociability	Both	Group Function	Sociability	Both

ADDITIONAL READING SUGGESTIONS

BECKER, HOWARD. 1956. "Interviewing Medical Students," *American Journal of Sociology*, 62 (September), pp. 199–201. Explains the problems encountered in interviewing medical students and offers practical advice applicable to other research areas.

CHAMBLISS, WILLIAM. 1972. *Box Man*. New York: Harper and Row. An example of research based almost totally on an intensive interview. Chambliss taped an interview with a professional thief, and most of the book consists of the thief's narrative.

CICOUREL, AARON. 1964. *Methods and Measurement in Sociology*, Chap. 3. New York: The Free Press. Discusses theoretical problems and underlying assumptions in the use of interviews. Especially useful in the discussion of the role of language in interviews.

DOUGLAS, JACK (ed.). 1972. *Research on Deviance*. New York: Random House. This collection represents writings of researchers who have gathered ethnographic data. Even though most of the collection focuses on problems in observation, much of the information is useful for interviewing groups that are in one way or another less accessible to the researcher than non-deviant groups.

10. Unobtrusive Measures

PHYSICAL EVIDENCE
—Eugene J. Webb, Donald
T. Campbell, Richard D.
Schwartz, and Lee Sechrest

EXTERIOR PHYSICAL SIGNS

MOST OF THE EXTERIOR PHYSI-
cal signs discussed are durable
ones that have been inferred
to be expressive of current or
past behavior. A smaller number are portable and shorter-lived.
The bullfighter's beard is a case in point. Conrad (1958) reports
that the bullfighter's beard is longer on the day of the fight than
on any other day. There are supporting comments among matadors
about this phenomenon, yet can one measure the torero's anxiety
by noting the length of his beard? The physical task is rather difficult, but not impossible in this day of sophisticated instrumenta-
tion. As in all these uncontrolled measures, one must draw inferences about the criterion behavior. Maybe it wasn't the anxiety at
all. Perhaps the bullfighter stands farther away from the razor on
the morning of the fight, or he may not have shaved that morning
at all (like baseball pitchers and boxers). And then there is the
possible intersubject contaminant that the more affluent matadors
are likely to be shaved, while the less prosperous shave themselves.

A less questionable measure is tattoos. Burma (1959) reports on
the observation of tattoos among some nine hundred inmates of
three different institutions. The research measure was the propor-

From *Unobtrusive Measures: Nonreactive Research in the Social Sciences*,
© 1966 by Rand McNally and Company, Chicago, pp. 115–127.

tion of inmates with tattoos: "significantly more delinquents than nondelinquents tattoo themselves." Of course, one could hardly reverse the findings and hold that tattooing can be employed as a single measure of delinquency. Returning to the bull ring for a moment, "There are many ordinary bullfighters, but ordinary people do not fight bulls" (Lea, 1949:40).

More formal classification cues are tribal markings and scars. Doob (1961:83) reports on a walk he and an African companion took through a Nigerian market.

> I casually pointed to a dozen men, one after the other, who had facial scars. My African friend in all instances named a society; then he and I politely verified the claim by speaking to the person and asking him to tell us the name of his tribe. In eleven instances out of twelve, he was correct. Certainly, however, he may have been responding simultaneously to other cues in the person's appearance, such as his clothing or his skin color.

In a report whose authors choose to remain anonymous (Anonymoi, 1953–60), it was discovered that there is a strong association between the methodological disposition of psychologists and the length of their hair. The authors observed the hair length of psychologists attending professional meetings and coded the meetings by the probable appeal to those of different methodological inclinations. Thus, in one example, the length of hair was compared between those who attended an experimental set of papers and those who attended a series on ego-identity formation. The results are clear cut. The "tough-minded" psychologists have shorter-cut hair than the long-haired psychologists. Symptomatic interpretations, psychoanalytic inquiries as to what is cut about the clean-cut young man, are not the only possibilities. The causal ambiguity of the correlation was clarified when the "dehydration hypothesis" (i.e., that lack of insulation caused the hard-headedness) was rejected by the "bald-head control," i.e., examining the distribution of baldheaded persons (who by the dehydration hypothesis should be most hardheaded of all).

Clothes are an obvious indicator, and A. M. Rosenthal (1962:20), wrote of "the wide variance between private manners and public behavior" of the Japanese:

> Professor Enright [British lecturer in Japan] and just about every

other foreigner who ever visited Japan have noted with varying degrees of astonishment that there is a direct relationship between the politeness of a Japanese and whether or not he is wearing shoes.

It is quite likely that this relationship reflects the selective distribution of shoes in the Japanese society more than any causal element, an example of a population restriction. The economically marginal members of the Japanese population should, one would think, be more overt in expressing hostility to foreign visitors than those who are economically stable—and possession of shoes is more probably linked to affluence than it is to xenophobia.

Shoe styles, not their presence, have been used as the unit of discrimination in the United States society where almost everybody does wear shoes. Gearing (1952), in a study of subculture awareness in south Chicago, observed shoe styles, finding features of the shoe to correspond with certain patterns of living. In general, the flashier shoe more often belonged to the more culture-bound individual. Similar concern with feet was shown by the OSS Assessment Staff (1948) when, because standard uniforms reduced the number of indicators, they paid special attention to shoes and socks as a prime indication "of taste and status."

Despite the general consensus on clothing as an indicator of status, little controlled work has been done on the subject. Flugel (1930) wrote a discursive book on clothing in general, and Webb (1957) reported on class differences in attitudes toward clothes and clothing stores. Another investigation shows many differences between clothing worn by independent and fraternity-affiliated college males. Within the fraternity groups, better grades are made by the more neatly dressed (Sechrest, 1965b).

Kane (1958; 1959; 1962) observed the clothing worn by outpatients to their interviews. He has considered pattern, color, texture, and amount of clothing, relating these characteristics to various moods, traits, and personality changes. In a more reactive study, Green and Knapp (1959) associated preferences for different types of tartans with need achievement; it would be of interest to see if this preference pattern were supported in clothing purchased or worn.

A southern chief of detectives has discussed using clothing clues as predictor variables. In a series of suggestions to police officers, he noted the importance of dress details. When Negroes are planning a mass jail-in, "The women will wear dungarees as they enter the meeting places" (Anonymous, 1965).

Jewelry and other ornamental objects can also be clues. Freud gave his inner circle of six, after World War I, rings matching his own. On another intellectual plane, observers have noted that in some societies one can find illiterates who buy only the top of a pen and then clip it to clothing as a suggestion of their writing prowess. One could observe the frequency of such purchases in local stores, or less arduously, examine sales records over time from the manufacturer, considering the ratio of tops to bottoms for different countries or regions. The observation method would have an advantage in that one could make coincidental observations on the appearance of those purchasing the tops alone, or isolate a sample for interviewing. The archival record of top and bottom shipments is infinitely more efficient, but more circumscribed in the content available for study.

As part of their study of the social status of legislators and their voting, MacRae and MacRae (1961) observed the houses lived in by legislators and rated them along the lines suggested by Warner (Warner, Meeker, and Eells, 1949). This house rating was part of the over-all social-class index produced for each legislator.

Observation of any type of possession can be employed as an index if the investigator knows that there is a clear relationship between possession (ownership) of the object and a second variable. Calluses, for example, can serve as an observable indicator of certain classes of activity. Different sports make selective demands on tissue, for example, and the calluses that result are reliable indicators of whether one is a squash player or a golfer. Some occupations may also be determined by similar physical clues.

With these measures used alone, validity is often tenuous. Phillips (1962) is unusual in giving multiple indicators of the changes in Miami resulting from the influx of a hundred thousand Cubans. Two years following the Castro revolution, he observed:

Bilingual streets signs (No Jaywalking; Cruce por la Zona para Peatones)
"A visitor hears almost as much Spanish as English."
Signs in windows saying "Se Habla Español"

Stores with names like "Mi Botanica" and "Carniceria Latina"
Latin-American foods on restaurant menus
Supermarkets selling yucca, malanga, and platanos
The manufacture of a Cuban type of cigarette
Radio broadcasts in Spanish
Spanish-language editorials in the English-language newspapers
Services held in Spanish by 40 Miami churches

Perhaps Phillips was overstating his case, but the marshalling of so much, and so diverse, observational evidence is persuasive. For a prime source in such studies of the unique character of cities, and their changes, there is that eminent guide, the classified telephone directory. It can yield a wide range of broad content information on the economy, interests, and characteristics of a city and its people. Isolating the major United States cities, which ones have the highest numbers of palmists per thousand population?

EXPRESSIVE MOVEMENT

The more plastic variables of body movement historically have interested many observers. Charles Darwin's (1872) work on the expression of emotions continues to be the landmark commentary. His exposition of the measurement of frowning, the uncovering of teeth, erection of the hair, and the like remains provocative reading. The more recent studies on expressive movement and personality measurement are reviewed by Wolff and Precker (1951:457–97). Of particular interest in their chapter is the emphasis on consistency among different types of expressive movement. They review the relation between personality and the following measures: facial expression, literary style, artistic style, style of speech, gait, painting and drawing, and handwriting. Not all of these studies are nonreactive, since the central criterion for this is that the subject is not aware of being measured.

Examples of using expressive movement as a response to a particular stimulus—i.e., stimulus-linked rather than subject-linked—are provided in the work of Maurice Krout (1933; 1937; 1951; 1954a; 1954b). Although this work was done in a laboratory setting, it was under façade conditions. That is, subjects were unaware of the true purpose of the research, considering the experiment a purely verbal task. There is a good possibility for application of

Krout's (1954a) approach in less reactive settings. He elicited autistic gestures through verbal-conflict situations, and his analysis deals primarily with digital-manual responses. An example of his findings is the correlation between an attitude of fear and the gesture of placing hand to nose. Darwin (1872) mentioned pupil dilation as a possible fear indicator.

Kinesics as a subject of study is relevant here, although as yet large amounts of data are not available. Birdwhistell (1960:54–64; 1963:123–40) has defined kinesics as being concerned with the communicational aspects of learned, patterned, body-motion behavior. This system of nonverbal communication is felt to be inextricably linked with the verbal, and the aim of such study is to achieve a quantification of the former which can be related to the latter. Some "motion qualifiers" have been identified, such as intensity, range, and velocity. Ruesch and Kees (1956) have presented a combination text-picture treatment in their book, *Nonverbal Communication*. An example of the impressionistic style of observation is provided by Murphy and Murphy (1962:12), who reported on the differences in facial expressions between young and old Russians: "While faces of old people often seemed resigned, tired and sad, generally the children seemed lively, friendly, confident and full of vitality."

Something of the detail possible in such studies is shown in Wolff's (1948; 1951) work on hands. In the first study, Wolff observed the gestures of mental patients at meals and at work, concluding, "I found sufficient evidence that correlations exist (1) between emotional make-up and gesture, (2) between the degree of integration and gesture" (1948:166). The second study was anthropometric, and Wolff compared features of the handprints of schizophrenics, mental defectives, and normals. The hands were divided into three major types: (1) elementary, simple and regressive; (2) motor, fleshy and bony; and (3) small and large. On the basis of an individual's hand type, measurements, nails, crease lines, and type of skin, she delineates the main characteristics of their personality, intelligence, vitality, and temperament.

Without necessarily endorsing her conclusions, we report the finding of a confused crease-line pattern peculiar to the extreme of mental deficiency. Other structural characteristics such as concave primary nails, "appeared to a greater or lesser degree in the hands of mental defectives . . . but were completely absent in the hands of the control cases" (Wolff, 1951:105).

A journalistic account of the expressive behavior of hands has been given by Gould (1951:1). Here is his description of Frank Costello's appearance before the Kefauver crime hearings:

> As he [Costello] sparred with Rudolph Halley, the committee's counsel, the movement of his fingers told their own emotional story. When the questions got rough, Costello crumpled a handkerchief in his hands. Or he rubbed his palms together. Or he interlaced his fingers. Or he grasped a half-filled glass of water. Or he beat a silent tattoo on the table top. Or he rolled a little ball of paper between his thumb and index finger. Or he stroked the side piece of his glasses lying on the table. His was video's first ballet of the hands.*

It is of interest that conversations of male students with females have been found to be more frequently punctuated by quick, jerky, "nervous" gestures than are conversations between two males (Sechrest, 1965b).

Schubert (1959) has suggested that overt personal behavior could be used in the study of judicial behavior. In presenting a psychometric model of the Supreme Court, he suggests that the speech, grimaces, and gestures of the judges when hearing oral arguments and when opinions are being delivered are rich sources of data for students of the Court.

On the other side of the legal fence, witnesses in Hindu courts are reported to give indications of the truth of their statements by the movement of their toes (Krout, 1951). The eminent American legal scholar J. H. Wigmore, in works on judicial proof and evidence (1935; 1937), speaks of the importance of peripheral expressive movements as clues to the validity of testimony.

That these cues can vary across societies is demonstrated by Sechrest and Flores. They showed that "leg jiggling" is more frequent among Filipino than American males, and held that jiggling is a "nervous" behavior. As evidence of this, they found jiggling more frequent in coffee lounges than in cocktail lounges.

The superstitious behavior of baseball players is a possible area of study. Knocking dust off cleats, amount of preliminary bat swinging, tossing dust into the air, going to the resin bag, and

* © 1951 by the New York Times Company. Reprinted by permission.

wiping hands on shirts may be interpreted as expressive actions. One hypothesis is that the extent of such superstitious behavior is related to whether or not the player is in a slump or in the middle of a good streak. This study could be extended to other sports in which the central characters are relatively isolated and visible. It should be easier for golfers and basketball players, but more difficult for football players.

From a practical point of view, of course, coaches and scouts have long studied the overt behavior of opponents for clues to forthcoming actions. (It is known, for example, that most football teams are "right sided" and run a disproportionate number of plays to the right [Griffin, 1964].) Does the fullback indicate the direction of the play by which hand he puts on the ground? Does the linebacker rest on his heels if he is going to fall back on pass defense? Does the quarterback always look in the direction in which he is going to pass, or does he sometimes look the other way, knowing that the defense is focusing on his eyes?

A police officer reported eye movement as a "pickup" clue. A driver who repeatedly glances from side to side, then into the rearview mirror, then again from side to side may be abnormally cautious and perfectly blameless. But he may also be abnormally furtive and guilty of a crime. Another officer, in commenting on auto thefts, said, "We . . . look for clean cars with dirty license plates and dirty cars with clean plates," explaining that thieves frequently switch plates (Reddy, 1965).

In a validation study of self-reported levels of newspaper readership, eye movement was observed when people were reading newspapers in trains, buses, library reading rooms, and the street (Advertising Service Guild, 1949). A number of interesting eye movement and direction studies have been conducted in controlled laboratory settings. Discussion of them is contained in the following chapter on observational hardware.

Physical Location

The physical position of animals has been a favored measure of laboratory scientists, as well as of those in the field. Imanishi (1960), for example, described the social structure of Japanese macaques by reporting on their physical grouping patterns. The dominant macaques sit in the center of a series of concentric rings.

For people, there are the familiar newspaper accounts of who stood next to whom in Red Square reviewing the May Day parade. The proximity of a politician to the leader is a direct clue of his status in the power hierarchy. His physical position is interpreted as symptomatic of other behavior which gave him the status position befitting someone four men away from the Premier, and descriptive of that current status position. In this more casual journalistic report of observations, one often finds time-series analysis: Mr. B. has been demoted to the end of the dais, and Mr. L. has moved up close to the middle.

The clustering of Negroes and whites was used by Campbell, Kruskal, and Wallace (1965) in their study of seating aggregation as an index of attitude. Where seating in a classroom is voluntary, the degree to which the Negroes and whites present sit by themselves versus mixing randomly may be taken as a presumptive index of the degree to which acquaintance, friendship, and preference are strongly colored by race, as opposed to being distributed without regard to racial considerations. Classes in four schools were studied, and significant aggregation by race was found, varying in degree between schools. Aggregation by age, sex, and race has also been reported for elevated trains and lunch counters (Sechrest, 1965b).

Feshbach and Feshbach (1963:499) report on another type of clustering. At a Halloween party, they induced fear in a group of boys, aged nine to twelve, by telling them ghost stories. The boys were then called out of the room and were administered questionnaires. The induction of the fear state was natural, but their dependent-variable measures were potentially reactive. What is of interest to us is a parenthetical statement made by the authors. After describing the ghost-story-telling situation, the Feshbachs offer evidence for the successful induction of fear: "Although the diameter of the circle was about eleven feet at the beginning of the story telling, by the time the last ghost story was completed, it had been spontaneously reduced to approximately three feet."

Gratiot-Alphandery (1951a; 1951b) and Herbinière-Lebert (1951) have both made observations of children's seating during informal film showings. How children from different age groups clustered was a measure used in work on developmental changes.

Sommer (1961) employed the position of chairs in a descriptive way, looking at "the distance for comfortable conversation." Normal subjects were used, but observations were made after the subjects had been on a tour of a large mental hospital. Distances among chairs in a lounge were systematically varied, and the people were brought into the lounge after the tour. They entered by pairs, and each pair was asked to go to a designated area and sit down. A simple record was made of the chairs selected.

The issue here is what one generalizes to. Just as the Feshbachs' subjects drew together during the narration of ghost stories, it would not be unrealistic to expect that normal adults coming from a tour of a mental hospital might also draw closer together than would be the case if they had not been on the tour. Their seating distance before the tour would be an interesting control. Do they huddle more, anticipating worse than will be seen, or less?

Sommer (1959; 1960; 1962) has conducted other studies of social distance and positioning, and in the 1959 study mentions a "waltz technique" to measure psychological distance. He learned that as he approached people, they would back away; when he moved backward during a conversation, the other person moved forward. The physical distance between two conversationalists also varies systematically by the nationality of the talkers, and there are substantial differences in distance between two Englishmen talking together and two Frenchmen in conversation. In a cross-cultural study, this would be a response-set characteristic to be accounted for.

Sommer's work inspired a study in Germany (Kaminski and Osterkamp, 1962), but unfortunately it is not a replication of Sommer's design. A paper-and-pencil test was substituted for the actual physical behavior, and 48 students were tested in three mock situations: classroom, U-shaped table, and park benches. Sechrest, Flores, and Arellano (1965) studied social distance in a Filipino sample and found considerably greater distance in opposite-sex pairs as compared with same-sex pairs. Other tests include measuring the distance subjects placed photographs away from themselves (Smith, 1958; Beloff and Beloff, 1961) and Werner and Wapner's (1953) research on measuring the amount of distance walked under conditions of danger.

Sommer (1960) noted how the physical location of group members influenced interactions. Most communication took place among neighbors, but the corner was the locus of most interaction. Whyte (1956) observed that air conditioners were dispersed in a nonrandom way in a Chicago suburban community, and Howells and Becker (1962) demonstrated that those who sat facing several others during a discussion received more leadership nominations than did those who sat side by side.

Leipold's (1963) dissertation carried the work further, paying special attention to the individual response-set variable of "personal space," the physical distance an organism customarily places between itself and other organisms. Leipold gathered personality-classification data on a group of 90 psychology students, divided them into two groups on the basis of introversion-extraversion, and administered stress, praise, or neutral conditions to a third of each group. He evaluated the effect of the conditions, and the tie to introversion-extraversion, by noting which of several available seats were taken by the subjects when they came in for a subsequent interview. The seats varied in the distance from the investigator. In one of his findings, he reports that introverted and high-anxious students, defined by questionnaire responses, kept a greater physical distance from the investigator (choosing a farther chair) than did extraverted and low-anxious students. Stress conditions also resulted in greater distance.

That random assignment doesn't always work is shown in Grusky's (1959) work on organizational goals and informal leaders —research conducted in an experimental prison camp. He learned that informal leaders, despite a policy of random bed assignments, were more likely to attain the bottom bunk. Grusky also considered such archival measures as number of escapes, general transfers, and transfers for poor adjustment. On all of these measures, leaders differed significantly from nonleaders. It must be remembered that this was an experimental prison camp, and the artificiality of the research situation presents the risk that a "Hawthorne effect" may be present. What would be valuable would be another study of regular prison behavior to see if these findings hold in a nonexperimental setting.

On still another plane, the august chambers of the United Nations in New York, Alger (1968) observed representatives at the General Assembly. Sitting with a press card in the gallery, he recorded 3,322 interactions among representatives at sessions of the

Administrative and Budgetary Committee. Each interaction was coded for location, initiator, presence or exchange of documents, apparent humor, duration, and so on. His interest was in defining the clusters of nations who typically interacted in the committee.

Using the same approach, it might be possible to get partial evidence on which nations are perceived as critical and uncertain during debate on a proposed piece of UN action. Could one define the marginal, "swing" countries by noting which ones were visited by both Western and Bloc countries during the course of the debate? Weak evidence, to be sure, for there is the heavy problem of spatial restriction. One can only observe in public places, and even expanding the investigation to lobbies, lounges, and other public meeting areas may exclude the locus of the truly critical interactions. This bias might be selective, for if an issue suddenly appeared without warning, the public areas might be a more solid sampling base than they would be for issues which had long been anticipated and which could be lobbied in private. That the outside observer must have a broad understanding of the phenomenon and parties he is observing is indicated in Alger's study. He comments on the high level of interaction with the Irish delegate, which was not a reflection of the political power of Ireland, but instead the result of the easy affability of the man. This affability might truly influence the power position of his country, and hence be an important datum in that sense, but it is more likely to confound comparisons if it is used as evidence on a nation.

Barch, Trumbo, and Nangle (1957) used the behavior of automobiles in their observational study of conformity to legal requirements. We are not sure if this is more properly coded under "expressive movement," but the "physical position" category seems more appropriate. They were interested in the degree to which turn-signalling was related to the turn-signalling behavior of a preceding car. For four weeks, they recorded this information:

1. Presence or absence of a turn signal
2. Direction of turn
3. Presence of another motor vehicle 100 feet or less behind the turning motor vehicle when it begins to turn
4. Sex of drivers.

Observers stood near the side of the road and were not easily visible to the motorists. There was the interesting finding that conforming behavior, as defined by signalling or not, varied with the direction of the turn. Moreover, a sex difference was noted. There was a strong positive correlation if model and follower were females, and also a high correlation if left turns were signalled. But on right turns, the correlation was low and positive. Why there is a high correlation for left turns and a low one for right turns is equivocal. The data, like so many simple observational data, don't offer the "why," but simply establish a relationship.

Several of the above findings have been verified and perturbingly elaborated by a finding that signalling is more erratic in bad weather and by drivers of expensive autos (Sechrest, 1965b). Blomgren, Scheuneman, and Wilkins (1963) also used turn signals as a dependent variable in a before-after study of the effect of a signalling safety poster. Exposure to the sign increased signalling about 6 per cent.

REFERENCES

Advertising Service Guild. 1949. *The Press and Its Readers.* London: Art & Technics.

ALGER, C. F. 1968. "Interaction in a Committee of the United Nations General Assembly." In J. D. Singer (ed.), *Quantitative International Politics (International Yearbook of Political Behavior Research).* 6 vols. New York: The Free Press.

ANONYMOI. 1953–60. "Hair Style as a Function of Hard-Headedness vs. Long-Hairedness in Psychological Research: A Study in the Personology of Science," unpublished manuscript. Evanston, Ill.: Northwestern University; Chicago: University of Chicago.

ANONYMOUS. 1965. "Civil Rights: By the Book," *Newsweek,* Vol. 65, No. 37 (March 1).

BARCH, A. M., D. TRUMBO, and J. NANGLE. 1957. "Social Setting and Conformity to a Legal Requirement," *Journal of Abnormal and Social Psychology,* 55, pp. 396–98.

BELOFF, J., and H. BELOFF. 1961. "The Influence of Valence on Distance Judgments of Human Faces," *Journal of Abnormal and Social Psychology,* 62, pp. 720–22.

BIRDWHISTELL, R. 1960. "Kinesics and Communication." In E. Carpenter (ed.), *Exploration in Communication.* Boston: Beacon Hill.

————. 1963. "The Kinesic Level in the Investigations of Emotions." In P. Knapp (ed.), *The Expression of Emotions in Man.* New York: International Universities Press.

BLOMGREN, G. W., T. W. SCHEUNEMAN, and J. L. WILKINS. 1963. "Effects of Exposure to a Safety Poster on the Frequency of Turn Signalling," *Traffic Safety*, 7, pp. 15–22.

BURMA, J. H. 1959. "Self-Tattooing Among Delinquents: A Research Note," *Sociology and Social Research*, 43, pp. 341–45.

CAMPBELL, D. T., W. H. KRUSKAL, and W. P. WALLACE. 1966. "Seating Aggregation as an Index of Attitude," *Sociometry*, 29, pp. 1–15.

CONRAD, B. 1958. *The Death of Manolete*. Cambridge: Houghton Mifflin.

DARWIN, C. 1872. *The Expression of the Emotions in Man and Animals*. London: Murray.

DOOB, L. W. 1961. *Communication in Africa*. New Haven: Yale University Press.

FESHBACH, S., and N. FESHBACH. 1936. "Influence of the Stimulus Object Upon the Complementary and Supplementary Projection of Fear," *Journal of Abnormal and Social Psychology*, 66, pp. 498–502.

FLUGEL, J. C. 1930. *Psychology of Clothes*. London: Hogarth.

GEARING, F. 1952. "The Response to a Cultural Precept Among Migrants From Bronzeville to Hyde Park," unpublished M.A. thesis. Chicago: University of Chicago.

GOULD, J. 1951. "Costello TV's First Headless Star; Only His Hands Entertain Audience," *New York Times*, March 1.

GRATIOT-ALPHANDERY, H. 1951a. "L'Enfant et le film," *Revue Internationale de Filmologie*, 2, pp. 171–72.

———. 1951b. "Jeunes spectateurs," *Revue Internationale de Filmologie*, 2, pp. 257–63.

GREEN, H. B., and R. H. KNAPP. 1959. "Time Judgment, Aesthetic Preference, and Need for Achievement," *Journal of Abnormal and Social Psychology*, 58, pp. 140–42.

GRIFFIN, J. R. 1964. "Coia 'Catch,' Kicking Draw Much Criticism," *Chicago Sun-Times*, October 27, p. 76.

GRUSKY, O. 1959. "Organizational Goals and the Behavior of Informal Leaders," *American Journal of Sociology*, 65, pp. 59–67.

HERBINIÈRE-LEBERT, S. 1951. "Pourquoi et comment nous avons fait 'Mains Blanches': premières experiences avec un film éducatif réalisé spécialement pours les mins de sept ans," *Revue Internationale de Filmologie*, 2, pp. 247–55.

HOWELLS, L. T., and S. W. BECKER. 1962. "Seating Arrangement and Leadership Emergence," *Journal of Abnormal and Social Psychology*, 64, pp. 148–50.

IMANISHI, K. 1960. "Social Organization of Subhuman Primates in Their Natural Habitat," *Current Anthropology*, I, pp. 393–407.

KAMINSKI, G., and U. OSTERKAMP. 1962. "Untersuchungen über die Topologie sozialer Handlungsfelder," *Zeitschrift für experimentelle und angewandte Psychologie*, 9, pp. 417–51.

KANE, F. 1958. "Clothing Worn by Out-Patients to Interviews," *Psychiatric Communications*, Vol. 1, No. 2.

———. 1959. "Clothing Worn by an Out-Patient: A Case Study," *Psychiatric Communications*, 2:2.

———. 1962. "The Meaning of the Form of Clothing," *Psychiatric Communications*, 5:1.

KROUT, M. H. 1933. *Major Aspects of Personality*. Chicago: College Press.

———. 1937. "Further Studies on the Relation of Personality and Gestures: A Nosological Analysis of Austistic Gestures," *Journal of Experimental Psychology*, 20, pp. 279–87.

—————. 1951. "Gestures and Attitudes: An Experimental Study of the Verbal Equivalents and Other Characteristics of a Selected Group of Manual Austistic Gestures," unpublished doctoral dissertation. Chicago: University of Chicago.

LEA, T. 1949. *The Brave Bulls*. Boston: Little, Brown.

LEIPOLD, W. D. 1963. "Psychological Distance in a Dyadic Interview as a Function of Introversion-Extraversion, Anxiety, Social Desirability and Stress," unpublished doctoral dissertation. Grand Forks: University of North Dakota.

MacRAE, D., and E. MacRAE. 1961. "Legislators' Social Status and Their Votes," *American Journal of Sociology*, 66, pp. 559–603.

MURPHY, G., and L. MURPHY. 1962. "Soviet Life and Soviet Psychology." In R. A. Bauer (ed.), *Some Views on Soviet Psychology*. Washington, D. C.: American Psychological Association.

OSS Assessment Staff. 1948. *Assessment of Men*. New York: Rinehart.

PHILLIPS, R. H. 1962. "Miami Goes Latin Under Cuban Tide," *New York Times*, March 18.

REDDY J. 1965. "Heady Thieves Find Wheeling Their Waterloo," *Chicago Sun-Times*, February 28.

ROSENTHAL, A. M. 1962. "Japan, Famous for Politeness, Has a Less Courteous Side, Too," *New York Times*, February 25.

RUESCH, J., and W. KEES. 1956. *Nonverbal Communication: Notes on the Visual Perception of Human Relations*. Berkeley: University of California Press.

SCHUBERT, G. 1959. *Quantitative Analysis of Judicial Behavior*. Glencoe, Ill.: The Free Press.

SECHREST, L. 1965. "Situational Sampling and Contrived Situations in the Assessment of Behavior," unpublished manuscript. Evanston, Ill.: Northwestern University.

SECHREST, L., and L. FLORES. (In Press.) "The Occurrence of a Nervous Mannerism in Two Cultures," *Journal of Nervous and Mental Disease*.

SECHREST, L., L. FLORES, and L. ARELLANO. 1965. "Social Distance and Language in Bilingual Subjects," unpublished manuscript. Evanston, Ill.: Northwestern University.

SMITH, H. T. 1958. "A Comparison of Interview and Observation Methods of Mother Behavior," *Journal of Abnormal and Social Psychology*, 57, pp. 278–82.

SOMMER, R. 1959. "Studies in Personal Space," *Sociometry*, 22, pp. 247–60.

—————. 1960. "Personal Space," *Canadian Architect*, pp. 76–80.

—————. 1961. "Leadership and Group Geography," *Sociometry*, 24, pp. 99–100.

—————. 1962. "The Distance for Comfortable Conversations: Further Study," *Sociometry*, 25, pp. 111–16.

WARNER, W. L., M. MEEKER, and K. EELLS. 1959. *Social Class in America*. Chicago: Science Research Associates.

WEBB, E. J. 1957. *Men's Clothing Study*. Chicago: Chicago Tribune.

WERNER, H., and S. WAPNER. 1953. "Changes in Psychological Distance Under Conditions of Danger," *Journal of Personality*, 24, pp. 153–67.

WHYTE, W. H. 1956. *The Organization Man*. New York: Simon and Schuster.

WIGMORE, J. H. 1935. *A Student's Textbook of the Law of Evidence.* Brooklyn: Foundation Press.

————. 1937. *The Science of Judicial Proof as Given by Logic, Psychology, and General Experience and Illustrated in Judicial Trials.* 3d ed. Boston: Little, Brown.

WOLFF, C. 1948. *A Psychology of Gesture.* London: Methuen.

————. 1951. *The Hand in Psychological Diagnosis.* London: Methuen.

WOLFF, W., and J. A. PRECKER. 1951. "Expressive Movement and the Methods of Experimental Depth Psychology." In H. H. Anderson and G. L. Anderson (eds.); *An Introduction to Projection Techniques.* N.J.: Prentice-Hall.

EXERCISES   Each of the following exercises involves
either the use or the discovery of an unob-
trusive measure or descriptive sign. The significance of such measures is that they are *nonreactive* and *given off*—that is, they are
not affected by the researcher's presence, nor are they for the benefit of the researcher. For example, interviews, experiments, and
participant observation all have potentially reactive effects on subjects. If a respondent believes that an interview may be used
against him in any way, he may tell the interviewer only those
things he feels will favorably impress the researcher. Hence, his
responses are a *reaction* to the method of gathering information.

On the other hand, unobtrusive measures are signs that indicate
a type of behavior or a behavior pattern, but are not meant to do
so. For example, Sherlock Holmes told Dr. Watson that he had
made a wise decision choosing a certain office for his practice, since
the steps to that office were more worn than were the steps to his
competitor's across the hall. Similarly, traffic patterns of pedestrians
can be determined by the shortcuts that are made across lawns.
The following exercises are designed to sensitize you to such measures and signs.

EXERCISE 1

Various occupations entail various uniforms, tools, and tasks
that indicate the occupational role. Make a list of occupations in
terms of various physical signs by which the occupation can be
recognized. Besides the more obvious physical signs, try to find
some more subtle signs as well. For instance, occupations entailing
physical work with the hands will result in the workers' having
larger fingers than workers in occupations requiring little physical
work with the hands. Auto mechanics frequently cut their hands
in their work and are likely to have numerous cuts and scars on
them. Miners, who also work with their hands, can be distin-
guished from construction workers in that construction workers
are more likely to be tanned. Classify the occupational signs as
clothing, *tools* and *artifacts*, or *task signs* left on the body from the
work.

EXERCISE 2

A measure of ethnic integration is the clustering of ethnic-specific stores dealing in goods and services preferred by, or characteristic of, various ethnic groups. If, for example, in one section of town many of the signs in store windows are written in Spanish, it can be assumed that the area is a segregated section of Spanish-speaking peoples such as former Mexicans or Puerto Ricans. The extent to which such signs, goods, and services are diffuse is an indication of integration, while clustering is a sign of segregation.

To find the extent of integration or segregation in your community or neighborhood, take a map and a set of colored pins and put a pin on the map for each ethnic sign you can find. Use a different color for each ethnic group. Some indicators will be fairly blatant, such as foreign-language signs, while other indicators will be fairly subtle, such as specific foods or services characteristic of an ethnic group. When you finish, you will find, if the different colors on your map are mixed together, that the area is integrated; if they are clustered, you will have found segregation.

EXERCISE 3

Signs of superstitions can be found in various gestures. For example, when some people spill salt, they will throw some of the spilt salt over their shoulder to ward off bad luck; some will knock on wood so that what is considered a good state of affairs will remain so. To find out what the various indicators of superstition are, interview people from various backgrounds and ask them whether they know of any gestures to bring good luck or ward off bad luck. Compile a list in terms of general superstitions as well as a list of gestures that are specific to certain groups or occupations. In this way, you will have developed a list of indicators that point to superstition as well as a set that can point to membership in various groups or occupations.

EXERCISE 4

People's relationships with one another can be determined by their spatial proximity. To get a sense of the distances people keep when together or separated, go to a public park and observe groupings. Note, for example, that, if two groups are next to one another, the distance between the groups is greater than the distance kept between members of the same group. This can be seen even more clearly if you observe couples sitting together. Compared with the distance the couples keep between themselves, the distance between one couple and the next is great. Try to make these observations on a day when the park will be crowded. On such days, the groups will have to sit closer, and you can determine the minimal amount of space they keep between one another. It will not be necessary to take precise measurements; attempt, rather, to estimate the differences in distance that strangers keep and acquaintances keep. In this way, you will become sensitive to distances as an indicator of social relationships.

ADDITIONAL READING SUGGESTIONS

Fast, J. 1970. *Body Language*. New York: Pocket Books. Explains various body gestures as forms of communication. Many of the interpretations may be questionable, but Fast does provide a highly readable resource on expressive movements.

Hall, Edward T. 1959. *The Silent Language*. Greenwich, Conn.. Fawcett. A detailed discussion of the various understandings of space, time, and other dimensions that different cultures hold. Provides numerous unobtrusive measures of cultural identity.

Petschek, Willa. 1970. "An Unblinking Look at the New York Private Eye," *New York*, 3 (November 23). Discusses numerous unobtrusive measures employed by private eyes. Several would have to be put in a more ethical context for sociological use, but the detectives have developed ingenious devices to measure various social conditions.

Webb, Eugene, Donald T. Campbell, Richard D. Schwartz, and Lee Sechrest. 1966. *Unobtrusive Measures: Nonreactive Research in the Social Sciences*. Chicago: Rand McNally. The most comprehensive work on nonreactive measures and indicators for sociological research. In addition, it provides a detailed discussion of how and why multiple measures, especially nonreactive ones, can be employed in social science research.

V: CONTENT ANALYSIS

IN INVESTIGATING APPARENT SUICIDES, DETECTIVES CAREFULLY ANA-lyze the suicide note, if any, to determine whether the dead person himself wrote it. For example, if the corpse was a well-educated person and the suicide note found pinned to his shirt contains several misspellings and mistakes in grammar, the detectives would begin investigating the possibility of murder. In the Zodiac case, the murderer sent several letters to the police, and the contents of the letters were analyzed for references that would help to identify the killer. For example, the Zodiac made references to exotic religious beliefs in some of his letters. These references were used as clues to place the Zodiac in certain parts of the world where such beliefs were practiced or to groups in the United States that held these beliefs. From letters, notes, and other written or transcribed documents, detectives are able to infer a great deal of information.

For the sociologist, content analysis has been used in describing cultural elements of societies. Such descriptions, in turn, are used for comparative analysis (Warwick and Osherson, 1973). Content analysis has also been found to be extremely useful in analyzing social change. Culture is reflected in the beliefs, sentiments, and moral themes of a society, and these cultural elements are reflected in various social writings, whether it be cave drawings or the daily newspaper. In the same context, as societies change, so, too, do the form and content of what people in those societies write. By comparing the different writings of a society over a period of time, the researcher is able to see changes in social behavior. For example, by looking at old magazines over a relatively brief period, it is possible to see changes in fashions, interests, technology, and politics. Abrupt changes in a society become apparent in examining various media before and after major events. For example, the Cuban press can be seen to have changed greatly after 1960, when Fidel Castro came into power, reflecting the sweeping changes made under his regime. Such a change is usefully compared to the more subtle changes, or to the lack of change, after an American Presidential election.

The term "content analysis" appears to denote merely a form of analysis, but actually it covers a number of methods of gathering data and several modes of analysis (Cicourel, 1964). For example, a researcher may count the number of favorable and unfavorable political editorials in a nation's newspapers as an indication of that nation's political policy regarding freedom of the press (Simon, 1969:279). Counting editorial comments and coding them as favorable or unfavorable constitute a method of gathering data. Here we shall discuss two forms of content analysis.

POPULAR MEDIA ANALYSIS

The character of a society is reflected in its popular media. Before the invention of the radio and television, popular media consisted primarily of newspapers and magazines. However, the same methods of analysis are applicable to the newer forms of radio and television as to printed media, except that access to past radio and television shows (in the form of recordings and tapes) is less available than access to old newspapers and magazines, which can be found in libraries.

The dimensions to be examined in analyzing the content of popular media depend on the research problem. Whatever the problem, data are generally gathered in terms of certain categories that are developed either beforehand or after preliminary examination of the content. For example, a researcher might want to compare two societies by comparing the contents of the newspapers with the highest circulation in each. He might find that economic, agricultural, and political issues dominate one newspaper, while sports, entertainment, and environmental concerns dominate the other. On the other hand, the researcher may begin with a definite dimension in mind and compare that dimension only. For example, he might examine stories about crime in terms of a punishment-and-treatment dichotomy.

The analysis of the contents of popular media can be either qualitative or quantitative, depending on how the data are organized. In comparing television news editorials, the researcher might develop a set of criteria designated as "conservative" and another set as "liberal." By counting the number of times conservative or liberal themes are a part of a station's editorials, the researcher can statistically compare stations as more or less conservative or liberal. On the other hand, the researcher may employ a qualitative approach, verbally explaining and comparing different types of editorials. The same kind of qualitative analysis employed in ethnographies, and the same kind of quantitative analysis used in surveys and experiments, moreover, can be employed in content analysis; and the use of one type of analysis or the other depends on whether the data are quantified or not.

CONVERSATIONAL ANALYSIS*

Conversational analysis is a new form of analysis in sociolinguistics. It may be considered a form of ethnographic or interactional analysis, but, because of the work done with written transcripts of conversations, it will be treated here as a form of content analysis. The essential purpose of conversational analysis is to determine the structure of conversations and the effect of the structure on the talk in conversation (Sacks, 1972). Most of the work done to date has focused on the sequential structure of conversations and has been based on data in the form of conversation transcriptions.

Conversational analysis relies on transcripts of recorded conversations. These transcripts are useful for analysis, since they "fix," or "freeze," the interaction. The analyst can go over the transcripts at his leisure to search for sequential structure and forms in the interaction instead of having to rely on notes taken during observations. Moreover, since interaction consists largely of people taking turns talking, most of it is preserved in the conversation itself.

In order to preserve the texture of the talk in conversations,

---

* The discussion here is greatly oversimplified; I suggest that the student who is seriously interested in conversational analysis read the work by Sacks (1972) cited in "Suggested Readings."

various transcription conventions are used. These conventions are like punctuation in written language, in that they indicate pauses, emphasis, and other elements that can be heard in conversations but not easily seen when normal grammatical punctuation is used. There is no universal set of conventions; the ones described here are only a partial list, developed by the writer.

Talk Turn	Refers to the turn the speaker has while (an)other(s) in a conversation listen(s) or interrupt(s)
/1–2 ... n/	Indicates the number of seconds between the preceding and present turns or silences in one speaker's talk; n is any positive integer
/ # /	Indicates very short interval, less than one second
/ /	Indicates the point at which the next speaker overlaps the person speaking. (Two speaking at once)
/	Indicates the point at which the following speaker interrupts and stops speaker
[ ]	Encloses the portion of an utterance that overlaps with the previous line
/j/	Indicates overlap; that is, there is no separation between speaker turns
but	Indicates emphasis
BUT	Indicates heavy emphasis

Example:
1. A   Hiya Joe. Whatja doin?
2. B /#/   Aww nutin much./1–2–3/ Why don't ja sit down//
3.   and hava bite/.
4. A /j/   [I gotta go over to th] library before it closes.
5. B /#/   Well uh /#/ it won't close for uh uh bout an
6.   hour. LOOK there's Pete! HEY PETE COMERE!

Once the conversation has been transcribed from a tape recording, the analyst has, as far as possible at least, a record of the conversation as it sounded on the tape in writing that can be analyzed.

The sequential structure of conversations can be analyzed by considering the whole conversation as it sequentially progresses from openers, to topics, to closings; or a conversation can be analyzed in terms of smaller sequences. However, the importance of such sequential structures is that, once the sequence has been initiated, only certain forms of responses can follow. That is, the structure of conversations is a causal factor of what occurs in conversations.

For example, the *question-answer sequence* (Q-A) is simply the sequence of an answer following a question (Schegloff, 1968). In the reading by Sanders (Chapter 12), the author shows how such a sequence was used in police interrogations. The interrogator would ask a question that conversationally obliged the person being interrogated to supply an answer. The interest for conversational analysis is not whether an answer to a question is correct, truthful, or even informative; rather, it is that, following a question, the next talk is in the *form* of an answer.

The *greeting sequence* is one in which a conversation is initiated when one member of the talk-group utters a greeting form and the other member(s) respond(s). These are usually a simple "Hi" followed by a "Hi" from the other, but more elaborate greeting sequences can also be found.

Finally, the *summons-reply sequence* (S-R) is one in which one person calls out to another and the other replies. For example, a boss may call his employee, "Hey, Jim," and the employee may respond with, "Yeah, whaddaya want?" These sequences can be found in all kinds of conversations, even though the content of the talk varies.

The two readings in this section represent the two forms of content analysis discussed. Chapter 11, by Winick, employs a combination of content analysis and questionnaires in exploring why teen-agers enjoy the humor in *Mad* magazine. The last reading is a conversation analysis incorporating the Q-A sequence to show how the police use conversational structure to get suspects to talk.

REFERENCES

CICOUREL, AARON. 1964. *Method and Measurement in Sociology.* New York: The Free Press.

SACKS, HARVEY. 1972. "An Initial Investigation of the Usability of Conversational Data for Doing Sociology." In David Sudnow (ed.), *Studies in Social Interaction*, pp. 31–74. New York: The Free Press.

SCHEGLOFF. E. A. 1968. "Sequencing in Conversational Openings," *American Anthropologist*, 70, pp. 1075–95.

SIMON, J. L. 1969. *Basic Research Methods in Social Science*. New York: Random House.

WARWICK, D. P., and S. OSHERSON (EDS.). 1973. *Comparative Research Methods*. Englewood Cliffs, N.J.: Prentice-Hall.

11. Popular-Media Analysis

TEEN-AGERS, SATIRE,
AND MAD
—Charles Winick

GOETHE ONCE OBSERVED THAT
nothing shows a person's character more than the things at
which he laughs. This thought
has recently been translated into psychiatry by measures of personality, based on a patient's ability to respond to humor (Redlich,
Levine, and Sohler, 1951) and on his favorite joke (Zwerling,
1955). How people respond to satire should be a revealing clue to
their character, because satire is the form of humor most concerned with comment on the norms of a society. Jonathan Swift's
epitaph on his Dublin grave, "Where savage indignation can no
longer tear his heart," suggests the nature of the satirist's work
expressing savage indignation, usually stemming from a firm sense
of morality. There have been times in a literature—as in the age
of Pope—when satire was the dominant literary form. Some satirists, like Lord Byron, have become international celebrities as a
result of their wit.

Although satire has often flourished in America since James
Russell Lowell first acclimated it, the writers and artists of today
do not seem to respond with satire; in contrast to the tradition
of Americans like Mark Twain, Thorstein Veblen, Kin Hubbard,
E. W. Howe, Robert Frost, and Sinclair Lewis.

From *Merrill-Palmer Quarterly of Behavior and Development*, Vol. 8 (July
1962), pp. 183–203.

Television performers have generally addressed their satire to peripheral themes, rather than to the central social concerns of our times. It is possible that sponsors have feared that claims made for their products would suffer if linked with the derision of satire. Another contributor to the decline in satire seems to be a decrease in the incidence of "wisecracks," an almost indigenous form of satire. Satirical movies are seldom made, or are usually unsuccessful commercially even when successful artistically. The character actors who provided humor and satire in movies have almost completely disappeared.

Although satirical magazines for adults flourish in other countries, the United States has no such magazines. Today the only satire magazine published in this country which has any considerable circulation is *Mad*, a magazine in comics format, which is geared toward adolescents.

Why adult satire has not been successful in the last several decades can only be a subject for speculation. The areas of national life in which ridicule is acceptable have diminished steadily. The preoccupation with un-Americanism, and, thus, with Americanism, can only be seen in perspective if we consider how we might feel if we heard of "Englishism" and "un-Englishism" and "Frenchism" and "un-Frenchism." James Thurber, who began as a satirist and spent his last years as a moralist, commented that it is almost as if patriotism were a monopoly by Americans (Thurber, 1958). Such a climate is not one that fosters satire. Another possible reason is that satire is like a soufflé. It must be done well; and there is no audience for an average performance.

Other reasons for the decline in American satire may reflect larger cultural trends. The American audience for even better-than-average satire may be smaller than the European audience, because Americans read less than Europeans. Even in the theater, American audiences do not go to satire, unless it is set to music, in contrast to European audiences, who enjoy the work of satirical dramatists. It is, therefore, less surprising that the only viable format for American satire is *Mad*, which is in comic-book format.

Satirical magazines other than *Mad* have only limited circulation. There are many college satire magazines; but few enjoy much extramural circulation. Many imitate *Mad*, while disdaining it. The *New Yorker* used to be a satirical magazine; but only a diminishing proportion of its content is satirical or even humorous. Perhaps the only format in which American satire has continued to appear over the decades is the editorial page political cartoons (e.g., Herblock). Some satirical cartoonists (e.g., Jules Feiffer, Saul Steinberg) have achieved commercial success.

The absence of a national, adult satirical magazine, at a relatively prosperous time like the present, is puzzling, because such magazines seem to flourish with prosperity. *Puck*, which established the traditional text and cartoon format of so many other satire magazines, was most successful during the Gilded Age. The satirical magazine *Life*, at its peak in the 1920s, had a circulation of 250,000 (Peterson, 1956:147–52). *Life* was a major vehicle for satirists, and ran articles on subjects like Anthony Comstock, trusts, and Christian Science. *Judge* also reached its top circulation of 250,000 in the 1920s. In the same decade, *Vanity Fair's* famous satirical "We Nominate for Oblivion" department was widely influential. One *Vanity Fair* cartoon, at the time of Japan's attack on Manchuria, showed the Japanese emperor pulling a rickshaw containing the Nobel Peace Prize. It was headed "Unlikely Happenings." The cartoon elicited a formal protest from the Japanese government. The *American Mercury*, which was a magazine of irreverence as well as of satire, reached a peak circulation of 77,000 copies in 1927, under H. L. Mencken's editorship. It is possible that satire could flourish in the 1920s because of the widespread awareness of institutions like "speakeasies" and "gangsterism" which so conspicuously flaunted current morality.

In that same period, *Ballyhoo* gleamed more brightly than any previous American satirical magazine. By the time of its sixth issue in 1931, *Ballyhoo* had reached a circulation of two million. It was read by adults and developed an array of rings, ties, and other objects sold by the magazine. The magazine inspired a successful Broadway show "Ballyhoo Revue." A number of advertisers paid to be satirized in the magazine. Thus, one manufacturer paid to have his radio identified as the one which gave you "all the crap in the world at your finger tips." *Ballyhoo* made a household word of "Elmer Zilch," a silly-looking man whose picture it displayed prominently. All the editors on the masthead were called Zilch. The creator of *Ballyhoo* could not account for its success (Anthony, 1946:126). Its success is probably attributable to a combination of a shock reaction to the depression, the public's reaction against advertising as the most visible symbol of our economy, and to the psychological spark of its "slapstick" approach.

MAD

Mad has some characteristics of *Ballyhoo*. Advertising and other media are among its major targets. It has a masthead on which "Fumigator," "Bouncer," and "Law Suits" are among the staff titles listed. It sells special identifying materials. It has a character somewhat like Elmer Zilch in "Alfred E. Neuman," who is a foolish-looking boy often shown in the magazine. He usually appears with the caption "What—Me Worry?" He is always grinning, has tousled hair and a missing tooth. The face was originally used in an advertising slide at the turn of the century and adopted by *Mad* several years ago. His name was given him by a member of the magazine staff. Neuman has become a symbol of the magazine, just as Zilch became associated with *Ballyhoo*. The name "Melvin" appears occasionally, as does an avocado plant called "Arthur," and a child in a cart. The nonsense word "potrzebie" appears from time to time in the magazine. On one recent cover, Alfred E. Neuman's girl friend, "Moxie," who looks much like him, is dressed as a drum majorette. She is beating a drum on which there is a picture of Neuman with a black eye. The drum belongs to Potrzebie High School, the Latin motto of which is "Quid, Me Vexari?" (i.e., "What—Me Worry?").

Mad started in 1952 as a comic book which lampooned other comics (e.g., *Superman*) and sold at the regular comic price of ten cents. It changed its format and raised its price to twenty-five cents in 1955. Its format of the extended comic magazine story differs from the text emphasis of earlier satire magazines, although its vocabulary level is fairly high. An average story has perhaps ten panels covering three pages, and an average issue has 17 stories. Some authors are well-known comedians like Steve Allen and Orson Bean. Its circulation has increased steadily and in 1960 reached 1,400,000, of which 97 per cent are sold on newsstands. The magazine receives over 1,500 fan letters a week. Surveys have indicated that the bulk of the readership is probably concentrated among high school students, although there is some readership in colleges and among adults (Gehman, 1960). Fifteen *Mad* anthologies have been published successfully. There are few areas of the country in which it does not enjoy some popularity, although it is most popular in urban areas. *Mad*'s stemming from comic books was probably responsible for its initially having more boy than girl readers, but both sexes are now equally represented among its readers. *Mad*'s ability to institutionalize satire and to develop an audience seemed to provide a clear-cut opportunity to study some parameters of satire's appeal to teen-agers.

CONTENT ANALYSIS

A content analysis of the magazine was conducted in order to determine the relative incidence of various kinds of subject matter. All eight issues published during 1959 were examined and each story was placed into one of eleven subject categories, which had been established on the basis of preliminary analysis of previous issues. Table I gives the incidence of each theme.

TABLE I   CONTENT ANALYSIS OF ISSUES PUBLISHED IN 1959

Theme	Proportion of total percentage
U.S. leisure time activity, other than media	21
Advertising	19
Magazines, newspapers, and radio	18
Television	10
Biographies of noted persons	10
Movies	6
Transportation	5
Politics and international relations	4
Business customs	3
Special groups in the population	2
Education	2
Total	10

Each of the categories shown in Table I represents a satirical treatment of a subject; laughing at it by using its established vocabulary or trappings. Although satire includes both the understatement of irony and the exaggeration of parody, there is less irony than parody in *Mad*. However, much of *Mad* is in the form of parody, since it treats the same subject as the original but burlesques its style. Thus, the category "Advertising" would include what appear to be real advertisements. Readers who know the original can easily recognize that the manner of presentation of the advertisement is satirical.

For example, one story classified as advertising was called "The Hip Persuaders," and presented "hip" versions of ten, very familiar, advertising campaigns, each one treated in one panel. One such advertisement showed a man wearing earphones with antennae coming out of his spectacles and about to put a wicked-looking pizza pie into his shining teeth. The headline read, "He lays on only *GLEEM*, the choppergrease for cats who can't sand after every scoff." The reader can respond to this on three levels. He can recognize the well-known advertisement which recommends a toothpaste for people who can't brush after every meal. He can also identify "hip" people who are in touch with the secret language of a deviant subculture. He can also comprehend the translation of the advertising slogan into "hip" language.

Another popular format for a *Mad* story is like Fielding's approach in *Jonathan Wild*, in which the actions of a highwayman are described in mock admiration, in the language usually bestowed on statesmen; and the satire consists in the linking of disparates.

An example of such high satire is "The National Safety Council's Holiday Weekend Telethon," in which a telethon is the theme. An announcer urges people to go out and get themselves killed in a highway accident, so that the Safety Council's quota for the holiday weekend will be met. Drivers are told that the program will pay their toll if they crash into another car while on a toll bridge. Children are told that they can contribute to the total even if they have no automobile by going out and playing on a highway after dark, when it will be easier for them to be hit. Similar appeals are used throughout the rest of the story (i.e., "The family that drives together—dies together"). As in *Jonathan Wild*, the mood is sustained; viewers of the telethon are urged not to tie up the lines by telephoning nonfatal accidents, because only fatal accidents can be used. As the story progresses, the number of deaths listed on the scoreboard mounts.

Over half of *Mad's* contents are concerned with leisure and adult mass media. The central role of media in socializing adolescents makes this major theme of *Mad* of special interest. The leisure and media activities and problems of adolescents, however, receive little coverage. Other adolescent problems are either not treated or treated without much gusto. Thus, the teen-age reader can enjoy his spectatorial role as he reads about how sick and silly is the rest of society. One possible reason for the relative absence of satirical material of direct interest to adolescents is that adolescents may have difficulties in perceiving comic elements in situations in which they are involved.

The teen-ager can laugh at those younger than himself, as well as those who are older. One article on magazines for younger children, for example, featured a magazine called "Pedal Trend, The Tricycle Owner's Magazine," with articles on customizing tricycles, the *Grand Prix de Disneyland* and similar subjects. Much of the satirical material on younger people is not separate but is worked into the details of the panels of stories on other subjects. Thus, one panel in a 14-panel story on "halls of fame" dealt with a copywriter who wrote advertisements for babies, with slogans, like "ask the kid who wets one." The artist who regularly draws a child in a cart in his stories never offers an explanation of why the child is there.

Personal Interviews with Readers

Although readers of *Mad* range from eight-year-olds to college students and adults, the most typical *Mad* reader is a high school student. Personal interviews were conducted in 1959 with 411 regular readers of *Mad* with a mean age of 16.2, in order to determine the readers' attitudes toward the magazine, pattern of reading, and participation in other typical activities of teen-agers. The respondents were asked questions on stories they would have published in *Mad* "if editor," what they liked most about it, how they read an issue, with whom they discussed it, how often they read magazines for teen-agers and comic books, and how they liked rock-and-roll music. The sequence of questions was rotated in order to minimize the effect of the sequence of questions. Background data on other and previous media use were also obtained.

Stories in Mad *if Editor.* The average respondent gave eight stories which he would run "if editor," with a range from four to 22. The responses were coded into the categories developed in the content analysis. Most respondents cited stories which had already appeared in *Mad*. Table II gives their specific choices.

TABLE II   WHAT READERS WOULD PUT IN *Mad* IF THEY WERE EDITOR

Theme	Proportion of total percentage
Advertising	17
Business customs	14
Leisure time activity, other than media	14
Movies	12
Alfred E. Neuman	11
Education	7
Biographies of noted persons	6
Television	5
Transportation	4
International relations	4
Special groups	3
Magazines, newspapers, and radio	2
Miscellaneous	1
Total	100

There was a high degree of agreement between what actually appeared in *Mad* and what the readers would put in the magazine. The only major category which *Mad* readers said they would like to see in the magazine and which had not been previously coded was Alfred E. Neuman. In the content analysis, there was no category for Neuman because he has not been the subject of stories, although often figuring in them.

Readers would, however, like more of some subjects and less of others. They want more satire on business customs, education and movies and less attention to other mass media. Respondents expressed no interest in seeing problems of adolescence like parents, vocational choice or sex, treated by the magazine. Its readers seem to prefer that matters close to them not be satirized, with the exception of movies and education, which are both relatively external institutions. The magazine occasionally carries articles on parents, in which parents and the family are presented as being relatively unattractive.

Cross-tabulations by sex, status, and school performance yielded no significant differences, except that more boys than girls selected the business customers area. Boys might be expected to be more aware of business. Their interest in business customs may reflect adolescents' special fascination with adult business behavior; much of which *Mad* has helped them to perceive as foolish and immoral.

The readers may regard such stories as clues and "how to" guides to the world of business which they may soon be entering. Some readers may want stories on business because of the inadequacies of high school instruction on business and their feeling that this is an important and mysterious area of American life that they do not understand. Others may want more on business, because the work done by their fathers is increasingly removed from the children's "ken" and less product-oriented, so that the children have a relatively dim impression of just what their fathers do in the business world.

The interest in movies reflects teen-agers' extreme "movie-going" activity; only the 15–19 age group has increased its movie-going in the last ten years (Opinion Research Corporation, 1957:12). The teen-age 11 per cent of the population accounts for approximately half of all movie tickets. Movies are important for teen-agers as the traditional "safe" date. It is also possible that the procedures whereby the movie stars of today are made into stars, have been so widely publicized that teen-agers are cynical about the techniques of making stars, and would like to see them satirized. There is often so little to say about the artistic qualities of some movie stars that their publicity stresses how they were "discovered," and teen-agers may wish to see more satire on this aspect of the movies.

The interest in education perhaps reflects readers' feelings that the subject should get more treatment in *Mad*, so that they might have a better vocabulary for laughing at it. Another possibility is that some teen-agers feel that their schools and teachers are quite inadequate, and that the sensationalist criticism of education in popular media is wide of the mark. *Mad*'s integrity might seem to these teen-agers to make it an ideal vehicle for candid and informed criticism of the schools.

Since the respondents are regular readers, their general acquiescence in *Mad* content is not surprising. It is curious that readers did not mention major social issues of our time, like "desegregation" and "atomic war," as subjects for satire. There seems to be a tacit understanding that there are some subjects which are best left alone, even satirically. The readers may sense that the traditional *Mad* procedure of satirizing both sides of a controversy would lead to obvious difficulties in the case of desegregation. Some may be apathetic about the issue while others may be so ego-involved in it that they would not want it satirized. Teen-agers may be so fatalistic about nuclear war that they could not face even a satirical treatment of the subject.

What Respondents Liked About Mad.   The reasons given by the respondents for liking *Mad* were coded into several categories. The average respondent gave approximately four reasons. The proportion citing each reason is shown in Table III.

TABLE III   WHAT READERS LIKE ABOUT Mad

Reason	Proportion of readers who cited reason (Percentage)
Makes fun of and satirizes things	44
It's funny, comedy	37
Stories on famous people	25
Like everything in it	24
Makes me laugh	22
Makes fun of itself	22
The ads	21
Tells how things work	19
Not afraid to attack things	19
It's crazy	19
The jokes	19
Alfred E. Neuman	18
Has current events	18
Well done, well written	17
Not like other magazines	17
The stories	16
It's fun	12
It's relaxing	8
It's silly	7
Cheers me up	2
Miscellaneous	2
Total	388

The respondents described the appeal of the magazine mainly in generalities and the third person. Relatively few responses refer to the reader's response in the first person ("relaxing, makes me laugh, fun, cheers me up"): In view of the complex and perhaps threatening nature of satire and of humor, it is hardly surprising that the readers did not verbalize many details of the magazine's appeal.

Over half of the reasons cited refer to the magazine's satirical and witty content.

One reason for liking Mad ("famous people, how things work") is its role as socializing agent. Some teen-agers may be learning skills for functioning in our society by acquiring the procedures for survival in America today which are spelled out in witty detail by Mad. They may, thus, covertly be learning rules for antisocial behavior, while overtly laughing at those engaged in such behavior. Mad has carried seventeen different articles with titles beginning "how to" and many other articles with similar themes. At their best, they range from the bitter satire of Schopenhauer's enumeration of the many ways to win a controversy without being right (1942:1–98) to the inspired buffoonery of Rabelais's Panurge's debate with a "great English scholar" (1952:306–10).

Reading Mad may thus be a kind of problem-solving activity. The teen-ager may feel that he is learning to emulate "gamesmanship" while laughing at it. He can be an inside "dopester" while chivying inside dopesters. It would be analogous to, for example, a reader of Ovid's Art of Love or Castiglione's Book of the Courtier studying them for the apparent purpose of ridiculing love-making and the courtier's life, respectively, but actually sopping up much "how to" information on these subjects. Thus, a recent Mad article on the "Practical Scout Handbook" is a parody of the Boy Scouts' Handbook in terms of various social situations. A discussion of scout teamwork urges the reader to keep on the alert for accidents, so that he can call an ambulance and then a lawyer. The reader is advised to act surprised if the lawyer offers him part of his fee, but to turn him in to the police for "ambulance chasing" if he doesn't. The reader can thus smile at the advice; which is typical of the literalist content of much of Mad. He can also experience dislike of people who behave in this way, while at the same time absorbing the advice. The same appeal can be seen, for example, in recent books which deplore prurience and consist largely of examples of prurience to which the reader can feel superior while enjoying them.

Few respondents said that they discuss the details of their enjoyment of the magazine with their peers. They said that they did often discuss it in general terms (i.e., "Did you see the last issue?" "Did you see the story on —?"). There appears to be no specific social context of teen-agers within which the magazine is unusually likely to be discussed.

A number of respondents (22 per cent) praised the consistency of the magazine, which manifests itself in *Mad's* making fun of or attacking itself in "house" advertisements. Such advertisements seem to say, "We can't criticize others without criticizing ourselves." A typical advertisement urges readers to buy a picture of Alfred E. Neuman, so that street cleaners may be kept busy gathering up the pictures when they are thrown out. An anthology from the magazine is called "The Worst From *Mad*" and refers to "sickening past issues" from which it is culled. The editors run their own pictures and laugh at them. These are examples of what many readers perceive as the infectious high spirits and enthusiasm with which the magazine is edited. Such enthusiasm seems to have a special appeal for young people, who are likely to respect competence in any form and apparently interpret the self-mocking advertisements as expressions of consistency and competence. The respondents commenting on how well written *Mad* was (17 per cent) also are praising the competence of the editors. The implication may be that the authors of *Mad* are professional enough to have absorbed all the skills of the people they are satirizing, but have chosen to use their expertise in making fun of society and even of themselves. Inasmuch as there is considerable agreement that a distinctive feature of juvenile delinquency is its celebration of prowess (Matza, 1961), it is possible that the teen-age reader perceives *Mad* as a kind of delinquent activity which has somehow become sucessful; and, thus, one way of demonstrating prowess by antisocial activity.

Relatively few readers (3 per cent) volunteered any features of the magazine which they did not like. These features were relatively independent of their enthusiasm for the magazine. Thus a reader liking a great many features might still mention some which he did not like. Alfred E. Neuman heads the list of least-liked features; one-half of those who expressed some dissatisfaction did so because Neuman "runs too often," "looks too dopey," and similar reasons.

Cross-tabulations—by sex, socioeconomic status, and degree of success at school—of the various reasons for liking the magazine did not yield any significant differences, with two exceptions: Alfred E. Neuman and current events.

Of the 74 respondents who cited Alfred E. Neuman as a reason for liking the magazine, 56 per cent were in the group which was not doing well at school. It can be speculated that the less successful students are more likely to identify with Neuman because he conveys a feeling of failure, defeat, defensiveness, and uninvolvement. His nonworry slogan has a "let the world collapse, I don't care" quality, and his appearance suggests stupidity. One fan admiringly said that, "If Alfred E. Neuman jumped off the Empire State building, he would be laughing." A few readers thought that Neuman was a functionary of the magazine, although he does not appear on the masthead. It is possible that his silliness and appearance of being someone who doesn't know any better helps to make the magazine more acceptable, by making its attack less committed.

An adolescent who is doing well at school might enjoy the magazine because of its "joshing" of the very symbols of status and achievement to which he is attracted. The less effective adolescent may like Mad because of Neuman, who represents fecklessness and nonachievement. The magazine may thus appeal to teen-agers at opposite ends of the scale of achievement for quite different reasons, while giving each one a chance to feel superior.

Most of the respondents (71 per cent) who commented on the magazine's basing its stories on current events, were in the group which was doing relatively well at school. The more alert readers, thus, seem to derive pleasure from their ability to recognize the relationship between an actual happening and its being satirized by Mad. A few called such consonance between Mad stories and current events to their parents' attention, perhaps as one way of making their parents feel that the magazine has some educational value. It might be speculated that the identification of such current events material may help to assuage guilt feelings which the magazine's satirical content may evoke.

Even though doing well at school does have some status among teenagers, it is more important for them to achieve good grades by appearing to do little work *without* making any special efforts to get good grades (Coleman, 1959). Adolescents' group norms operate to keep effort down. Therefore, if a Mad reader can scoff at his elders and society, by seeming to learn something about current events, he is deriving multiple dimensions of satisfaction.

How to Read an Issue. Another question put to respondents was intended to determine their traffic through the magazine. Over half (62 per cent) of the regular readers go through *Mad* soon after getting it. Twenty-eight per cent read the magazine in two or three sittings. Ten per cent read it intermittently. Readers often reread their favorite articles.

The large proportion of respondents who read *Mad* through is another confirmation of the loyalty of its readers, which is not unexpected in view of adolescents' fierce loyalties to group, team, and school.

It can be speculated that one way in which the group can give vent to nonconformism is by regular readership of a magazine which largely mocks the adult world. This is a world which the magazine's readers have not yet engaged directly, but which they are approaching during a period when they are trying to learn who they are and what their feelings are. By enjoying satire on this adult world, they can approach it while mocking it. They can also mock the world of younger children.

This ability of adolescents to take a socially acceptable medium, the format of which involves conformity to group norms—like a comic magazine or rock-and-roll—while using the medium to express hostility and aggressiveness, is in line with what is known about adolescents' needs. They want both, to belong and not belong, to have and have not, to enjoy but also to attack.

The very name of *Mad* implies not only aggression ("mad at") but also the foolishness ("mad as a hatter") of much civilization. This kind of ambivalence—enjoying media which imply conformity while at the same time using them to rebel against it—is a special kind of escape, with is strongly developed in adolescents.

Adolescence has long been known to be a period of contradictions and of the growing awareness of contradictions. Materialism and idealism, egoism and altruism, and sociability and loneliness are among the contradictory feelings which are likely to be emerging simultaneously. A major problem of adolescents is how to express their hostility while seeming not to do so. One noted expression of this conflict was "Hound Dog," probably the most successful single phonograph record ever made. This rock-and-roll record sold 5,500,000 copies, almost all to teen-agers. Its lyrics represent pure hostility, although the format in which it is expressed is the socially acceptable one of the rock-and-roll record. Elvis Presley, the nonpareil exemplar of the rock-and-roller's hostility toward the adult world, is the first performer in history to make a long-playing record that sold over one million copies. Another example of adolescents' ability to use media in this way is the extent to which they will *seem* to read all of a school circulated magazine (i.e., *Reader's Digest*) which has both serious and humorous material, but will pay attention to the jokes and cartoons, and largely ignore serious material.

This ability to express aggressiveness seems to have found some relatively recent outlets, but the *presence* of the aggressiveness has often been noted by other investigators. The most intensive study ever made of adolescent fantasy—using cartoon-like picture stimuli —found that its major theme was aggression, which was described as "practically universal" (Symonds, 1949). Even "mild" boys and girls told extremely aggressive stories, with considerable destructive violence. There were over three times as many themes of "aggression" expressed by the adolescents studied, as "eroticism," the next most popular theme. Anxiety, Oedipal conflict, moral issues, success striving and turning stories into jokes, were other common themes; all of these elements can be found in *Mad*.

A study conducted before the "heyday" of comic books suggested that high school students are less likely to respond to pictorial humor than to verbal and intellectual humor (Harms, 1943). *Mad* would seem to represent a combination of these elements. The use of the comic format may help to remove some sting from the aggressive content for some readers because of the association of comics with "kid stuff." Another reason for the special appeal of the comic format is suggested by previous studies of adolescent humor, which report that visual presentation of humorous material facilitates the ability of adolescents to respond to it (Omwake, 1937). Many adolescents have had much experience with the comic format in their preadolescent years. The great majority (89 per cent) of the respondents had read comic books before *Mad*. A convincing case could probably be made for the comic book's having supplanted the fairy tale as a major carrier of our culture's ethos to young people! *Mad*, along with some other comic books, is not permitted in schools by many teachers and even by some parents in their homes, thus adding the lure of the forbidden to the magazine.

During the interviewing, a number of respondents referred to *Mad* as "our magazine." They meant that *Mad* expressed their point of view so effectively that they had almost a proprietory feeling about it. *Mad* reinforces membership in the teen-agers' peer group—it's the "thing to do." As one respondent said, "All the kids read *Mad*. The cats and the frats both make it." This suggests that the less, as well as the more, staid teeners enjoy it. There is so much interest in *Mad* that one fan has published a complete cross-index to the magazine (Bernewitz, 1961). It is likely that this in-group feeling is strengthened by the several personalities in the magazine who are never explained: Neuman, Arthur, the plant, the child, and potrzebie. A number of the respondents mentioned that they had "discovered" these features by themselves. Their having done so seemed to contribute to their feeling of being a member of an in-group.

Practically no respondent referred to the magazine's commercial success, which did not seem to have made much of an impression on readers. Many explicitly commented on the extent of peer-group readership as a positive feature. "Most of the other kids read *Mad*" and "we swap old copies back and forth," were typical comments. The wide readership of the magazine by other teen-agers helps to legitimize its appeal; especially in the face of the considerable opposition to it by parents and other institutionalized figures of authority. Readership of *Mad*, thus, reinforces membership in a kind of ritual nonconformity.

This use of media to obtain membership in an in-group of outsiders is one way in which the adolescent can make tolerable his need both to assent and dissent. It is perhaps this sensitivity and response to the near intolerable which has helped to make what is now called "sick" humor, an established part of adolescent humor. Stories like "I stepped on my mother because I wanted a step-mother" have been told by teen-agers for decades. A similar kind of gallows humor appeared in World War II among French adults faced with the extreme situation of the Resistance. It is probably no accident that this kind of "sick joke" has appeared among American adults coterminously with the near-intolerable situation of the threat of atomic annihilation.

A special appeal of a magazine of satire like *Mad* is that *the satirist can say things which even a reformer or critic cannot easily* say. *It may be easier to laugh at something than to discuss it objec-tively.* The adolescent both wants to make contact with the sym-bols of success in the outside world, as some do by autograph collecting and fan clubs, and, at the same time, wants to believe ill of them. *Mad* provides its readers with an oportunity to "go away a little closer" from some important American institutions.

This hostility seems to have a special need to find expression in high school and college students. They enjoy the absurd and satirical, as well as the opportunity to release pent-up emotional energy, and feelings of superiority (Kambouropoulou, 1930). Satire may have a special appeal to relatively young people, because it can be viewed psychoanalytically, as a reflection of the inner dependence of childhood, which is projected onto noted individ-uals and institutions, in order to attack them (Bergler, 1956:161–65). Satire is often described metaphorically as "biting," because it is a method of communication for persons who respond orally. It can be regarded as a weapon of the weak; and adolescents may regard themselves as being relatively weak. *Mad* offers an oppor-tunity for a kind of counterphobic, defensive reaction to social institutions. The adolescent readers of the magazine face the prospect of going out into the adult world, not with anxiety but with an opportunity for gratification through laughter, as they achieve symbolic mastery over the adult world by continually assur-ing themselves that its institutions and personalities cannot be taken seriously (Wolfenstein, 1945–69:336–50). The gratification comes from re-enacting mastery over anxiety (Kris, 1938), for which the *Mad* story provides the occasion. It is traditional to say that adolescents "quest for new people to love and new forms of functioning." By its exposés of the latter, *Mad* gives its adolescent readers new targets for their ambivalence.

ENTHUSIASM SCORE

Even within a group of such regular readers of the magazine, it was considered useful to obtain a measure of comparative degree of enthusiasm. Each interview was read through independently by two analysts, who considered how the magazine was read, what the respondent said about it, the respondent's feeling tone about the magazine, and the extent of his ego involvement in it. The inter-viewee was rated on a scale with one representing the lowest and ten the highest score. The range of scores was from 4 to 10, with an average of 8.0.

Boys had an average enthusiasm score of 8.7, girls of 7.8. The upper-class readers had a score of 8.6, middle-class readers also averaged 8.6, and lower-class readers 7.1. The group which was doing relatively well at school averaged 8.2, the average students 8.4, and the poorest students averaged 7.5 on enthusiasm. The difference between the poorest students and each of the other two groups was significant.

The readers whose families are faring better economically and who are better students, thus seem to like *Mad* better. Why? We might speculate that these students are likely to be expecting, consciously or otherwise, to be assuming more active and significant roles in their society and community once they leave school and college. Similarly, boys are likely to be more aware of their potential involvement with, and functioning in, the community than girls, because the boys face decisions on jobs and military service The very closeness of these groups to the opportunity of function ing in our society may make them more than usually alert to the dissonances and moral ambiguities of society. It is this kind of alertness which makes satire possible.

It is no coincidence that our wealthiest universities have also spawned some of the best college satire and humor magazines (e.g., Columbia *Jester*, Vassar *Igitur*, MIT *Voo Doo*, Stanford *Chaparral*, Harvard *Lampoon*). The student body at the Yale Law School in New Haven, which is perhaps as sensitized to power as any American student body, created *Monocle*, a political satire magazine. Thus, universities with students likely to achieve power also have publications which sneer most enthusiastically at manifestations of power. These publications represent one method of absorbing role strain on the part of groups other than the lower-class marginal groups, which have traditionally showed strain in adolescence. How cautious even such elite groups may be, can be seen in a recent issue of *Monocle*, in which over *half* the contributors use pseudonyms. The editors dedicate the issue to the contributors' skill in selecting pen names! It is a vivid commentarv on satire in our time, and a magazine of satire in which most of its authors do not wish to be identified. The caution of these con tributors to Yale's *Monocle* makes especially relevant George S Kaufman's observation that "satire is what closes in New Haven "

Another possibility for the greater interest in *Mad* of the higher socio-economic groups and better students is that satire is the end result of indignation, and indignation is based on the awareness of standards. The higher status and education group may be more aware of the standards which contemporary society is implicitly said to be violating by *Mad*, because of its greater exposure to literature, other art forms, and other facets of society.

The existence and success of *Mad* does not necessarily mean that from an adolescent's point of view there is more to satirize today than there has been in the past. What it does mean is that this particular kind of satire has found a market at this time, because it serves some significant function for the teen-agers who are its primary market. There have been some changes in the life situation of teen-agers that probably contribute to their greater receptivity to satire. The number of teen-agers increased from 15 to 20 million during the 1950s. They currently spend $10 billion a year and are the targets of many marketers, so that they are more aware of marketing. They save their money less than previous generations did, start dating earlier, and marry earlier. Teen-age girls spend $300 million on cosmetics each year. The first magazine specifically for teen-agers, rather than for boys or girls, appeared in 1955.

The 1950s appeared to provide a climate that was especially hospitable for the approach of a satirical magazine. Cynicism among the middle classes was certainly a significant characteristic of the post–World War II national mood; to which, on another level, the late Senator McCarthy responded. *Confidential* strengthened this mood by becoming the most successful magazine in American history, with its exposés of "irregularities" among the famous. This combination of factors may have helped to contribute to the mood of criticism of society, which is necessary for satire. A clue to how teen-agers feel about the morality of their elders can be obtained from the comments of teen magazines on the charge that their leading television master of ceremonies, Dick Clark, had accepted "payola." None of the magazines that commented on the charge had anything adverse to say about Clark, because they saw nothing wrong in payola.

The teen-agers of the 1950s are the "war babies" of the World War II period. Not only were their fathers often away, but their mothers were likely to be working. Even after the war, many teen-agers of the 1950s may have grown up in suburban communities, where fathers were at home less often than the fathers of previous generations. The effect of moving from one place to another, which 20 per cent of the population engages in each year, may be related to the feelings of deracination that many teen-agers experience; and that may have contributed to teen-agers' feeling more critical of their elders, and closer to each other.

Inevitably, the success of Mad and the new sick comedians during the same decade suggests some comparison between the two. Mad and the new comedians are both nihilistic, and level their burlesque at so many targets that they hardly seem to have any time or energy left to deal with alternatives to the lunacy they attack. They must both therefore continue to charge harder at their targets. They both engage in irony and reinforce their audience's feeling of being "in." Both see corruption everywhere. Both enjoy attacking mass media. The sick comedians, however, regularly attack intolerance, domesticity, religion, and self-improvement, which are seldom butts of Mad. Although politics represents a target for the sick comedians, it constitutes a small proportion of Mad's content. Mad actually does not comment on substantive political matters, but deals with personalities in politics. Thus, it might joke about President Eisenhower's golf or President Kennedy's haircut, but not about their policies.

It is curious that, with the possible exception of the sick comedians, satire has not found a market among adults since Ballyhoo. In a democracy in which the dissident voice may be a sign of healthy differences in points of view, and awareness and examination of alternatives, Mad has not only entertained dissident theories but made them feel at home and helped to get them into millions of homes. Its very success, however, may have a boomerang effect. As Mad achieves greater success and recognition as a vehicle for teen-agers, adults may reinforce their image of satire as a juvenile medium. Satire as an adult format may thus become less possible in this country for this generation. Another possibility, of course, is that the millions of teen-agers who have read Mad may develop into adults who will constitute a ready audience for sick comedians and other satire. It is also possible that the reason teen-agers enjoy Mad is that the school has sensitized them to standards, but today's nonschool, adult world is so normless that adults cannot respond to an art form that implicitly is based on departures from the norm. Yet another possibility is that the magazine's continuing attacks on so many targets will give its satire almost a good-natured quality, and thus ultimately blunt its impact. For at least the next four years, however, it appears likely that Mad will maintain its unique status of being respected, if not quite respectable.

REFERENCES

ANTHONY, N. 1946. *How to Grow Old Disgracefully.* New York: Eagle Books.

BERGLER, E. 1956. *Laughter and the Sense of Humor.* New York: Intercontinental Medical Book Corp.

BERNEWITZ, F. von. 1961. *The Complete Mad Checklist.* Silver Spring, Md.: Author.

COLEMAN, J. S. 1959. "Academic Achievement and the Structure of Competition," *Harvard Educational Review,* 29, pp. 330–51.

GEHMAN, R. 1960. "It's Just Plain Mad," *Coronet,* Vol. 48, No. 1, pp. 96–103.

HARMS, E. 1943. "The Development of Humor," *Journal of Abnormal and Social Psychology,* 38, pp. 351–69.

KAMBOUROPOULOU, P. 1930. "Individual Difference in the Sense of Humor," *American Journal of Psychoanalysis,* 37, pp. 268–78.

KRIS, E. 1938. "Ego Development and the Comic," *International Journal of Psychoanalysis,* 19, pp. 77–90.

MATZA, D. 1961. "Subterranean Traditions of Youth," *Annals of the American Academy of Political and Social Sciences,* 338, pp. 102–18.

OMWAKE, L. 1937. "A Study of the Sense of Humor," *Journal of Applied Psychology,* 21, pp. 688–704.

Opinion Research Corporation. 1957. *The Public Appraises Movies.* Princeton: Author.

PETERSON, T. 1956. *Magazines in the Twentieth Century.* Urbana: University of Illinois Press.

RABELAIS, F. 1952. *The Portable Rabelais.* Translated by Samuel Putnam. New York: Viking Press.

REDLICH, F., J. LEVINE, and T. P. SOHLER. 1951. "A Mirth Response Test," *American Journal of Orthopsychiatry,* 21, pp. 717–34.

SCHOPENHAUER, A. 1942. "The Art of Controversy." In *Complete Essays of Schopenhauer.* New York: John Wiley & Sons.

SYMONDS, P. M. 1949. *Adolescent Fantasy.* New York: Columbia University Press.

THURBER, J. 1958. "A Subversive Conspiracy," *Realist,* Vol. 1, No. 1, pp. 25–26.

WOLFENSTEIN, M. 1954–69. "A Phase in the Development of Children's Sense of Humor." In Ruth S. Eissler et al., *The Psychoanalytic Study of the Child.* Vol. 4. New York: International Universities Press.

ZWERLING, I. 1955. "The Favorite Joke in Diagnostic and Therapeutic Interviewing," *Psychoanalytic Quarterly,* 24, pp. 104–14.

EXERCISES

This set of exercises deals with two of the many ways in which popular media can be analyzed. On the one hand, popular media can be used as a source of information that has little to do with the type or form of the media themselves as the subject of analysis. For instance, the vital statistics in newspapers can be used to analyze various trends in a community, or, if viewed over time, used as indicators of social change. On the other hand, the form and distribution of the media can be the subject of analysis rather than a direct source of information. Winick used the themes in *Mad* magazine in this way. The first exercise deals with using popular media as a direct source of information, and the other three exercises deal with analysis of the form and distribution of media.

EXERCISE 1

In this exercise, the medium to be employed is the daily newspaper, and the information to be analyzed is the number of applications for marriage licenses. Under "Vital Statistics," "The Daily Record," or some similar title, newspapers provide information dealing with civil, criminal, and governmental records. Included in this information are the names and ages of couples applying for marriage licenses. For this exercise, record the ages of the men and women who have taken out a marriage license and compute the mean, median, and mode for the ages of the men and women. Use a sample of a year in case one age group is overrepresented in certain months. This will necessitate your going to the library and looking up the information from the old newspapers kept there. If your library has microfilms of very old newspapers, compare the average ages of marriage over the years to see whether the marriage age has gone up or down. If it has, this will indicate that some form of social change has occurred.

EXERCISE 2

This exercise will involve a little detective work.

One indicator of a society's values and interests is the media the population reads or views. The more popular a certain theme, the more this theme can be taken as a characteristic interest of the society. To find these interests, locate the subscription rates of the forty most popular magazines and the viewer ratings of the forty most popular television programs. Analyze the magazines and the television programs in terms of themes or contents and compile a list. For instance, you may find that the most popular television programs are comedies, or that magazines dealing with domestic matters (i.e., household management) have the greatest circulation. The detective work will involve finding these subscription rates and television ratings.

EXERCISE 3

The purpose of this exercise is to compare two popular magazines, *Playboy* and *Reader's Digest*, to find what themes predominate in each. In this way, you will be able to see two very different trends in American society, one traditional and conservative, the other modern and liberal. The fact that both have very high subscription rates attests to their popularity, and the fact that they are very different in their treatment of values points to a pluralistic society.

To carry out this exercise, a group approach would be the most expedient, since the contents of several issues will have to be examined. Since both magazines are issued monthly, twelve copies of each would give a year's sample, and this should be sufficient. Each student will be given one copy of each to analyze in terms of the subjects discussed, the general themes of the contents, and whether the treatment of each issue represents a conservative or liberal viewpoint. Also, a list of key issues, such as race relations, women's liberation, pollution and the environment, and any other topical issue should be examined to see how each publication treats these issues. If one or the other magazine ignores an issue that the other has several articles or stories about, this, too, should be noted.

After each student has examined and analyzed his copies, this information should be pooled with that from others who analyzed other issues. Finally, the results of the two groups should be compared to find what two very different lines of interest dominate American society.

EXERCISE 4

Like the analysis of *Mad* magazine, this exercise deals with the content of a communication medium. Even though the form of the medium is different, the same techniques will be employed. The problem is to find whether there is any relation between the form and content of television commercials and the type of program sponsored by the advertiser.

To make this analysis, take a random sample of television programs, using a television program directory as the source of the sample. Then record on an "analysis form" (see below) the type of program; the program topic; the audience that would be assumed to view such a program; the sponsor's service, product, or message; the form of propaganda used; and whether the commercial appealed to reason.

Below is a list of types of propaganda typically employed by advertisers.

Band Wagon:	Appeals to join everyone else and become popular
Testimonial:	A well-known person of high status recommends product, service, or cause
Slogan:	A phrase is repeated over and over so that viewers will remember the commercial
Demonstration:	The virtues of the advertiser's wares or service are demonstrated
Entertainment:	The commercial is entertaining but says little about the product, except to associate it with the entertainment
Straight Claim:	The advertiser simply claims his service is the best. (Differs from testimonial in that no celebrity is used.)
Favor:	The commercial tries to present the advertiser as doing a favor for the consumer

Once you have collected your data, see whether certain kinds of propaganda are used (1) with one type of audience more than others, (2) with one type of product, service, or cause more than others, and (3) with one type of program more than others. This will give insight into not only types of propaganda in relation to what the advertiser is selling but also how the sponsor views the audience, what the society sees as valuable, and some of the reasons you may be purchasing one thing over another.

Analysis Form

Time and day of program
Name of program
  Program format:
    a. Movie
    b. Regular series
    c. News
    d. Special (specify)
    e. Cartoon
    f. Other (specify)
  Program topic:
    a. Variety
      1. Musical
      2. Comedy
      3. General
    b. Law
    c. Medicine
    d. Police or private detectives
    e. Western
    f. Situation comedy
    g. Nature
    h. Travel
    i. Soap opera
    j. Drama
    k. Comedy
    l. Adventure
    m. Other (specify)
Audience (estimate audience):
  a. General
  b. Adult
  c. Children
Sponsor's service, product, or message:*
  a. Product
  b. Service
  c. Message
Form of Propaganda:†

* If more than one sponsor use separate forms.
† Sponsor may use more than single form.

a. Band Wagon
b. Testimonial
c. Slogan
d. Demonstration
e. Entertainment
f. Straight claim
g. Favor
h. Other (specify)
Appeal to reason?
a. Yes
b. No

The analysis form should be typed on duplication masters, and enough forms should be made so that there is a form for each commercial. Because of the amount of television viewing necessary, it is suggested that this be done as a group project.

ADDITIONAL READING SUGGESTIONS

ALBRECHT, M. C. 1956. "Does Literature Reflect Common Values?" *American Sociological Review*, 21, pp. 722–729. Discusses the extent to which the content analysis of literature can be used as a cultural indicator. This is an especially good article if one plans a historical or comparative analysis using literature as a data resource.

BERELSON, BERNARD. 1952. *Content Analysis*. New York: The Free Press. A valuable resource on how content analysis can be employed in dealing with sociological problems. Also explains how the analysis is executed.

NIXON, R. C. 1924. "Attention and Interest in Advertising," *Archives of Psychology*, 11, pp. 1–68. A useful analytic tool for the content analysis of propaganda in commercial advertising. You might want to consult this article for Exercise 4 of Chapter 11.

12. Conversation Analysis

PUMPS AND PAUSES:
STRATEGIC USE OF
CONVERSATIONAL
STRUCTURE IN
INTERROGATIONS
—William B. Sanders

Introduction

MY PURPOSE HERE IS TO SHOW how the sequential structure of conversations is strategically employed by police in their interrogations. On the one hand, the sequential structure of conversations suggests that certain strategies are more efficient than others in getting a suspect to talk. On the other hand, if certain strategies are found in police interrogations, their usage will reveal various sequential structures of the conversation. Thus, it will be necessary first to show what strategies are suggested by the conversational structure and how they operate as strategies, and secondly to show how these strategies, to the end of forcing a suspect to talk, reveal certain conversational structures. The latter task is the more important in that it points to the consequences of the sequential structure of conversations in general and can be applied to forms of conversation other than interrogations.

Interrogations as Q-A Sequences

To begin this analysis, I will take Schegloff's (1968) question-answer (Q-A) sequence as the prototype of an interrogation. Basically, the interrogator asks the questions, and the suspect answers them. It should be noted that, in police manuals on interrogation, the interrogator is cautioned to control the talk, and his control can be summed up by the euphemism often heard in police dramas, "I'll ask the questions" (Kidd, 1940:73).

Not "just any talk" in an interrogation is sufficient for the interrogator. He attempts to keep the suspect on the right track, and the questions he asks can be taken to be efforts to direct the talk to salient issues. However interesting this might be, the issue of relevance *per se* will be ignored, here; our focus will be, rather, on questions as mechanisms for keeping the talk going. Likewise, answers given by suspects can be viewed as evasive or straightforward, truthful or false, excuses, justifications, boasts, admissions, or any other type of response; but our interest here is not in the content of responses. Rather, the replies will be examined in structural juxtaposition to questions.

In addition to showing that questions structurally demand replies and are therefore useful strategies for "forcing talk," I want to show that, once a question has been asked and the suspect begins to talk, the interrogator "pumps" the talk with nonquestion talk and grunts, which function to leave the "talk-turn" with the suspect. Secondly, pauses or gaps will be shown to be strategies that force the suspect to keep talking. That is, if the suspect ceases to talk before the interrogator is ready for him to stop or before he decides to ask another question, the lack of response by the interrogator leaves the suspect with an awkward silence which he is obliged to fill with talk.

In order to show this clearly, I will impress transcription conventions that should highlight the matters of interest while ignoring other transcription conventions. The first convention is the "numbered pause," illustrated by parenthetically numbering the pauses from "1" to "n" (the number of seconds in the pause). For example, an eight-second pause would look like this: (1-2-3-4-5-6-7-8). For briefer pauses, one second or less, standard conventions will be used; for example, /#/ denoting an interval of less than one second, and /*/ denoting an interval of approximately one second.

A second convention employed indicates difference between what I have referred to as a "pump" and what is normally taken to be a turn. Turns will be indicated by placing a "Q" (interrogator) or an "A" (suspect) in the left-hand margin on the line where either speaker's turn begins. "Pumps," or utterances designed to keep the speaker's talk going, will be indicated by equal signs (=) placed before and after the pump and by underlining the pump at the place in the speaker's turn where it occurs. For example, the pump in the following segment is done by Q in A's turn.

. . . for a shotgun, which ah everybody in the shop knows about it. = *Uh huh*= And then ah /*/ they already. . . .

The Q-A sequence, taken as an utterance pair (Schegloff, 1972: 77) in conversational organization, poses the following proposition: If the first half of the pair is observed in the conversation, the second half will follow. That is, if a question is asked, the next talk in the sequence will be an "answer." Schegloff has pointed out the expectation that, if the next talk is not formulated as an answer to the question, the question will be asked again. A nonanswer—i.e., talk that is something other than answer or silence—is to be taken as an event. One form of nonanswer talk after a question has been discussed by Schegloff (1972) as an "insertion sequence," which seems to be taken as an "answer in the process of development" by the questioner. Even though the talk following the question is not an answer, it points to one in the sense that it can readily be seen as leading up to an answer.

The focus of this paper is not on the appropriateness of the response but, rather, on the fact that a question has the property of *action selection* (i.e., a question selects the next action in the conversation, an answer) and of *speaker selection* (i.e., the question directed to a particular person selects that person to speak next). Whether or not the suspect is evasive and the question has to be repeated is only tangentially interesting. The fact of response to a question and recognition of the obligation to fill in awkward silences, indicated by who speaks after a long pause, are the main events of interest in this analysis.

Another relevant feature of the Q-A sequence is that a question and only a question can *assign* silences. As soon as a question is asked, the silence "belongs" to the next speaker and not to—never to—the questioner. On the other hand, an answer that does not include a question, as insertion sequences do, can never leave the next speaker—in this case, the questioner—with the silence. Any silence after one question is asked and before another question is asked will be the nonquestioner's silence, whether or not he has given what he takes to be an answer, since an answer can always be construed to be incomplete (Garfinkel, 1967:40). In this way, the questioner can force the other to talk. In interrogation situations, where the questioner is the interrogator, the silences always belong to the suspect; he is always obliged to talk, and the interrogator never is.

The silence in the pauses will be shown to belong to the suspect, in that he does the talking before *and* after the pauses. Similarly, the pumps can be seen to be done by the interrogator but in the suspect's talk-turn. This can be seen, in that the pumps do not alter the suspect's talk, except by keeping him talking. The following transcript segment of an interrogation illustrates this feature.

The first transcript begins after incidental procedural matters have been discussed with the suspect. I will take it to be the "beginning" of the talk concerning the incident for which the suspect was arrested.

TRANSCRIPT 1

```
1          Q. Do you want to tell me about the weapon? Where
2             you got it? When you got it?
3  /#/  A. Ah (1-2-3-4-5-6-7) it was just about two weeks
4             =Uh huh= (1-2-3) before Christmas (1-2-3-4) and
5             I bought it from this at the gun shop /#/ ah,
6             (1-2-3) Whewww six, six-hundred block I can't
7             remember the exact address. Six (1-2-3-4) six
8             something ah (1-2-3-4) Parksburg.
9  /#/  Q. Six-hundred block Parksburg?
10 /#/  A. I think that's it.
11 /#/  Q. Do you know the name of the shop?
12 /#/  A. Ah (1-2-3) something about I think it's Crafts.
13            He doesn't have a sign up there or anything /#/
14            ah (1-2) but it's Crafts Gun Shop I believe
               =Uh huh=
15            Bennings is the man's name.
16         Q. Bennings?
17         A. (1-2) No, Bekins =Bekins=
18         Q. (1-2) And you bought the gun there?
19 /#/  A. Yeah.
20         Q. About two weeks before Christmas?
21         A. (1-2-3-4) And ah he held it for five days and then
```

In the transcript segment, the first point to be noticed is that there is some talk after every question. Secondly, of the 38 seconds of silences in the talk, all but two seconds belong to the suspect (A). Both of these observations support the contention that questions force the talk and the silences on the recipient of the question. Between lines 3 and 8, some 25 seconds of silences take place, all followed by A's talk. Moreover, the pauses on lines 4 and 6 appear to be at points of possible utterance completion, suggesting that, even if A attempted to give the turn to Q, he could not do so, since, as I have argued, the silences belong to the recipient of the question, and it is up to the questioner to decide when *his* question has been answered. Until then, he can leave the silences with the recipient of the question.

The pump that occurs in the first response by A is in a position that does not appear to be a possible utterance completion. Because it does not occur at a possible completion point, it strengthens the argument that such "minimal responses" may be something other than talk-turns, as I am attempting to show. It appears to be there in relation to the first pause, which lasted a full seven seconds, and it appears to be in A's turn. The first pause, in other words, prompted the interrogator to pump A's turn as soon as A started talking instead of waiting for a possible completion point, which would seem to be after the word "Christmas" in line 4. At the first point of possible completion, A stops; but, since there is an awkward silence, he tacks on ". . . and I bought it from this at the gun shop."

Another interesting feature of the transcript segment occurs on line 17. It appears that the interrogator wanted the suspect to keep on talking, but what was meant to be a pump turned out to give the interrogator the silence; thus, the "pump" functioned as a "stopper." (Stoppers will be discussed later.) He realized this quickly, however (two seconds of silence), but, perceiving that he had to say something, ended up asking the suspect what he had just been told. The interesting feature is that he *did* say something in order to keep the suspect talking, and what he used was a question. A's response in line 19 did not go anywhere, so Q quickly followed with another question, which gave the silence and the turn back to A, resulting in a lengthy account of how he came to get the gun. (Only part of the reply is in the transcript segment.)

The point, however, was not to elicit new information, since the interrogator had just been told when the suspect had bought the gun. This gave the silence to the suspect (four seconds), and he did begin talking.

The next segment is near the end of the interrogation. The interrogator's question is of a procedural nature, so that no inference can be made that the suspect was intoxicated during the interrogation. (The suspect said he had had two beers before the interrogation.) It appears that the interrogator is attempting to end the interview, but he nevertheless gets a lengthy reply from the suspect. The pumps here do not seem to be intended as pumps, but, structurally, they function that way. There are several pauses where the interrogator could have taken a turn as possible utterance completion points, but for some reason he let the suspect keep on going.

Transcript 2

```
 1      Q. Do you think the alcohol is affecting you in any way?
 2 /#/  A. No this /#/ whole /#/ deal is a like I said I never
 3         realized ah I jus (1-2-3) be put in this position
 4         jus fer =Yeah= cause I was (1-2) ah (1-2) course
 5         I did lie when he asked me if I'd been convicted
 6         of a felony. I told him no /*/ but ah (1-2) I mean
 7         ah /*/ I didn't buy it from jus anybody ej ah y'know.
 8         =Yeah= I did buy it from a gun shop =Yeah= and like
 9         I said eh juh this is all easily be checked out I
10         tell ya eh juh ah /#/ the gun for a shotgun which
11         ah everybody in the shop knows about it =Uh huh=
12         and then ah /*/ they already gave it back to me
13         because the way it didn't shoot straight and like
14         I said duh eh the guy that I bought it from ah (1-2)
15         he'll verify that I brought it back and complained
16         about it not shootin' good too and ah /*/ well every-
17         thing I said y'know. I know heh huh =Yeah= heh /*/
18         I got eh /*/ it all ah (1-2-3-4) wheww like I said
19         I didn't know ah I didn't realize I could be (1-2)
20         took to jail for a felony fer (1-2-3-4-5-6) the way
```

21	the way ah (1-2) christ // I would huv never bought

21   the way ah (1-2) christ // I would huv never bought
22   the thing to start with the ah = Yeah =
23 / j / Q. [Have you ever]* Have you ever seen me before?

This last interchange does not seem to be an attempt by the interrogator to get the suspect to talk. Talk does occur, however, and in relation to the same structural features as in Transcript 1. Following the question, the suspect talked, filled in silences, and was pumped by the interrogator, even though the interrogator may not have intended his "= Yeah =" to be a pump.

The significance of this transcript is that after the question, in the context of the entire interrogation, the interrogator *immediately* gets the information answering his question when A responds with "No. . . ." The rest of the suspect's talk is largely irrelevant to the question. Thus, it can be inferred that the interrogator did not attempt to make or trick the suspect into talking. Rather, the suspect's talk was encouraged structurally. The sequential structure of the Q-A sequence not only forces the obligation to talk, but the speaker in the answer half of the Q-A sequence can talk in the response to the question for as long as he wants, and the questioner is conversationally obliged to listen.† Hence, not only does a question force talk from a recalcitrant conversationalist, it also gives the floor to a talkative speaker, which may prove difficult to regain. This difficulty can be seen in line 21, where Q has to overlap A then repeat his next question in line 23 after A finally stops in line 22.

There are six pumps that appear to keep the talk going, with the exception of the last one, at the very end of A's talk. It might seem that this last pump is not a pump at all, and this brings into question the notion of a pump as opposed to the notion of a turn. (Any utterance can be treated as a turn.) However, it should be pointed out that the last pump occurs after an overlap, where the interrogator attempted to introduce a new question. Secondly,

---

* The brackets indicate that this portion of the conversation overlapped at the point indicated by double slashes (//).

† The difficulty of regaining the floor after having asked a question has been experienced by sociological interviewers. Most of the emphasis in teaching interviewing techniques is in how to get the subject to answer questions, but very little has been done to explain how to stop subjects once they have started.

there is no gap between Q's final "= Yeah =" and his next question. It can be seen either as a preface to his question, and therefore misplaced in the transcript, or as a verbal period on A's talk. It does not appear to be a preface, since on the tape it sounds similar to the other pumps, and there is a marked difference in the tone of the question compared to Q's final "= Yeah =." It appears, rather, that Q's turn begins with "Have," and A's turn ends with = Yeah =."

Since I have argued that pumps function to keep the speaker's talk going, and since, from examining the transcripts, the other pumps appear to do so, this last one is troublesome. On the one hand, it is clearly not the beginning of Q's turn; on the other hand, it clearly stops A's turn as a speaker at a place that does not appear to be a point of possible utterance completion. Moreover, it does not do what a pump is supposed to do; thus, it must be something else. The "something else" will be called a "stopper," since it functions to stop the other's talk and gives the listener a chance to slip in and take his turn. It is only coincidental that the "same" word is used as a stopper as is used for a pump. The real importance is not what word is used as a pump or stopper but how they are used in the sequential structure of the conversation. (In Transcript 1, the repeating of the speaker's last word functioned as a stopper in line 17.) Stoppers are devices to stop the other's talk, so that the listener may take his turn as a speaker; they are not the initiators of the listener's turn, or "starters."

Summary and Conclusion

At the beginning, we proposed that the sequential structure of conversations can be employed strategically by police in their interrogations. We noted the strategies that are suggested by the conversational structure, how they operate as strategies, and, more important, how they reveal the structure of conversations. First, it was shown that questions force the talk-turn on the recipient of the question by leaving him with the obligation to fill in any silences following the questions. This structural feature suggests the Q-A sequence as a strategic device in interrogations, in that it obliges the suspect to talk. Moreover, it was shown that the questioner could "pump" the respondent, obliging him to answer the question without taking the turn and the obligation to talk away from him. In turn, the successful use of the Q-A strategy revealed how the sequential structure of the Q-A sequence operates in conversations. Thus, one could expect to find the same structural forms in any conversation in which the Q-A sequence is used. Radio and television talk-show hosts, guests at cocktail parties, teachers attempting to stimulate class discussion, and other conversation situations in which the actors feel compelled to keep the talk going employ the Q-A sequence to the end of avoiding interactional silence and directing the obligation of talking to another party.

REFERENCES

GARFINKEL, HAROLD. 1967. *Studies in Ethnomethodology*. Englewood Cliffs, N.J.: Prentice-Hall.

KIDD, LT. W. R. 1940. *Police Interrogation*. New York: Basuino.

SCHEGLOFF, EMANUEL A. 1968. "Sequencing in Conversational Openings." *American Anthropologist*, 70, pp. 1075–95.

———. 1972. "Notes on a Conversational Practice: Formulating Place." In David Sudnow (ed.), *Studies in Social Interaction*, pp. 74–119. New York: The Free Press.

EXERCISES   The purpose of this set of exercises is to
give the student rudimentary experience in
taping conversations, transcribing the tapes, and analyzing the
transcriptions. The importance of conversation analysis lies not
so much in the taping or transcription of the tapes as in the search
for the social structure of conversations and their effect on what is
said and how it is said. This type of analysis is quite complex and
requires extensive training. However, the first step is to get the
conversation down on tape and then transcribe the tapes to reflect
the texture of the conversation. The following exercises are meant
to introduce this new and promising area of research in sociology.

EXERCISE 1

First, tape a segment of a television talk show on which there is
a lively exchange of talk between the host and one or more guests.
Next, tape a segment of a movie or another television program
that involves actors delivering lines from a script. Now take segments of the two tapes that have ongoing discussions between
two or more participants. The segments should be no more than
five minutes long, for even this small amount of talk will reveal
aspects of interest and will require a good deal of transcription.
Once the transcriptions are completed, using the transcription
conventions presented in the introduction, determine which conversation contains the most overlaps, interruptions, and pauses. In
normal conversations and unrehearsed discussions, there should be
more interruptions and overlaps, and unequal amounts of time in
the pauses between speakers' turns. Whereas the actors have their
conversations laid out in advance, conversationalists create theirs
as an ongoing process. The differences between actual conversations and dramatized ones can be clearly seen in terms of these
aspects.

EXERCISE 2

In the study of police interrogations, it was seen that interro-
gators could employ the sequential structure of conversations to
force a talk-turn on the suspect. Talk-show hosts can use the same
strategy in getting their guests to speak. Whenever the talk starts
to lag on a talk show, you should find the host asking a question.

This can be seen by analyzing the transcription of the television talk show in terms of the Q-A sequence.

EXERCISE 3

A class discussion will be used as the source of data for this exercise, to analyze the points at which speakers change in a conversation.

Choose a class in which discussions are common. Ask the instructor if you may tape some class discussions and, when you set up your tape recorder, explain what you are doing to the class. Have the tape recorder present and running for several sessions, so that students and instructor have a chance to get used to it and overcome any inhibitions they might have about speaking "for the record." Then, once you feel that the discussions are the same as before you introduced the recorder, transcribe a segment of the tape.

The analysis here involves finding where one speaker stops talking and another begins. The points where speakers change should normally be "completion points," or those places in talk where a thought has been completed. You will notice that, in any talk, there are several possible completion points where another speaker could have taken a talk-turn, and these points can be located by first identifying the forms of completion points where speakers change. Similarly, overlaps can be used. Often where overlaps occur, the speaker who was overlapped will finish his thought even though another has begun to talk. Generally, however, you should find that one speaker's thought has been completed, and then, without a gap or overlap, another speaker will take over.

ADDITIONAL READING SUGGESTIONS

SACKS, HARVEY. 1972. "An Initial Investigation of the Usability of Conversational Data for Doing Sociology." In David Sudnow (ed.), *Studies in Social Interaction*. New York: The Free Press. Examines how transcriptions from conversations can be used for sociological research. Provides an analytic framework and underlying logic for conversational analysis.

SCHEGLOFF, EMANUEL A. 1968. "Sequencing in Conversational Openings," *American Anthropologist*, 70, pp 1075–95. A very good discussion of the structure of the question-answer sequence in conversational openings. It should be consulted when completing the exercises using Q-A sequence analysis.